Sound and Sight

Sound and Sight

POETRY AND
COURTIER CULTURE IN THE
YONGMING ERA (483–493)

Meow Hui Goh

STANFORD UNIVERSITY PRESS
STANFORD, CALIFORNIA

Stanford University Press
Stanford, California

Printed in the United States of America on acid-free, archival-quality paper

Library of Congress Cataloging-in-Publication Data

Goh, Meow Hui.
  Sound and sight : poetry and courtier culture in the Yongming era (483-493) / Meow Hui Goh.
      p. cm.
  Includes bibliographical references and index.
  ISBN 978-0-8047-6859-7 (cloth : alk. paper)
  1. Chinese poetry--Northern and Southern dynasties, 386-589--History and criticism. 2. Sensuality in literature. 3. Senses and sensation in literature. 4. China--Court and courtiers. I. Title.
  PL2319.G64 2010
  895.1'1209--dc22   2010018634

Typeset by Bruce Lundquist in 10.5/14 Adobe Garamond

For Keoni

Contents

Acknowledgments ix

Conventions xi

Prologue
Shengse: Sound and Sight 1

CHAPTER 1 Individual Talent and the "Worthy One" 7

CHAPTER 2 Knowing Sound 21

CHAPTER 3 Seeing a Thing 40

CHAPTER 4 In the Garden 57

CHAPTER 5 Leaving the Capital City 80

CHAPTER 6 In and Out of the Landscape 100

Epilogue 120

Abbreviations 127

Notes 129

Selected Bibliography 155

Character List 171

Index 183

Acknowledgments

The research for this project was supported by a post-doctoral fellowship from the Center for East Asian Studies, Stanford University, which allowed me to produce the first draft of this book. A Humanities Publication Subvention Grant from the College of Humanities at OSU was crucial in making this publication possible. Through the years, my research had also been supported by the Assistant Professor Research Fund, also from the College of Humanities, and various funding from the Department of East Asian Languages and Literatures at OSU. To these institutions, I want to express my deepest gratitude. Many friends and colleagues have guided and supported me along the way. Specifically, I want to thank Robert Joe Cutter, whose tireless mentoring and warm friendship mean so much to me, and also Mark Bender, Kirk Denton, Ronald Egan, David R. Knechtges, Paul W. Kroll, Young Kyun Oh, Patricia Sieber, and Stephen West. I am also grateful to Leonard Kwok-kou Chan, Wang Kuo-ying, and Yuan Xingpei for giving me my early training in Chinese literature. The prompt and warm assistance of Stacy Wagner, Acquisitions Editor at Stanford University Press, Jessica A. Walsh, her editorial assistant, Mariana Raykov, Production Editor at the Press, and all their staff ensured the smooth and timely publication of this book; the careful and thoughtful editing of Richard Gunde, my copyeditor, greatly improved the overall quality of this book. The comments and insights of the anonymous readers at the Press helped correct mistakes and strengthen arguments. My friend Alex Burry was kind enough to help with proofreading, and my colleague Shelley Quinn patiently suggested many stylistic changes. I owe these wonderful people my sincere thanks. My parents and my three brothers and their families deserve to know that their love and care for me, coming from the distant island of Singapore, have always been a main source of strength for everything that I do. Keoni has been by my side through the ups and downs, reading my chapters when I needed him to, making dinners and doing the laundry when I was caught up in work. This book is dedicated to him, my first reader and my loving and inspiring companion in life.

Conventions

I use the *pinyin* system for romanizing Chinese throughout this book. In quotations, I have changed other forms of romanization, when they are used in the original, to *pinyin*. As for the names of authors and the titles of works, I have kept the original forms of romanizing.

The Chinese characters of the terms and phrases given in *pinyin* in the main text are listed in the Character List, which can be found in the back pages.

All translations, unless otherwise specified, are my own.

Sound and Sight

Prologue

Shengse: Sound and Sight

The Chinese word *shengse* ("sound and sight") essentially refers to all objects of the five senses. However, it has a long history of negative connotations. Zhonghui, a minister pivotal to the founding of Shang (ca. 1600–ca. 1045 B.C.E.), for example, once proclaimed that the virtues of his king included "not going near sound and sight" (*buer shengse*).[1] A similar sense of the word was again invoked when Kuang Heng, the Western Han (206 B.C.E.–C.E. 8) scholar and minister, admonished Emperor Cheng to "refrain from 'sound and sight'" (*jie shengse*).[2] In these two examples, *shengse* connoted sensual pleasure, which was considered a distraction—even a threat—that had ramifications not only for the individual, but for the state as a whole as well. Therefore, it is not surprising that the first definition listed for *shengse* in the major dictionaries of classical Chinese is "unorthodox music and the beauty of women" (*yinsheng yu nüse*).[3] These, however, are only two of the items on a long list of *shengse*. Rich food, strong fragrances, and ornate decoration, among others, were all considered potentially dangerous sensual pleasures, and they had provoked serious warnings in anecdotal stories, historical commentaries, and philosophical discourses.[4] Even *shengse* displayed in the context of moral instruction were discouraged at times. In the *Liji* (Record of Rites), for example, Confucius (551–479 B.C.E.) is cited as saying,

> "Sound and sight" are not the means by which [a ruler] transforms the common people. The *Shi* states, "The carriage of virtue is as light as a feather." Yet a feather still has markings. "The manner in which Heaven on the High propagates [its virtue] is soundless and odorless"—that is perfect.[5]

In this statement, *shengse* is simply appearance: the surface form that can be seen, heard, touched, smelled, or tasted. From the Confucian perspective, the ideal state of moral influence is "soundless and odorless" (*wu sheng wu xiu*), that is, a state void of *shengse*. The imperative to be wary of, avoid, or even eliminate *shengse* revealed in the Chinese textual tradition is fundamentally a moral one and was often interpreted to guide political rule.

In light of the discussion thus far, what does it mean when poetry is said to exhibit "sound and sight"? I have borrowed the word *shengse* from the Qing dynasty poet and critic Shen Deqian (1673–1769), who made this comment about the trajectory of poetry at the onset of the Southern Dynasties (420–589): "By the time of the Song dynasty [420–479], 'nature and feeling' were gradually eclipsed in poetry, while 'sound and sight' were completely unleashed. This was a turning point in the course of poetry."[6] The Song dynasty and the following dynasties, the Qi (479–502), the Liang (502–557), and the Chen (557–589), are collectively called the Southern Dynasties. The group of poets to be discussed in this book lived right in the middle of this fascinating period and has been regarded as the main "instigators" of its poetic trend in "sound and sight." When Shen Deqian discussed *shengse* in opposition to *xingqing* ("nature and feeling")—a poetic quality he probes and emphasizes throughout his *Shoushi zuiyu* (An Assortment of Comments from Talking about Poetry)—he obviously did not intend to use it for appraisal.[7] By *shengse*, Shen Deqian was referring to a broad range of poetic traits that he observed in Southern Dynasties poetry, including the descriptive landscapes of Xie Lingyun (385–433), the unconventional imagery of Bao Zhao (c.a. 414–466), the elegant diction of Yan Yanzhi (384–456), and much more. Ultimately, he was making the point that Southern Dynasties poets had shifted their attention to the "surface" or "exterior" forms of poetry, and, as a result, had "eclipsed" the genuine expression of "nature and feeling," which presumably came from "within."

Shen Deqian's disapproval of the poetic trend in "sound and sight" is more obvious when he compares Tao Yuanming (Tao Qian; 365–427) side-by-side with Xie Lingyun. Tao Yuanming, known for a tranquil and natural style, is the only Southern Dynasties poet whom Shen Deqian unequivocally celebrates:

> Tao Yuanming's poetry immediately feels natural and others cannot surpass its genuineness and truthfulness. Xie Lingyun's poetry came from manipulation and went against that which was natural; but others cannot surpass its novelty and gracefulness. Tao Yuanming's poetry exceeds others for it has no crafting, whereas Xie Lingyun's exceeds others exactly because of its crafting.[8]

If we pay attention to Shen Deqian's tone, we will hear that the difference between Tao Yuanming's and Xie Lingyun's poetry is not a simple contrast between a bland and easy style and a more stylized and explicit one. Their difference has moral and philosophical implications about "genuineness," "truthfulness," and "naturalness," qualities that are opposed to "crafting," "manipulation," and "unnaturalness." Fundamentally, Shen Deqian was concerned about the overt display of artistry, which he obviously treated with great caution and suspicion. His evaluation of Southern Dynasties poetry continues:

> Among Qi writers, few were good. . . . During the Liang of the Xiaos, the "Exchange Poems" of the rulers and their subordinates were quite skillfully composed, but their description of beautiful women and romantic love had caused the literary style and taste of their day to become more and more decadent. . . . From the Liang to the Chen and then to the Sui [581–618], poets were only interested in embellishing their lines.[9]

Like a historian commenting on the fall of a kingdom or a philosopher reflecting on the moral decline of a society, Shen Deqian portrayed the trajectory of Southern Dynasties poetry as a fatal degeneration. He warns at one point: "When it comes to articulating one's aim and making known the worthy teachings and yet one relies only on coloring and polishing, then one has lost the true meaning of being a poet from the start" (*yanzhi zhangjiao, wei zi tuze, xian shi shiren zhi zhi*).[10] Once "sound and sight" were completely unleashed, it became a downward slope; the moment it headed in the direction of "sound and sight," Southern Dynasties poetry already lost its way.

It is not unusual that Shen Deqian should conflate literary criticism with moral judgment and political interpretation. More than a millennium earlier, the prince-poet Cao Pi (187–226) had declared that "literary composition is a great achievement that concerns the ruling of a state" (*wenzhang jingzuo zhi daye*).[11] This statement is widely viewed as a landmark recognition of literature as literature in modern scholarship; but it is equally, if not more, significant in its clear articulation of the political and didactic relevance of literature. Shen Deqian's remarks about Southern Dynasties poetry only highlight the attention paid to the moral and political implications of literature in the case of our particular subject. In the Chinese collective memory, the Southern Dynasties were at their best "a stable time [presided over by a court] at a corner" (*pianan*) and, at their worst, plagued by the "illegitimacy" of their rule, they were an era of political dysfunction and military weakness.[12] Lasting more than 150 years, the Southern Dynasties saw the succession of the four dynasties whose capital city, Jiankang (modern Nanjing), was located just south of the lower Yangzi delta, while the Northern Dynasties (420–589)—themselves constituted by more than ten states over the course of the period—loomed large to the north. In 589, when the Chen dynasty was conquered by Yang Jian (later Sui Wendi; 541–604), who had consolidated his power in the north, this period of north-south division was brought to an end. Casting the period's political failings onto its culture and literature—or, rather, seeking to explain these failings *through* its culture and literature—the Tang minister Zheng Tan (d. 842) bluntly argued that "the reason the Northern and Southern Dynasties had failed in their rule was that they allowed literary splendor to surpass real substance."[13] In this case, the "sound and sight" that originated from literature had caused the demise of an entire age. This is not only the imagination of "premodern" commentators. The hero of modern Chinese literature, Lu Xun (1881–1936), for example, once characterized pre-Han and Han writers of *fu*, a poetic form famous for its verbose and ornate style, as "playthings among sounds, sights, dogs, and horses" (*wei zai shengse gouma zhijian de wanwu*).[14] And as recently as 2007, at a talk on Southern Dynasties poetry, I heard criticism of the period's poets for their "narrow" and "materialistic" lifestyle, which was assumed to be the source of their formalistic pursuits in poetry.[15]

Without doubt, the central figures in this study were well versed in the literary tradition suffused with moral and political meaning. That makes the following questions even more significant: What did "sound and sight" mean to these poets? How did they come to guide the poetic trend in "sound and sight"? It is a mistake, I believe, to see their poetics only as surface or exterior forms, or to assume that the environment within which they pursued "sound and sight" was simply "narrow" or "materialistic." This study will highlight their identity as courtier-poets by situating their poetics within the courtier culture of the day. That perspective draws on a broad range of issues that collectively will produce a more complex image of the courtier-poet. Ultimately, this book argues that their pursuit of "sound and sight," which emphasized a process of grasping the phenomenal world in a meticulous manner, reflects a hybrid concept of personal worth that was unique to their time and far more significant in Chinese literary and cultural history than critics have acknowledged. Seen through this lens, the issue of "sound and sight" can be defined literally—it is about *how* one sees and hears. Tracing their unique way of seeing and hearing, this book will reveal how a group of early medieval courtier-poets ushered in a truly new and influential poetics.

Due to their activities during the Yongming reign period (483–493) of Qi Wudi (Xiao Ze; r. 483–493), this group of courtier-poets is called "the Yongming poets." In Chapter One, I will outline two contexts important to their poetics: the shifting socio-political environment and the growing influence of Buddhism in Southern Dynasties courts. The merging of the two contexts, this chapter argues, resulted in a hybrid concept of personal worth that was channeled increasingly into poetry.

Chapter Two focuses on the issue of "sound." The Yongming poets are best remembered for inventing a new form of poetic prosody, which used the concept of "four tones" (*sisheng*). To explain what their prosodic invention meant to them, I will look at how the Yongming poets pursued, displayed, and received poetic sound patterns within their courtier community. From that perspective, we will see how they created a new notion of cultural excellence.

Chapter Three looks at "poems on things" (*yongwu shi*), a poetic sub-genre popularized by the Yongming poets. Earlier studies view these poems as a kind of social verse written out of expediency, while, for instance, attending a gathering at a prince's mansion or waiting on the emperor at a banquet. My discussion will reveal a keen interest in observing things, such as a drizzle or a neglected plant, that are difficult to grasp or are easily overlooked in these poems. Cynthia L. Chennault has suggested that these poems were a means for the courtiers to present and negotiate their "personal merit" before their patrons and fellow courtiers.[16] Building on her suggestion, I will discuss how the freshness of seeing had become a crucial part in that process.

The issue turns to the perception of space in Chapter Four. The Yongming poets wrote about the "garden" (*yuan*) more prominently than earlier poets. During the Southern Dynasties, the *yuan* was being portrayed more and more as a private space that one "returned to" (*gui* or *huan*), signaling a withdrawal from officialdom and an inward turning towards one's "true nature." In that context, the Yongming poets' depictions of gardens further reflected a unique spatial experience, wherein wilderness became organized "nature," which in turn is transformed into the Buddhist void. In this fluid space, they contemplate the practical issue of self-preservation, the aesthetic imitation of nature, and the struggle for Buddhist enlightenment.

Chapter Five observes the Yongming poets as they take leave of the capital city on official assignments. The perception of motion—riding on a carriage out of the city or sailing on a boat into the distant unknown—takes center stage in their travel poems. Fatefully bound to their identity as courtiers, they conflate the idea of *xiang* or *guxiang* ("hometown") with that of *jingyi* ("capital city"), sometimes successfully, sometimes in tortured ways. The most interesting moment is when the place where they have taken up a post suddenly seems more like "hometown" than the capital city they have left behind.

Chapter Six follows them in and out of the natural landscape. Contrary to popular imagination, their identity as courtiers did not confine the vision of the Yongming poets only to rare things, ornate objects, or artificial settings within the court, as evidenced by their large corpus of landscape poems. Writing after Xie Lingyun, the first master of landscape poetry, they offer a much-needed opportunity for understanding the changes in landscape representation during the Qi-Liang period. Engaging with natural landscape as courtiers, they also pose the question of whether or not "mountains and rivers," an antithesis to officialdom, can be "obtained" (*de*)—and, if so, how to obtain it.

This book pursues two paths. It follows a series of *shengse*—sound, sight, space, and motion—in the poems of the Yongming poets. At the same time, it trails them as they take the center stage of their courtier community, negotiate their self-image before their princes and emperors, retreat temporarily to their private gardens, take leave of the capital city, and move in and out of the natural landscape. By overlapping the two paths, so to speak, I present the issue of "sound and sight" in a completely new light, challenging the old perception of the Yongming poets and their courtier culture and, fundamentally, the common practice of reading classical Chinese poems for semantic meaning only.

Individual Talent and the "Worthy One"

Introduction

Referring to Shen Yue (441–513), Wang Rong (467–493), and Xie Tiao (464–499) as the Yongming poets—an extension of the so-called Yongming style (*Yongming ti*), a new prosodic form attributed to them—is a practice developed by modern scholarship. The lives of these three courtier-poets were certainly not confined to the Yongming reign period. While Wang Rong's death did coincide with the end of Yongming, both Xie Tiao and Shen Yue survived it; particularly in the case of Shen Yue—he was already in his forties when the Yongming reign period began, and he lived for another two decades after its end. Shen Yue's long life, which lasted seventy-two years and spanned three dynasties (Song, Qi, and Liang) at a time "when the average age of his contemporary courtiers at death was less than forty,"[1] was indeed extraordinary. More importantly, the significance of these court-ier-poets and their works far transcends a single reign period or a single dynasty. When Richard B. Mather rendered "Yongming" literally as "eternal brilliance" in the title to his two-volume translation of their poems, he was already hinting at their far-reaching impact.[2]

But what was so "brilliant" about them? In the common account of Chinese literary history, they are recognized mainly, if not solely, for their creation of the Yongming style. An outstanding achievement without doubt, for the Yongming style marks not only the beginning of Chinese tonal prosody, but also a rare moment in Chinese literary history when a "creation" or even an "invention" can be substantively identified; but the Yongming style continues to evoke a sense of unease in literary critics. The *Liang shu* (Liang History) comments: "By the point [Wang Rong, Xie Tiao, and Shen Yue created the new prosodic form], [the literary trend] turned to adhering to 'sounds and rhymes,' causing a widespread preference for ornateness and superfluousness, so much so that it surpassed that which came before them."[3] Compounding the impression that the Yongming style was "ornate and superfluous" was its association with the Palace style (*Gongti*), which, flourishing about half a century later, has come to be viewed as a kind of pleasure poem meant for sensuous depiction of court ladies. The genius poet Li Bai (701–762), for example, said on one occasion, "Since the Liang and the Chen, [poetry] has become licentious and vulgar in the extreme. And Shen Xiuwen [Shen Yue] had promoted 'sound regulation' on top of that. If the ancient way (*gudao*) were to be revived, who but I would be the one [leading the way]?"[4] By the Tang dynasty (618–907), it was apparently necessary to reject the "ills" of Southern Dynasties poetry—whether "licentiousness," "vulgarity," or "sound regulation"—if one were to claim the moral high ground of the "ancient way."

The question facing us is not what the Yongming style was, but what it was *about*. While this question will be answered more fully in Chapter Two, here it suffices to say that it was about the perception of sound. If not for their probing of the questions How does one differentiate sounds? How does one refine one's hearing? the Yongming poets would not have created a new poetic form so distinctively marked by sound patterning. In that sense, their association with the later Palace style can be seen in a completely new light. As revealed in a recent study by Xiaofei Tian, the Palace style, misunderstood for a long time as being about "women and romantic passions," was in fact intensely visual and concerned a new way of seeing.[5] In light of her argument and my own, we can say that the Yongming style and the Palace style collectively reflect a broader concern for human sensory perception during the Qi and Liang periods. In fact, the association between the two styles was not that one concerned sound and the other sight; rather, they were both concerned with sound *and* sight. Not only were the

Yongming poets attempting to hear with precision and clarity, but to see with equal facility as well. Their coming signaled a new awareness among Chinese cultural elites about one's ability to hear and see. And it was not only in the Palace style, which is also known for its prosodic form, that their influence was evident:[6] for the entire period leading up to the formation of the so-called Regulated poetry (*Lüshi*), which became very popular in the Tang and continued to be composed in large numbers even as recently as the early twentieth century, the poetic issue of sound and sight remained a crucial one, as Chinese poets continued to probe the freshness of poetic imagery and prosodic patterning.[7]

Before entering their world of sound and sight, I want to situate it within the courtier culture of their day, particularly concerning a new and eclectic idea of personal worth. Through this idea, we will see why poetic "sound and sight" had unique relevance to the Yongming poets.

Individual Talent

The contemporaneous critic Zhong Rong (468–518), commenting on the popularity of their prosodic invention, described Shen, Wang, and Xie as "three worthies, all sons and grandsons of respected dukes (*guigong zisun*), who attained literary distinction as youth."[8] That the three should come to be viewed as belonging to a single elite group is itself indicative of a shifting socio-political structure wherein "literary distinction" was gaining importance.

By some measures, it was a stretch for Zhong Rong to characterize Shen Yue as "a son and grandson of respected dukes." A descendant of the Shens of Wuxing (in modern Zhejiang), a southern gentry family with a military background and members who were not even literate, Shen Yue was the first in his family to rise to prominence.[9] By contrast, Wang Rong was a descendant of the Wangs from Langye (in modern Shandong), whose deco-rated family history includes aiding the move of the Western Jin (265–316) to the south and helping to establish the Eastern Jin (317–420); and Xie Tiao came from the reputed Xies of Chenliu (in modern Henan), follow-ing a long line of influential courtiers and renowned writers.[10] Just over a century earlier, when the Simas of the Eastern Jin were relying heavily on preestablished family prestige and social status for their rule, members of reputable northern émigré families—like Wang Rong and Xie Tiao's ances-tors from five or six generations before—were the most favored in court and dominated the most powerful positions.[11] Members of southern gentry families, on the other hand, were considered inferior to the northerners and were sidelined from official appointments.[12] When Liu Yu (later, Song Wudi; r. 420–422), a southerner who made his way up from a position as a low-ranking military officer, ended the rule of the Sima family and founded the Song dynasty, the northern émigré families lost their absolute socio-political control.[13] The new court environment became such that native southerners, northern émigré clansmen, and military strongmen co-existed, alternately collaborating and competing.[14] That Shen Yue should rise to be one of the highest-ranking courtiers, influencing court politics and revered as "the godfather of literature of the present age" (*dangshi cizong*), certainly tells a unique story for his time. That Wang Rong's grandfather Wang Sengda (423–458), a defiant "son from a prestigious family" (*gui gongzi*), was put to death after having openly disrespected the Liu imperial family, and that Xie Tiao himself was married to the daughter of Wang Jingze (435–498), an illiterate general, are equally revealing of the shifting socio-political structure inside the Southern Dynasties courts.[15]

Several studies have provided detailed accounts of the recruitment system as it pertained to the changes in the socio-political structure from the Eastern Jin through the Southern Dynasties. Here, I want to highlight an argument for "individual talent" (*rencai*) made by Shen Yue amid these changes. His perspective was retrospective in that he always found support for his argument in an idealized Confucianistic past. For example, in the preface to a section called "The Favored and the Fortunate" ("En xing") in his *Song shu* (Song History), he writes:[16]

> "The true man and the mean man" (*junzi xiaoren*)—this is a comprehensive way of differentiating people. Follow the Way and one is a true man; deviate from it, and one is a mean man. Being a butcher or an angler is to have an inferior vocation; being a wall-builder is to do lowly labor; and yet Taigong rose to become the founding Master of the Zhou and Fu Yue left the legacy of a Shang minister.[17] Those were times when it did not matter if within one's family there was a succession of dukes and marquises or an inheritance of bronze vessels for feasting; the ones who were brilliant were promoted and those who were not were demoted, as only talented men were given appointments. By the time of the two Hans, such a path to appointment was not altered, as evinced by the fact that Hu Guang [*zi* Boshi; 91–172], whose family were farmers for many generations, ascended to the position of Counselor Duke; and that Huang Xian [*zi* Shudu], the son of an ox-curer, was venerated in the capital city.[18]

In Shen Yue's view, "the way of Zhou and Han" (*Zhou Han zhi dao*) was one in which "those who were talented ruled over those who were obtuse" (*yi zhi yi yu*).[19] As we will see in Chapter Five, he would romanticize such a time in the past again. The narrowing and stagnation of the recruitment system since the Wei-Jin period, according to him, were caused by the practice of appointing officials based solely on family status:

> Amid the failing and chaos at the end of the Han, Emperor Wu of Wei [Cao Cao; 155–220] was seeking to establish [the Wei] and there were many urgent affairs in his army. Instituting the "Nine Ranks System" at the time, he used it to measure the superiority and inferiority of talents, and not the high or low statuses of clans and families. The system was then preserved and continued, eventually becoming the standard. From the Wei to the Jin, since the "Nine Ranks System" could not be substituted, the arbiters in the prefectures and commanderies ranked their people according to their talent; and yet, with so many talented people in the world, promotions and replacements were rare. This was because [official appointments] had come to be based solely on the succession among members of established families, who were using the appointments to compete among themselves. The vulgar men in the prefectures and commanderies, weighing their own timely benefits, simply went with the tide of the day as they decided how many grades and ranks to bestow. As Liu Yi [d. 285] said of the situation, "among the lower ranks there were none from the prestigious families, and among the higher ranks there were no lowly clansmen."[20] As time went by, the practice became more rigid, to the point that those who wore official robes and caps made up only two ranks; and eventually there were the so-called inferior masses.[21]

To be sure, even though his argument was "progressive," Shen Yue never directly opposed "having those from prestigious families rule over those from humble ones" (*yi gui yi jian*).[22] Taking into account other statements that he made, his position was a nuanced one: on the one hand, he saw the practical need of maintaining the division between the two broad social classes, the commoners (*shu*) and the gentry (*shi*);[23] on the other hand, he repeatedly argued for more open and talent-driven appointment opportunities for members of the gentry class. As far as the later argument is concerned, his key idea was that "individual talent" was more important than family prestige. By the time Liang Wudi (Xiao Yan; r. 502–548) was in power, several measures aimed at making the recruitment system more inclusive and more talent-driven were implemented, and the idea of "individual talent" expressed in Shen Yue's preface from two decades before was further institutionalized.[24] The question arises: How was individual talent to be measured?

There are many telltale signs to indicate that during the Southern Dynasties the measure for talent had shifted significantly to literary distinction. Yao Cha (533–606), who served as Imperial Secretary for the Ministry of Personnel (Libu Shangshu) during the Chen dynasty, was the first to observe the shift: "If one were to look at the recruitment of talented people during the two Hans, one would see they gave priority to the study of the classics. In recent eras, the enlistment of people has been based primarily on literary and historical studies (*wen shi*)."[25] Yao Cha made this comment when he was explaining why both Jiang Yan (444–505) and Ren Fang (460–508) were able to secure prominent appointments and enjoy widespread fame even without family prestige and connections. Both, he noted, could compose "grand and embellished language that agreed with [the literary taste of] the time."[26] Yao Cha's observation was certainly supported by other signs: even during the earlier years of the Southern Dynasties, when the National University (Guozi xue) had not yet been completely rebuilt, an academy for *wenxue* ("literary learning") was established;[27] and, as noted by Luo Xinben and others, the period's examination system placed more emphasis on a candidate's literary skill.[28] Beyond the recruitment and appointment processes, there was also intense interest among the cultural elites in composing prose and poetry, compiling anthologies, evaluating literary histories, and critiquing literary works and writers, culminating in the rich production of literary texts that surpassed earlier times.[29]

The more specific argument for the period, in other words, was individual talent based on literary distinction. The three Yongming poets, "who attained literary distinction as youth," fully embodied this concept of individual talent. "Literary distinction," a rather broad and vague term, no doubt could encompass every aspect of the literary activities stated in the preceding paragraph. To understand what it meant to the Yongming poets, we have to bear in mind that what they specifically represent is literary distinction achieved by a courtier. Facing the courtiers were first and foremost their imperial patrons, that is, the princes and the emperors. Their respective biographies make it clear that they stood out before these patrons because of their literary distinction:

> At the beginning of the Qi, Shen Yue was Private Secretary for Invading the Enemy (Zhenglu jishi), as well as magistrate of Xiangyang Prefecture [in modern Hubei; Xiangyang ling]. The prince whom he served was Crown Prince Wenhui [Xiao Changmao; 458–493]. When the Crown Prince moved

into the Eastern Palace [in the capital city], he made Shen Yue Commandant of the Infantry (Bubing xiaowei) and put him in charge of documents and records, the Department of Longevity (Yongshou sheng), and the collation of books in the palace library. At the time, there were many scholars in the Eastern Palace, but Shen Yue was particularly favored by the Crown Prince. Every time he went to see the prince, he did not leave until the night was casting long shadows.[30]

Wang Rong was swift and eloquent with literary language, and he was especially good at composing in haste. When he composed a work, he only had to hold up his brush and it would come through. [Xiao] Ziliang [the Prince of Jingling; d. 494] was particularly fond of him and their relationship was exceptional.[31]

When [Xiao] Zilong [Prince Sui; 474–494] was in Jingzhou [in modern Hubei], he was fond of literary composition and had held several literary gatherings. Because of his literary talent, Xie Tiao was especially admired and loved by the prince. They would spend their time together, not leaving each other day or night.[32]

The three prince-patrons were, respectively, the first, second, and eighth sons of Emperor Wu of Qi. They were, particularly the Prince of Jingling, the most enthusiastic and successful patrons of literary talents during the Qi dynasty. In fact, the number of retainers and the range and extent of works and activities that the Prince of Jingling was able to amass were unsurpassed by any other imperial patron throughout the Southern Dynasties. His literary salon was where the three Yongming poets and many of their fellow courtiers gathered:

The Prince of Jingling set up the Western Villa (Xidi) to recruit literary talents. The emperor [i.e., Xiao Yan, later Liang Wudi], along with Shen Yue, Xie Tiao, Wang Rong, Xiao Chen [478–529], Fan Yun [461–503], Ren Fang, Lu Chui [470–526] and others all socialized with one another there; they were called the Eight Friends (Bayou).[33]

While the Eight Friends were the most prominent members of the prince's coterie, the literary men and courtiers associated with his coterie numbered more than sixty.[34] Based on the descriptions just given, one might say that while the courtiers served at the pleasure of their princes—and, by extension, the emperor—the Yongming poets and their fellow courtiers faced a court environment more fluid and energetic than ever before. They clearly had to compete for their princes' attention, which meant their audience also included their fellow competitors—other courtiers at large. The competition among the courtiers gave rise to many well-known anecdotes, such as these two:

> At the time, Wang Rong of Langye, being exceptionally talented, thought himself to be unmatched by his contemporaries. When he saw Ren Fang's prose, he became listless as if losing himself.[35]

> Since Ren Fang was known for his literary talent, people at the time spoke of "Ren Fang's prose and Shen Yue's poetry" ("Ren bi Shen shi"). Ren Fang detested it when he heard this. In his late years, he shifted his attention to writing poetry, attempting to surpass Shen Yue. Since he used allusions excessively, his language lacked a natural flow. He mistakenly thought the literary men in the capital city admired him for that and ended up making his language even more forced. Therefore, there was talk that his talent had been exhausted.[36]

As the tale of Ren Fang suggests, it was important for a courtier to read the response of his peers correctly, for it could help steer one's talent in the right direction and prevent its eventual loss. One might notice from the earlier citation about the Eight Friends that one of them—Xiao Yan—later ascended the throne. By then, following the unexpected death of Crown Prince Wenhui in 493, the Prince of Jingling, and Prince Sui, along with Wang Rong and Xie Tiao, had all died prematurely. Amid the complicated and dangerous struggles for court power, Shen Yue, who was highly adept at decoding court politics, survived to draft the edict that legitimized Emperor Wu of Liang (i.e., Xiao Yan), his fellow courtier at one point, and went on to live and write for many more years.[37] The fluidity of the power structure meant that competitors were also collaborators. The fact that their fellow courtiers were as much their intended audience as their patrons is evidenced by many poems discussed in the chapters to follow.

Literary distinction also had "transcendental" value. Given the political reality of their time, the Yongming poets probably felt this Confucian notion acutely.[38] In terms of military strength, the states in the south were no match for those in the north. The Northern Wei (368–534), in particular, not only lasted more than twice as long as any southern state, but also defeated its southern rivals in numerous battles.[39] Even though the southern courts did not recognize the legitimacy of the northern states, they dealt with them seriously and came to terms with their own constraints. Diplomatic exchanges between the northern and southern states continued throughout the entire period; and, in such a context, courtiers with literary distinction were the face of the southern states. An episode involving Wang Rong is particularly revealing:

> In 493, Emperor Wu, considering Wang Rong smart and eloquent, had him serve concurrently as Director of Receptions to receive Fang Jinggao and Song Bian [452–499], two foreign envoys. When Song Bian saw that Wang Rong was young, he asked, "How old is the Director of Receptions?" Wang Rong said, "I've long passed half the age of fifty." Song Bian went on to say, "I heard in the court that you wrote the 'Preface to Poems on the Qu River.'" Fang Jinggao added, "Back in the north I heard that this work of yours exceeded that of Yan Yannian [Yan Yanzhi], and I really wish I could read it." Wang Rong thus showed it to them. Two days later, Song Bian said to Wang Rong at the Hall of Jasper Pool, "In the past I read the 'Essay on the Fengshan Ceremony' by Sima Xiangru [179–117 B.C.E.] and understood the virtue of Emperor Wu of Han. Now, reading your 'Preface to Poems on the Qu River,' I can see from it the greatness of the King of Qi." Wang Rong said, "How can the splendor and glory of an imperial house really parallel those of Emperor Wu of Han? But I am even more ashamed of my humble work, which is in no way comparable to Sima Xiangru's work."[40]

In this episode, the rivalry between the Northern Wei and the Southern Qi plays out most fully in the exchange about Wang Rong's age: while Fang Jinggao and Song Bian no doubt were seeking to tease Wang Rong about his youth, the latter was quick to retort with clever language. As their conversation turned to a preface written by Wang Rong two years earlier—elegantly composed, this preface remains one of his most famous works—a different dynamic emerged.[41] The northern courtiers, having kept themselves informed of the recent works by the southern courtiers, had already heard of Wang Rong's preface. Like Yan Yanzhi before him and Yu Xin (513–581) after, Wang Rong's literary reputation was known in the northern court—a fact that caused the young courtier known for his arrogance to respond humbly.[42] The admiration of literary accomplishment transcended the political enmity on the two sides; as such, through his literary talent, a southern courtier was able to find a form of universal recognition. In this context, universal recognition was synchronic, but the same context probably helped spur it diachronically as well.

As often noted, Southern Dynasties poets and literary commentators were particularly interested in the notion of literary history. A key concept in their construction of literary history was "novelty and transformation" (*xinbian*). Xiao Zixian (489–537), the compiler of *Nan Qi shu* (Southern Qi History), expressed it best when he wrote: "In regards to literary composition, it is dreadful to only follow the past; if the poet does not exhibit novelty and transformation, he cannot exceed his predecessors and dominate the scene" (*zaihu wenzhang, mihuan fanjiu, ruo wu xinbian, buneng daixiong*).[43] In light of this concept of *xinbian*, Southern Dynasties commentators saw literary history move like tidal waves: generation after generation of writers engulfed their predecessors with ever-newer literary forms and styles.[44] Their attention was on the salient differences that made each prominent writer or generation of writers stand out. The Yongming poets and the critics of their time certainly perceived their prosodic invention from such a point of view, as revealed in this comment in the *Liang shu*: "During the Yongming reign period of the Qi, the literary men Wang Rong, Xie Tiao, and Shen Yue began to use the 'four tones' in their literary composition in order to create 'novelty and transformation.'"[45] Against their collective sense of literary history, Southern Dynasties courtiers were particularly aware of how literary distinction might bring them recognition beyond their own time; as a result, their pursuit of literary innovation was very pronounced, as if it was an attempt to be the tidal wave of their time.[46] Their intended audience may thus include those whom they envisioned in the future. As the courtier's definitive trait, literary distinction possessed meaning and value for him at all levels. As he openly displayed his literary talent, he might catch the attention of his prince or emperor, send a coded message to his fellow courtiers, or even spread his name and transmit it to posterity.

"The Worthy One"

While the ideal of "individual talent" permeated the court environment of the Southern Dynasties, another conception of personal worth was also emerging. The source of this concept was found not in an idealized past, but in a new force in Chinese court culture: Buddhism.

The most identifiable patron and adherent of Buddhism in the first half of the Southern Dynasties was the Prince of Jingling. He is remembered for organizing the largest Buddhist convention of the period, launching several compilation and translation projects of Buddhist scriptures, hosting numerous renowned monks, composing Buddhist essays and poems, and more.[47] As key members of his literary coterie, Shen, Wang, and Xie became active supporters and participants in his various Buddhist initiatives.[48] After the Yongming reign period, Shen Yue continued to practice Buddhism and produce works in the area under Emperor Wu of Liang, who aspired to be a Buddhist king.[49] While this book is not a complete study of the influence of Buddhism on the court culture or the poetry of the Qi-Liang period, it will outline an important issue in that regard—one that can be traced to the Buddhist concept of "the worthy one" (*xianzhe*) as explicated by Shen Yue.

During the Southern Dynasties, the proponents of Buddhism often found themselves having to affirm the relevance and legitimacy of the Buddhist doctrine of karma and the Buddhist path to enlightenment within the Chinese cultural context. In one such effort—apparently prompted by the shocking assertion by a courtier that "body and spirit go into extinction together" and hence the irrelevance of karmic retribution[50]—Shen Yue contemplates what makes us human and, as he continues, what differentiates us from each other:

> What causes [the separation between] the worthy one (*xian*) and the obtuse one (*yu*)? It is all due to the possession of knowledge or lack thereof. The obtuse one knows little, and the worthy one knows much. As the myriad things combine and multiply, those from all quarters ponder their immensity; and, while their temperament may be illuminated or obscured, the wonder of Truth is always profound and subtle. When they follow the path to seek the Truth, each person being different from others due to his illuminated or obscured temperament, they eventually end up in the superior or the inferior ranks. From then on, the grades and ranks become steeper and steeper, with those at the top exhausting the original source and seeking to the farthest limit. Pushing each other forward and looking up to one another, they respond to whatever can be exhausted; as their path has been exhausted, then no subtlety is left without having been fully comprehended.[51]

What Shen Yue calls "the worthy one" and "the obtuse one" here he would later call "the saint" (*sheng*) and "the ordinary person" (*fan*); while they all "embody spirit" (*han ling*), he notes, the "saint" exists through eternity while the "ordinary person" alone vanishes into extinction.[52] He describes the difference as the ability "to know" (*zhi*) or the temperament (*qingxing*) that is either "illuminated" (*xiao*) or "obscured" (*mei*). For a moment, he seems to be describing a quest among "the worthy ones," with each propelling the other into engaging in a more and more subtle form of "knowledge."[53]

From the Buddhist perspective, the most vital "knowledge" is to know the illusory nature of the world; that is, to know that what might appear real or permanent is only an illusion. How does one grasp this truth? In Shen Yue's Buddhist discourse, the process of grasping this truth is never "sudden" (*dun*).

What really distinguishes "the worthy ones," Shen Yue suggests, is their ability to continue to refine their perception, so that "no subtlety is left without having been fully comprehended." In another *yi* ("arguments"), he would describe the process as a life-long accumulation that could continue into the next life:

> If the merit of molding and smelting accumulates gradually in this life, then the fruition obtained in the next life will cause the Truth that is perceived to become more refined. Knowledge that has become more refined will have its fruition in further futures until Buddhahood is eventually reached—the process never severs and never stops.[54]

"Molding and smelting" (*taolian*) or "practice" (*xiu*), as Shen Yue would argue in yet another *yi*, is an exertion of "effort" (*li*) that will not go to waste.[55]

The program that Shen Yue had outlined for "the worthy ones"—the able practitioners of Buddhism such as himself—readily reflects the influence of the Chengshi school of Buddhist scholasticism. By all accounts, this school was very influential among the members of the imperial family and courtiers of the Qi and Liang dynasties, and Shen Yue's Buddhist thought is "thoroughly consistent with its teachings."[56] The Chengshi school based its teachings on the *Chengshi lun* (*Satyasiddhiśāstra*), authored by Harivarman (ca. 310–390) and translated by Kumārajīva (344–413) in 411–412.[57] Divided into 202 sections (*pin*) in its transmitted form, the *Chengshi lun* delineates a course of incremental progression based on varying levels of cognitive power and mental quality.[58] It teaches, for example, that

> there are two types of people in the world: "the wise ones" and "the obtuse ones." Those who are not good at differentiating the *skandha*, the *dhātu*, and the various *āyatana*, and the *dvādaśāṅgika-pratītya-samutpāda* and other *dharmas* are called "the obtuse ones"; and those who are good at differentiating them are called "the wise ones."[59]

The phrase "good at differentiation" (*shan fenbie*) highlights the school's particularly analytical and systematic approach to enlightenment, which, at its most basic level, involves the following kind of analysis:

> The wheels and other parts are combined and hence named "cart"; the five *skandha* are combined and hence named "person."[60]

> If in fact there is fragrance in the wind, then the fragrance should be within the wind—just like fragrant oil, wherein the fragrance should be within the oil; but that is not the case.[61]

The key is to analyze the components of all perceptions, thereby "destructing" them. At a certain level, the Chengshi school maintained that all perceptions were real and could not become empty until they were completely broken down through repeated analysis.[62] Therefore,

> analyzing those five objects [i.e., five objects of the senses: form, sound, smell, taste, and touch], the school reduces them to molecules, and further reduces them to even finer atoms, and by thus repeating the process the school finally attains the finest elements. . . . Going one step further, the school attains the void.[63]

The course of incremental progression in the *Chengshi lun* has, from low to high, three levels—extinguishing the *jiaming xin* ("mind of provisional reality"), and then the *fa xin* ("dharma mind"), and finally the *kong xin* ("mind of emptiness").[64] Advancing from one level to the next required that a person first gain insight into the emptiness of all perception, then of perceiving itself and of oneself, and finally of emptiness itself. Ji Zang (549–623), the pioneering Sanlun theorist, sharply criticized the Chengshi school for its "hīnayānist approach" of "dismantling the dharmas to exemplify emptiness" (*chai[xi] fa mingkong*),[65] to the effect that the school waned in the Sui; its popularity in the Qi and the Liang, however, speaks to the relative strength of its analytical and systematic approach at a time when Buddhism was achieving widespread influence among Chinese elites.

The influence of the Chengshi school can perhaps explain Shen Yue's unusual awareness of the intricate processes of the mind. As noted in earlier studies, Shen Yue had produced one of the best analyses of *nian* ("thought-instant," which often has the dual meaning of "concentrated thought" [*smṛti*] and "moment" [*kṣaṇa*] in Chinese usage), that minute working of the mind. Through the analysis, Shen Yue explains why one's progress towards enlightenment is impeded:

> If within a single thought-instant there are yet other thoughts (*yi nian er jian*), then there is no recourse for it to become complete. Since there is no means by which it can become complete together with others, chaos and entanglement invade the mind in alternation. One single thought-instant has not yet become complete (*yi nian wei cheng*) and other minor thoughts have already arisen along with one another. The minor thoughts that have arisen along with one another, like those before them, cannot become complete together with others.[66]

In his final analysis, Shen Yue merges the relative "forgetting" (*wang*) of Daoism and the fundamental "emptiness" (*kong*; Skt. *śūnyatā*) of Buddhism: "To be free of shallowness or confusion comes from Double Forgetting (*jianwang*).[67] With this Double Forgetting, one attains Total Illumination (*jianzhao* ["emptiness"])."[68] Nevertheless, his dissection of the stream of thought into individual "thought-instants" clearly reflects the analytical and systematic approach of Buddhism. As we shall see, Shen Yue's interpretation of the Buddhist process of "refinement"—achieved by directing the mind to the analysis of a smaller and smaller area—strikingly recalls the portrayal of sound and sight in the poems he and his fellow courtier-poets composed. Xiaofei Tian insightfully traces the new way of seeing in the Palace style to the Buddhist concepts of concentration (*ding* or *zhi*; Skt. *śamatha*) and illumination (*zhao*), citing in particular Shen Yue's analysis of *nian* in the form of "a succession of thought-instants,"[69] which I have also discussed here. The Palace style poets' captivated view of a brief moment of illumination, their intense gaze that turns to illusion, and their eyes' interplay with light, shadow, and reflection, Tian argues, reveal a profound concentration of the mind in the Buddhist sense.[70] In this study, we shall see that the Buddhist perspective had come into play in the form and process of Chinese poetry even before the Palace style.

Seen through a complex lens, the underlying dynamic—and perhaps contradiction as well—between the exuberance of "individual talent" and the acute grasp of "the worthy one" might reveal itself to be the truly new trajectory of early medieval Chinese poetry. At the core of this poetry, in other words, was a hybrid concept of personal worth. On the one hand, this concept was motivated by a Confucian worldview that defined individual talent as it related to a larger community and to the needs of the state; on the other hand, it had taken on a Buddhist perspective, which gave new meaning and value to the ability to notice, perceive, and analyze refined things and subtle phenomena. Increasingly channeled into poetry, this new idea of personal worth was central to the self-expression and self-representation of the Yongming poets.

Knowing Sound

The Han dynasty writer Yang Xiong (53 B.C.E.–18 C.E.) famously coined the derogatory epithet "worm carving and seal engraving" (*diaochong zhuanke*), which has been used by Chinese commentators to denounce the "empty" pursuit of artistry in literature.[1] In the original context, Yang Xiong was speaking specifically about *fu*, a poetic genre famous for its verbose and ornate style. But the overarching resonance of his comment—from Confucius' warning against "glib speech and pleasing appearance" (*qiaoyan lingse*) to traditional and even some modern scholars' trivialization of literary technique—gives special weight to a statement made by Shen Yue. Replying to his challenger Lu Jue (472–499), he wrote:

> How did it happen there was something so wonderful as this and yet the sages did not esteem it? It was probably because adroitness in tuning sounds and rhymes was not appropriate for moral instruction. It was not considered urgent by the sages and the men of wisdom in establishing their teaching. For this reason, Yang Xiong compared it to "worm carving and seal engraving," saying that "a mature man would not do it."[2]

The "wonderful" thing that Shen Yue was referring to was none other than the new prosodic form that he and his fellow Yongming poets had invented. Alluding to Yang Xiong's remark, his awareness of the prejudicial attitude toward what he was promoting, and his obvious disagreement, were refreshingly new. Victor H. Mair and Tsu-lin Mei postulate that Chinese tonal prosody can be traced to a Sanskrit poetics that was filtered through numerous Buddhist chanting practices and translation projects of the early medieval period.[3] How did such a diffusion of prosodic technique effect a rethinking of poetic form and artistry among the Chinese cultural elites, such as that reflected in Shen Yue's remark? In that connection, this chapter asks a simple question: What did their prosodic pursuit *mean* to the Qi-Liang courtier-poets, who, though no doubt deeply influenced by Buddhism, were nonetheless not members of the Buddhist clergy? An answer to this question will be suggested through glimpses into how these courtiers exhibited their prosodic skill in the court or simply in personal exchanges among themselves. From that perspective, it becomes clear that it was through the process of poetic prosody—from creating and reciting, to decoding sound patterns—that their pursuit was fully manifested.

Four Tones and Eight Defects

Before proceeding to the main argument, a few words need to be said about the issue of "four tones and eight defects" (*sisheng babing*), which since the Tang have been recognized as the core of Shen Yue's prosodic theory.[4] The problem is not with the "four tones," which was clearly a linguistic and prosodic concept that Shen Yue and his fellow poets were using and promoting. In fact, Shen Yue and his acquaintance Zhou Yong (d. 488) were among the earliest known persons to have compiled a type of lexicon, called *shengpu* ("tone register"), based on the concept.[5] However, the attribution of the so-called eight defects to Shen Yue is problematic, even though it has become a conventional practice to describe his poetic prosody as based predominately upon them.[6] These "eight defects" are no more than eight rules regulating the placement of specific types of sound, including initials, finals, and tones, in a poem.[7] Victor Mair and Tsu-lin Mei have traced the Chinese concept *bing* ("[poetic] defect") to Sanskrit *doṣa*, but exactly how the concept was disseminated in China is still not entirely clear.[8] Let me simply make three points. First, *Bunkyō hifuron* (A Discussion of the Secret Treasury of the Literary Mirror) by Kūkai (774–835), the only surviving source that describes the "eight defects" in detail, only cites Shen Yue as *one of several commentators* on five of these "defects."[9] Second, Shen Yue makes no mention of any of them or even the concept of "defect" (*bing* or *shengbing*) at all in his surviving writing about poetic prosody. Third, Xiao Zixian, a historian who lived very close to Shen Yue's time, has given a simpler account of his prosodic invention:

> Shen Yue and the rest all used *gong* and *shang* in their literary compositions. They treated "level," "rising," "departing," and "entering" as the "four tones"; and, making use of them to create tonal prosody, they did not allow any addition or reduction. The world called it the "Yongming style."[10]

> 約等文皆用宮商，以平上去入為四聲，以此制韻，不可增減，世呼
> 為「永明體」．

In his criticism of their prosodic practice, the contemporaneous critic Zhong Rong mentioned only two defects—*fengyao* ("wasp's waist") and *hexi* ("crane's knee")—without attributing their invention to the Yongming poets.[11] But the Tang historian Li Yanshou, by whose time the discussion and works about "defects" had proliferated, would have it that

> Shen Yue and the rest all used *gong* and *shang* in their literary compositions. They treated "level," "rising," "departing," and "entering" as the "four tones"; and, making use of them to create tonal prosody, **they formed [the rules] "level head," "raised tail," "wasp's waist," and "crane's knee."** They wanted the sounds and rhymes within the five syllables [of a line] to be completely different, and the *jue* and *zhi* sounds to be distinct between the two lines [of a couplet].[12] They did not allow any addition or reduction. The world called it the "Yongming style."[13]

> 約等文皆用宮商，將平上去入四聲，以此制韻，有平頭、上尾、蜂
> 腰、鶴膝．五字之中，音韻悉異，兩句之內，角徵不同，不可增
> 減．世呼為「永明體」．

There is not only a clear interpolation of the names of the defects in Li Yanshou's statement, which retains almost word-for-word the earlier account by Xiao Zixian, but also an unequivocal attribution of the defects to Shen Yue and his peers. However, even in this reconstituted statement, only four of the "eight defects" are mentioned. That Shen Yue and his fellow poets were using "four tones" to create poetic prosody is without question. Shen Yue seemed to have been engaged in interpreting and even promoting several of what were later called "eight defects," but he was not the only one doing so during his time. The attribution of the "eight defects" to Shen Yue is at best tenuous. More importantly, to study and judge his prosody based solely on a set of rules only obscures its complex meaning, framing it once again in the old argument that he was engaging in "worm carving and seal engraving."[14]

"Knowing Sound"

The Yongming poets called those who shared their ability to control sound *zhiyin* ("one who [truly] knows sound").[15] In earlier times, the epithet was not meant for one who understood the sound of poetry or of language, but for one who understood music. The most famous *zhiyin* story, told in the *Lüshi Chunqiu*, is that of the great zither player Bo Ya and the one person who could truly understand his music, Zhong Ziqi. When Zhong Ziqi died, Bo Ya broke his zither and never played again.[16] The story speaks to a cultural ideal that combined aesthetics, human relationships, and moral integrity. The bond between the musician and his *zhiyin* (if he was lucky enough to chance upon one) was deeply personal and highly exclusive; the experience they shared through the musician's music was ungraspable by others, the non-*zhiyin*. At the same time, that ideal was based on a set of "objective" values that shaped the distinctive character of the Chinese elite culture, including treating music as the highest form of aesthetics and treating male friendship and loyalty as crucial to a man's life. Constantly evoking the idea of *zhiyin*, the Yongming poets were not simply attempting to counter the resistance they met from certain quarters or to raise their own profile; their clever use of the epithet revealed their new interpretation of a prevailing cultural ideal.

It is easy to forget that "four tones" was a novel concept that could generate awe, admiration, confusion, and contention in the early medieval period. The tone of a Middle Chinese syllable was a suprasegmental element that affected its shape, pitch, and possibly length, and the four categories of tones that Shen Yue and his peers had identified were variously named "level" (*ping*), "rising" (*shang*), "departing" (*qu*), and "entering" (*ru*).[17] The unique sound quality of their language, as they had come to realize, was caused by the effect of tones. According to Shen Yue's description, the interaction among the "four tones," when they were successfully "crafted" in a poem, sounded like this to their ears: *gao xia di ang* ("high and [then] falling, low and [then] rising").[18] Being attuned to sound based on this new concept often became a form of display in the Southern Dynasties courts;

and whether one "knew sound" or "did not know sound" was relevant to one's personal image in the eyes of others. A widely circulated anecdote has it that Emperor Wu of Liang once posed the question to the court official Zhou She (469–524): "What are the 'four tones'?"[19] Modern scholars are quick to point out that Emperor Wu must have known what the "four tones" were, since he was active in the same literary coterie as the Yongming poets about a decade before his enthronement.[20] Closer to his day, Emperor Wu's question was enough to arouse gossip, giving him the reputation of being "a king who does not know the 'four tones.'"[21] Recounting a slightly different version of the anecdote, Liu Shanjing of the Sui added that people at the time "sighed at how Xiao the Sovereign lacked understanding" (*tan Xiaozhu zhi buwu*).[22] Emperor Wu's "ignorance" was in stark contrast to the wit of Zhou She, who, according to the anecdote, gave this answer: "The Son-of-Heaven is sage-like and wise." Zhou She's wit is only revealed when one analyzes the four words he said:

	天	子	聖	哲
Translation:	Son-of-Heaven		sage-like	wise
Transcription:[23]	*than*	*tsiQ*	*syeingH*	*trat*
Tone:	level	rising	departing	entering
Tone pattern:[24]	—	/	\	^
	A	B	C	D

This response stood out because it was a loaded performance, displaying not only knowledge and wit, but also confidence and appropriateness; and all of that led back to a distinctive individual image. Zhou She, as it turned out, would be remembered as one of only a handful of courtiers noted for their ability in "sounds and rhymes" (*yinyun*) in the standard histories of the Southern Dynasties. In an elite culture where family genealogy and family education were dominant forces in one's training, Zhou She's legacy led directly back to his father, Zhou Yong, who shared Shen Yue's reputation as a pioneer of the concept of "four tones" and of "tone register."[25] An eccentric semi-recluse who nonetheless was a regular presence at various literary gatherings hosted by the Prince of Jingling, Zhou Yong produced melodious "words and rhymes" (*ciyun*) that were said to have made his audience "forget their fatigue."[26] One account has Zhou Yong saying to the high-ranking official Wang Jian (452–489), who had just asked him what he ate while living by himself in the mountains:[27]

| 赤 | 米 | 白 | 鹽, | 綠 | 葵 | 紫 | 蓼 |

Translation:
    Red rice and white salt, green mallow and purple knotweed.

Transcription:

| *tshyeik* | *meiQ* | *beik* | *yam* | *luk* | *gwi* | *tsiQ* | *laoQ* |

Tone:

| entering | rising | entering | level, | entering | level | rising | rising |

Tone pattern:

| ^ | / | ^ | - | ^ | - | / | / |
| **D** | B | **D** | A | **D** | A | B | B |

Notice that the first half of Zhou Yong's answer contains two "entering" tones—that is, "abrupt and hasty" (*zhicu*) ending sounds, as in *-p, -t, -k* (also called glottal stops).[28] Here, Zhou Yong primarily uses this tone to create a contrast with other tones, resulting in an exaggerated sound quality that can still be heard in Cantonese and other modern Chinese southern dialects. The second half of his answer begins with yet another entering tone, but it is followed by a level tone and two rising tones—the overall effect is an obvious contrast to the abruptness and hastiness of the first half of his answer. The distinctive sound quality of Zhou Yong's answer must have been particularly memorable to his listeners. Without the many challenges, exchanges, discussions, and displays surrounding the novel concept "four tones" that must have taken place in the courts and the literary circles of the day, the Southern Dynasties would not have survived in Chinese collective cultural memory as a period of distinctive innovation and experimentation in prosody. To be "one who knows sound" at the time was to be at the forefront of an emerging form of literary skill and knowledge.

What Shen Yue did was to display that new literary skill and knowledge through poetry. Having discovered the suprasegmental elements that caused a group of Chinese syllables to sound different from other groups, Shen Yue simply translated the concept into a broad guideline for poetry composition. He presented his proposal in a famous essay included in the *Song shu*, the history that Emperor Wu of Qi charged him to compile.[29] His idea was, in fact, very simple: one should use syllables that have different tones and avoid those with the same tone within a line, as well as between the two lines of a couplet. This principle ensured that the sounds would "alternate" or "mutate," giving rise to the sense that they were not stagnant, but constantly changing, as the lines unfolded. If rhythm is "the unbroken continuity of a flux," then his prosodic idea signified a major awakening to rhythm in a fresh, new way.[30] In the end, giving no more than a general guiding principle on how to elevate sound change in a poem, his proposal left open the possibility of creating many different tone patterns. Consequently, what emerged from his (and his fellow poets') poetics was not tonal prosody as a highly regulated form, but rather, tonal prosody as a distinctive concept. However, given the novelty of the concept, being able to comprehend, practice, and appreciate it required delicate and meticulous skill. It was only between two people who "knew sound" that its manifestation could be fully realized.

At the height of their prosodic movement, the Yongming poets apparently aroused much enthusiasm in the literary circles in and around Jiankang, the capital city, attracting admirers and followers. As Zhong Rong remembered it, "those learned men who admired them sought only refinement in their literary composition; fastidiously tuning the small details in their tone patterns, they attempted to outdo each other."[31] However, an episode that supposedly took place during Shen Yue's late years, when he had retired to a suburb, gives us better insight into how his prosodic idea actually worked. At the time he was drafting what would turn out to be one of his most celebrated works, "*Fu* on Living in the Suburbs" ("Jiaoju fu").[32] Totaling an impressive 450 lines, the transmitted version of this elegant *fu* begins by recounting Shen Yue's own personal history, tracing back to his fifteen generations of ancestors, and ends on a note of reflection upon his own life. The episode has Shen Yue inviting Wang Yun (481–549), a younger poet whom he admired greatly and took under his wing during his later years, to his residence to read through the draft. According to the account, "When Wang Yun read on to *tshi ngiek lan gwan* ['the joined arc of the Female Rainbow'], Shen Yue clapped his hands in great excitement and said: 'I always worried that others would read *ngiek* ('rainbow') as *ngiei*!'"[33] Now, why is *ngiek*, and not *ngiei*, the "correct" pronunciation? The different pronunciations do not affect the meaning of the word in question (it means "rainbow" in either case); the difference is only in the ending sounds (-*ek* versus -*ei*), with the former consisting of an "entering" tone and the latter a "level" tone. The narrator of the account offered no further explanation, but a fuller story will emerge once we link it back to Shen Yue's prosodic ideas. Another line that is syntactically parallel to it follows the line in question:

Lines 323–324:

Riding the joined arc of the Female Rainbow,	駕雌蜺之連卷
I drift along the endless flow of the Heavenly River.[34]	泛天江之悠永

Below are the two tone-patterns of these two lines that resulted from reading the word for "rainbow" in two different pronunciations.

Reading for "rainbow":	*ngiek*	*ngiei*
Tone-pattern:		
Line 323	\ - ^ - - /	\ - - - - /
Line 324	\ - - - - /	\ - - - - /
Tone-pattern by letter:		
Line 323	C A **D** A A B	C A A A A B
Line 324	C A A A A B	C A A A A B

The reading *ngiek* would give the two lines their only "entering" tone, without which their sounds would certainly be less elevated, as would be the case if the reading *ngiei* was adopted. Shen Yue's preferred reading obviously created a tonal contrast (represented as "AD") between the two syllables *tshi ngiek* ("Female Rainbow") in line 323 as well as a tonal contrast ("AD" versus "AA") between the two syllables and their matching syllables (i.e., *than kong*; "Heavenly River") in the next line. This reading, hence, fulfilled the prosodic idea of elevating the sound change within a line and between the two lines of a couplet. As the account goes on to depict, when Wang Yun comes to line 336 in Shen Yue's *fu*, he becomes so taken by its rhythm that he is "beating the time and praising it" (*jijie chengzan*).[35] As Richard Mather points out,[36] Shen Yue was describing "the celestial landscape of his own spiritual quest" in the part of his *fu* that contains the line:

Lines 333–338		Tone pattern	
Magnificent, precipitous,	巍峨崇崒	- - - ^	A A A D
Their tall branches brush the sun.	喬枝拂日	- - ^ ^	A A D D
High-soaring, towering,	巋嶷昭嵉	- ^ - -	A D A A
Their fallen rocks pile up to the stars.	墜石堆星	\ ^ - -	C D A A

| Sharp and steep, rugged and abrupt, | 岑崟峛屹 | - - ^ ^ | A A D D |
| Some sunken, some level.[37] | 或坳或平 | ^ - ^ - | D A D A |

Notice that except for one single syllable (the first in the fourth line, denoted as "C") all the other syllables in the six lines have either the "level" tone or the "entering" tone. The two types of tones were distinctively different from each other. As mentioned before, the "entering" tone was an "abrupt and hasty" sound; the "level" tone, by contrast, was a sound that could be indefinitely prolonged in a level manner.[38] In the lines given, the stark contrast between the "levelness" of the "level" tone and the "abruptness" of the "entering" tone perfectly matches the image of the austere landscape. As the last line goes: "Some sunken, some level" (as noted above, the tone-pattern of this line is " ^ - ^ - "). In addition, the single "departing" tone ("\") in the syllable *drwiH* (which means "fallen") of line 336—the line that completely engrosses Wang Yun—adds a fitting and timely twist to the sound symbolism. Fully vindicated, Shen Yue is said to have told Wang Yun: "'One who knows sound' (*zhiyin zhe*) is rare, and true appreciation has since vanished. The reason I invited you is exactly for these few lines."[39] Through this exchange, regardless of how fictional its account might be, their entire prosodic pursuit still came alive to a later audience. What transpired through the meeting of the two *zhiyin* was the recasting of a cultural ideal through a new form of knowledge. Even though it retained a deeply personal quality and an exclusive aura, the intricacy and meticulousness involved in the process reflect a very different kind of aesthetic sensibility and a transformation of the old cultural ideal. Most strikingly, the display of a few verse lines, or even of a single tone, would now determine if that intellectual, aesthetic, and personal process of "knowing sound" had succeeded or failed. In light of the fact that the specific work under discussion here is a *fu*, it is also important to note that while Shen Yue and his fellow poets' prosodic principle has only been narrowly understood in the context of their *shi* ("lyric poetry") in modern scholarship, their attempt was to apply it broadly to all literary forms.[40]

In an earlier literary tradition, the most crucial idea in artistic expression and appreciation was *zhi* ("what is intently on the mind"), which often spoke to one's moral essence or high-minded aspirations in a Confucian or Daoist sense.[41] According to *Lüshi Chunqiu*, "When Bo Ya began to play the zither, his mind went to a high mountain. Zhong Ziqi said: 'You are great at playing the zither! Marvelous and magnificent, just like Mount

Tai.'"[42] Mount Tai (in Shandong) is where Confucius once stood and, look-ing down, realized how small the world is.[43] Mutual mental transportation to Mount Tai was what transpired between Bo Ya and Zhong Ziqi through his music; guiding their interaction was *what* the mind was intent on or *where* the mind was going. The object or destination of the mind, with its strong moralistic overtone, was central to earlier artistic expression and appreciation. In light of this tradition, what Shen Yue proposed was signifi-cantly different. In his *Song shu* essay, he concludes that "the lofty language and marvelous lines" in earlier literature were achieved only unwittingly and not through *si* ("conscious thought"), which he sees as the force behind the process of *truly* "knowing sound."[44] As trivial as it might seem to some, his fastidious attention to a single tone reflects just this line of thinking. The differentiation of the "four tones" among the syllables, the crafting of distinctive sound patterns in a poem, the "accurate" decoding and apprecia-tion of sound and sense in poetry recitation were all exercises in "conscious thought." He speaks as a *zhiyin* in a letter to Wang Yun:

> When I look at the poems that you sent me, I find them truly exquisite mod-els. Their harmonious sounds spread over the pages, and light and shadow are cast through every character. . . . As their combined brilliance shines forth brightly, the orchids sway and the jades tinkle. On the true meaning of "attaining harmony," how can that gained through the reeds of a mouth or-gan compare to yours? All that should be attained by effort of thought (*sili*) is realized to the fullest in these poems. I sigh with admiration as I recite and ponder over them, lingering back and forth and becoming oblivious of my own thoughts (*wang nian*).[45]

Unlike the earlier aesthetic of *zhi*, Shen Yue's idea of "conscious thought" or "effort of thought" did not speak specifically to a reflection upon a moral ideal or a morally ideal act, but directly to the *process* of the mind. Its man-ifestation through the creating and decoding of intricate sound patterns bespeaks the attentive, cognitive, and sensory qualities of the process. The third-century poet Lu Ji (261–303) had already articulated the notion that sound changes in poetry were "inconstant" (*wuchang*) and thus difficult to control.[46] Two centuries later, Shen Yue would argue for a new aesthetic ideal based on the mind's ability to overcome the problem identified by Lu Ji. In Shen Yue's new aesthetic, the meeting of two *zhiyin* was the interac-tion of two minds that shared the unique ability to grasp the changes from one tone to the next in a flow of sounds.

The Process of Grasping Sound

The conventional way of reading premodern Chinese poetry is particularly unsuited to the understanding of the Yongming style. Instead of approaching the poems written in the style as "silent readers of mute texts,"[47] we should imagine them in a process in which sound, imagery, and meaning all unfold together. Often enough, that process of unfolding is itself the meaning of Yongming-style poetry. Earlier studies have found "little meaning" in the three short poems that I have chosen for the discussion to follow, but I see them as "sound poems" whose meaning can only come alive if we imagine the interaction between their words and their sounds and between the poet and his intended audience.

In the following poem, the cries of gibbons come through the night:

Shen Yue, "Listening to Gibbons' Cries at Stone Dike Rapids"	石塘瀨聽猿	Tones
Kau! *Kau*! Gibbons in the night cry out;	噭噭夜猿鳴	C C C A A
Coat upon coat, morning mists are merging.	溶溶晨霧合	A A A C D
I know not how far or how near the sounds are,	不知聲遠近	D A A B C
But see only mountains piled upon mountains.	惟見山重沓	A C A A D
Having rejoiced in the calls from the eastern ridges,	既歡東嶺唱	C A A B C
I pause to wait for answers from the western cliffs.[48]	復佇西巖答	D B A A D

Under the coat of the night and the approach of "morning mists," Shen Yue's view is reduced to the silhouette of overlapping mountains, and with these mountains acting as "sound walls," he "does not know" (*buzhi*) how far or near the sources of the sounds are. In the end, he *grasps* the alternating pattern in the animal sounds, and he celebrates it. This act of grasping is that of the mind overcoming; it indicates the success of attention. However, there is another level of "grasping sound" in the poem. As often noted, nasal sounds such as *m, n, ny, ng* can create a particularly strong sense of consonance when they echo one another. Among the poem's 30 syllables, 16 of them have nasal endings.

噭 噭 夜 猿 鳴
    -n -ng
溶 溶 晨 霧 合
-ng-ng-n

不 知 聲 遠 近
-ng -n -n

惟 見 山 重 沓
-n -n -ng

既 歡 東 嶺 唱
-n -ng -ng -ng

復 佇 西 巖 答
-m

Obviously, Shen Yue wanted to exaggerate the effect of nasal sounds in this poem (and one can still hear it, even in Mandarin Chinese). Even more interestingly, he would have the nasal endings alternate with the glottal stop *-p* (an "abrupt and hasty" sound, i.e., the entering tone) at the end of the lines:

嗷嗷夜猿鳴
-ng

溶溶晨霧合
-p

不知聲遠近
-n

惟見山重沓
-p

既歡東嶺唱
-ng

復佇西巖答
-p

The alternation between *-ng/-n* and *-p*—still loud and clear in Cantonese—can be likened to the "call and answer" among the gibbons. In other words, an audience that has comprehended this alternating sound pattern would then have taken part in the poet's experience of grasping the gibbons' cries. Through "successful" reading, the two layers of unfolding—the poet's grasping of the gibbon's cries and the reader's grasping of the poet's sound pattern—would be integrated into one unified act, completing the meaning and the purpose of the poem. One can only imagine that in Shen Yue's day, reciting or listening to this poem must have been an alluring experience.

The most common type of "sound poem" found in Shen Yue's corpus is about musical instruments, which were popular subjects in earlier *fu*, a genre known for its rhetorical force. On first appearance, Shen Yue's *shi* on musical instruments are only highly compressed versions of earlier *fu*. However, their "compressed" form reveals a different and more intricate verbal art. A good example is his poem about the twelve-stringed zither, *zheng*. Much like the previous one, this poem unfolds as a "live" experience.

Shen Yue, "On the Twelve-Stringed Zither"	詠箏詩	Tones
The zither of Qin emits excellent music;	秦箏吐絕調	A A B D C
Its jade bridges spread clear melodies.	玉柱揚清曲	D B A A D
While its strings accordingly tighten and break away,	絃依高張斷	A A A A C
Its sounds continue on with those magical fingers.	聲隨妙指續	A A C B D
I only hear the music winding around the beams—	徒聞音繞梁	A A A C A
How would I know that her face is like jade?[49]	寧知顏如玉	A A A A D

The "excellent music" stands in contrast to the "clear melodies," and the focus on the player's fingers further intensifies the sense of listening and watching. The third line captures the entire sensory experience:

絃 依 高 張 斷
Its strings accordingly tighten and break away

Tone pattern:　— — — — \
　　　　　　　A A A A **C**

Through *duan* ("break away"), the line disrupts the continuation in the "level" tone. In this unusual tone-pattern, one not only "hears" the breaking away of *zheng* music, but also "sees" and even "feels"—through the movement in one's mouth when pronouncing the line—the fingers letting go of the strings. Shen Yue has this exaggerated form of sound pattern continue through the last couplet:

徒 聞 音 繞 梁
I only hear the music *winding* around the beams—

— — — \ —
A A A **C** A

寧 知 顔 如 玉
How would I know that her face is like *jade*?
— — — — ^
A A A A **D**

Again, there is only one non-level tone in each of the two lines. Confucius was said to be so captivated by the *Shao* music that he heard in Qi that for three months he "did not know the taste of meat" (*buzhi rouwei*).[50] In these lines, the poet declares he "does not know" the performer's face is as beautiful as jade. This moment of "not knowing" (if we believe him) belongs to "one who knows sound." The dual meaning of "knowing sound" ("knowing music" and "knowing the sound of poetry") plays out wonderfully in this poem.

Wang Rong's poem set in the zither room would take the dual meaning of "knowing sound" further. Simply being present in the room, he "hears" music.[51]

Moving My Mat to the Zither Room: Writing at the Instruction of the Director of Instruction   移席琴室應司徒教   **Four Tones**

The snowy cliff looks as if it has retained the moon;   雪崖似留月   D A B A D
The lichen path appears to be covered in clouds.   蘿徑若披雲   A C D A A
Gurgling, rapids-over-the-rocks rush down;   潺湲石溜寫   A A D C B
Twittering—I hear the mountain rain.   綿蠻山雨聞   A A A B A

Unlike the last poem by Shen Yue, these lines by Wang Rong do not present a musical performance.[52] Instead, it is a *meditation* about music: simply being present in the zither room—perhaps with the sound of a zither playing in the background, perhaps without music at all—the poet encounters a series of natural scenes. In the first couplet, his mind's eye sees two (or four?) soundless images. The verbs *si* and *ruo* (both can mean "alike" or "as if") suggest an illusive quality, as if the poet is uncertain about his "vision." In the second couplet, he not only "sees" but also "hears" the "music," suggesting a deepening of his meditation. As the poem moves from silent to sounding images, its syllables also begin to sound:

Gurgling, rapids-over-the-rocks   潺   湲   石   溜   寫
    rush down;   *-an* *-an*
Twittering—I can hear the mountain   綿   蠻   山   雨   聞
    rains.   *man* *man* *-an*   *men*

The first two syllables in line 1, *dzran ghwan* ("gurgling"), are a pair of rhyming binomes (words of two syllables that rhyme). In addition, they are matched in line 2 by *man-3by man-2a* ("twittering"), a pair of alliterative binomes (words of two syllables that have the same initial sound). In addition, the four syllables in the two pairs of binomes all begin and/or end with a nasal sound. Through the echoes of nasal sounds—*-an -an man man -an men*—the sounds of syllables, music, and nature all come forth at once, creating a particularly rich and transformative aesthetic experience. Xie Tiao creates the same effect in a poem about listening to a friend playing the zither:

Wind rustling through the woods fills my ears,	蕭	瑟	滿	林	聽
		-n	- m		-ng
As soft murmurs sound from the mountain streams.[53]	輕	鳴	響	潤	音
	-ng	-ng	-ng	-n	-m

The succession of nasal endings—*-n -m -ng -ng -ng -ng -n -m*—conjures up several forms of sound imagery. They are the consonance among the syllables, the rustling wind and the *murmuring* streams, as well as the music flowing from his friend's zither. He who truly knows sound, the Yongming poets seem to be suggesting, listens deeply in that he listens not only with his ears, but with his mind as well.

"Refinement"

Even though we do not speak or read like Shen Yue and his fellow courtiers, it is not too far-fetched to imagine their process of "reciting and pondering over" (*yinyan*) a poem as being similar to how we might appreciate, say, contemporary American poet Natasha Tretheway's "Myth."[54] That one may find oneself being carried away by a sounding poem is probably a universal experience, even though what that means to the individual might differ across time and place. It might seem like a common term, but Shen Yue would insist on calling the "euphonic sounds" that he was after *jing* ("refined" or "refinement")—a word that turned out to be particularly charged in his discourse. In his *Song shu* essay, as noted earlier, he maintains that earlier poets achieved "euphonic sounds" only "unwittingly" and not through "conscious thought."[55] When rebuked by the younger official Lu Jue on this point, he argues, "Whether or not [a work] has attained euphony, there is in addition the difference between refinement (*jing*) and crudity (*cu*)."[56] To Shen Yue and his fellow *zhiyin*, the difference between "refinement" and "crudity" was very subtle (as in a single tone) and yet fundamental. This was the point that he made repeatedly to Lu Jue: a poet who *truly* "knew sounds" would not attain great euphony at one instance, only to lapse into an "off-key tune" in another (he cited Cao Zhi [192–232] and Lu Ji as examples of this), just as a great musician would not mix in "undisciplined and dissonant sounds" in his song.[57] "Refinement" was the result—as well as the direct reflection—of the conscious, attentive, and persistent mind, which grasped sound in the most meticulous and intricate way. In this regard, I would argue that Shen Yue indeed was proposing that "consciously contrived effects are superior to those that are achieved spontaneously."[58] But what was the thinking that motivated Shen Yue to challenge the derogatory epithet "worm carving and seal engraving" openly and to promote a poetics that associated the idea of refinement with the process of the mind, specifically in connection with sense perception? Here one detects the influence of Buddhism.

Shen Yue would cite the paradigm of "refinement versus crudity" again in a very different context: "From the ordinary person to the saint, the meaning of embodying spirit is the same. However, in all matters there is [the difference between] refinement (*jing*) and crudity (*cu*), and therefore among people there are the ordinary person and the saint."[59] This statement is the conclusion to one of several *yi* that Shen Yue had written in response to a debate on the Buddhist thesis "the spirit does not become extinct" (*shen bumie*).[60] As discussed in Chapter One, Shen Yue was a strong proponent of the thesis; in this *yi*, he seeks to explain why, even though they both embody "spirit," the "saint" exists through eternity while the "ordinary person" alone vanishes into extinction. The difference lies in "refinement," which, as one may recall from Chapter One, is the gradual process of gaining "knowledge" into "emptiness" by directing the mind to the analysis of a smaller and smaller area in a particularistic way. That Qi-Liang interpretation of the Buddhist mind recalls in a striking way the concept and process of creating "refined sound" in poetry as advocated by Shen Yue and his peers. The mind's ability to engage in the subtle analysis of sound into "four tones" is important and its grasp of a single tone in a stream of sounds matters—as Shen Yue reveals in his landmark discourse on *nian*, the Buddhist mind strives to be rid of chaos and entanglement by grasping a single thought-instant in a stream of thoughts (see Chapter One). In this connection, it is also noteworthy that, in his letter to Wang Yun, Shen Yue says that the process of "reciting and pondering over" the well-crafted poems from the latter has caused him to *wang nian* (literally, "forget his own thought-instants")—the state that will, based on his final analysis on *nian*, lead to "total illumination" (see Chapter One). Evidently, his poetics of sound was not only the recasting of a cultural ideal through a new form of knowledge; it also reflects how the Buddhist perspective had come into play in the form and process of poetry, fundamentally transforming the old cultural ideal.

The Buddhist backdrop against which Shen Yue and his fellow courtier-poets sought to "refine" poetic prosody can be observed from another angle: Buddhist discourse and practice appeared to have provided a different argument than that represented by the derogatory epithet "worm carving and seal engraving." The best evidence of this is found in Zhou Yong, the celebrated *zhiyin*, who also happened to be a devout Buddhist. In a spirited exchange with Zhang Rong (444–497), a defender of Daoism, Zhou Yong argues: "That Buddhism captivates our feeling and spirit through its teaching and mutates *sounds and prosody* in its language is all due to '*se* is not having'; hence, it surpasses all the other schools."[61] *Se* (Skt. *rūpa*; "form") is "not having" because it is the congregation of *yin* (Skt. *hetu*; "causes") and *yuan* (Skt. *pratyaya*; "conditions") and is not real in and of itself. Even though its interpretation and method of discourse are thorny issues that have important implications for the history of medieval Chinese Buddhism, the thesis is often traced to one of its early exponents, Zhi Dun (314–366).[62] What is particularly relevant to this discussion is that Zhou Yong included the issue of prosody (as well as other forms of artistry) in the discourse on the thesis. By pointing out that Buddhism "mutates sounds and prosody in its language," he reminded us of the "intricate and marvelous sounds" (*weimiao yinsheng*) of Buddhist chanting often depicted in early medieval sources, such as Huijiao's entries on the sūtra masters (*jingshi*) in the *Gaoseng zhuan*.[63] In one such entry, Tan Qian (fl. 445) is said to be "skillful in chanting the sūtras and has endless sounds and rhymes."[64] While at first the Chinese might indeed have been "completely unprepared for and utterly bedazzled" by "the meticulousness and seriousness" with which their Buddhist teachers of Indo-Iranian origins conducted their chanting, recitation, and singing, by early medieval times, there certainly were "home-grown" experts who were giving meticulous and serious attention to fine-tuning Chinese prosody and prided themselves on their ability to do so.[65] In that context, it is worth citing another passage that remembers Zhou Yong as the *zhiyin*:

> Zhou Yong's voice and wording were clear and yet exquisite; once he began to speak, words would flow endlessly. Melodies of the notes *gong* and *shang*,

and wording as beautiful as red and purple—he would open his mouth to speak, and these would be formed into sentences instantaneously.[66]

As Tang Yongtong interprets it, "if *se* is not having, then there is no need to exclude having (*waiyou*) or to exclude not having (*waiwu*)."[67] Depending on where one stands, it might even be argued that *se* is "real" and even necessary for the attainment of Emptiness. Living at a time when Chinese Buddhism was toiling over the Two Truths (*Erdi*)—the Mundane Truth (*Sudi*) that held that all *jiaming* ("provisional reality") were not empty and the Ultimate Truth (*Zhendi*) that viewed all *jiaming* as empty—and witnessing the sprouting of the idea of a third Truth, the courtiers of the Yongming era might indeed have taken a more flexible stand or even multiple stands when it came to the issue of *se*.[68] If nothing else, the concept "*se* is not having" certainly released them from the pejorative attitude toward the pursuit of form and artistry in poetry. Both Zhou Yong's and Shen Yue's open and engaging pursuit of "sound refinement," which brought Zhou Yong his reputation of being a charismatic rhetorician and Shen Yue his reputation of being a master of poetic "sounds and rhymes," proved that they had more than shifted away from the tradition of trivializing and demeaning the overt display of artistry.

That Buddhism should play a crucial role in the rethinking of form and artistry in early medieval China should not surprise us. Rather, it is the manner by which the Buddhist influence manifested itself that is the most fascinating and yet also the easiest to overlook. Instead of direct articulation of a Buddhist thought or idea in a poem (there are certainly examples of this), this chapter has examined how the Yongming poets assumed a Buddhist perspective in the process of their poetry. That process has now vanished into abstraction, leaving only little traces in many "mute texts."[69] For the courtier-poets of Qi-Liang times, however, that process was the immediate, concrete, and natural means by which they searched for meaning and excellence within their community of emperors, princes, and courtiers. As an exceptional example of this process, the Yongming style reminds us of how what is now seen as only an empty form or a dry technique once functioned intrinsically as poetry itself. When critics closer to their day criticized the Yongming poets for their "superfluous" (*mi*) or "severe" (*yan* or *ku*) style, these critics probably also had in mind *how they conducted poetry*. Their fundamental dissatisfaction was with how the Yongming poets toiled over a single tone or with how they insisted on making a clear distinction among the "four tones." As that process disappeared into time, memories of their "superfluousness" or "severity" were being re-substantiated by increasing attribution of "rules and defects" or other relevant signs that one may find by reading their poems as "mute texts." We can never escape the silence that has befallen us, but whether we imagine the poets and their poems as silent or not makes a great difference to our understanding of them. As we shall see, their "sight" poses similar challenges to us.

THREE

Seeing a Thing

The most commented on of the Yongming poets' works are their *yongwu shi* ("poems on things"). The idea of *yongwu*, as works that adopt this kind of title—"*yong*-something"—clearly show, is to focus on a single object, and not a scene comprising various elements as in a landscape *fu* (*shanshui fu*) or a landscape poem (*shanshui shi*). *Yongwu* involves a more isolated encounter—one that is between the poet and a single object. Even though *yongwu* is a thematic category of *fu*, which emerged much earlier, and many *shi*-like pieces about a single object are also found in earlier *ming* ("inscriptions") and *song* ("appraisals"), *yongwu shi* did not become popular until the Yongming poets and their fellow courtiers produced them in great numbers. Why, one might wonder, did the encounter with a single object, presented in a few lines and easy language, seem to captivate these courtier-poets?

One assumption that has been made about the Yongming poets' *yongwu shi* is that their "narrow focus" somehow mirrors the courtiers' life of ease within the court or coterie environment.[1] In light of this view, it is challenging to find the best characterization for the things that they depict: Are they mostly "trivial" and yet "rare" or "man-made" objects that were exclusive to the palace setting?[2] Below is a sampling of the titles of the

Yongming poets' *yongwu shi*, which should suffice to call that characterization into question.[3]

1. "On Azure Moss"
2. "On Dodder"
3. "On Sweet Flag"
4. "On the Pear Tree Flowers above the Pond"
5. "Listening to the Singing Cicadas: By Imperial Command"
6. "Attending a Banquet: On a Mockingbird"
7. "On Wind"
8. "On Remaining Snow"
9. "Courtyard Rain: Responding to an Imperial Command"
10. "Composing Together about an Object Seen from One's Seat"
11. "Composing Together about a Plaything by One's Seat"
12. "The Embroidery along the Collar"
13. "The Sandals Beneath Her Feet"

The things listed in these titles can be roughly grouped in three categories: minor plants, birds, or insects (the first six); natural phenomena (the next three); and objects of daily life (the last four).[4] Compared with some of the items dominantly featured in the *yongwu fu* ("*fu* on things") from earlier courts, such as a "red parrot" (*chi yingwu*) and "dancing horses" (*wuma*), these things seem quite ordinary.[5] As these titles accurately reflect, the "object" most commonly chosen by the Yongming poets for depiction is one of or related to nature. If their *yongwu shi* are any indication of the court milieu at the time, characterizations such as "artificiality," "ornateness," "triviality" or "narrowness" do not adequately reflect it. After all, what kind of court would exchange a "red parrot" for a mockingbird? Or, as the poem to be discussed next may suggest, take a leaf for a tree?

Reading a Leaf

The *yongwu shi* of the Yongming poets can indeed be considered a kind of social verse. By that, I am referring to the belief that many of these poems were composed at social gatherings, often a banquet at court or a meeting hosted by a prince or a courtier. That several poets had composed on the same object or on a series of objects and several titles indicated the social occasion upon which the composition took place certainly supports the belief.[6] In that sense, these *yongwu shi* can be particularly indicative of what the court environment was like, thus helping us imagine our poets in it. Cynthia Chennault has argued that these *yongwu shi* were a means for the courtiers to present and negotiate their "personal merit" before their patrons and fellow courtiers.[7] Building on her argument, I will look more closely into how that process worked and what it meant to courtiers specifically.

A popular *yongwu* topic for the Yongming poets was the *wutong* (paulownia), which certainly was no ordinary tree. It was "prized as an ornamental tree whose star-shaped, greenish yellow flowers exhale a delicate fragrance,"[8] not to mention its reputation as "the phoenix tree," befitting the phoenixes and simurghs that perched on it, or as the precious tree whose wood made the best zithers.[9] However, Shen Yue and Xie Tiao would have none of these in their poems about the tree. To appreciate what their unassuming poems may suggest about the nature of their *yongwu* and the court milieu of their time, one needs to consider how subtle signs of politics were read by them and their contemporaries.

It is impossible to overemphasize the importance of observation in a court environment. One's fortunes and even one's life hinged on that ability. According to one opinion, Wang Rong's demise was caused exactly by his lack of careful observation. The incident that culminated in his death was a crisis moment that revealed the Qi court at its most unsparing. This is a brief account: When Crown Prince Wenhui died from an illness on February 2, 493, an intense struggle for his replacement erupted in the court. In July, when Emperor Wu became very ill, he summoned the Prince of Jingling and the prince's personal guards to his palace to care for him. As a newly appointed general in the prince's army, Wang Rong was in charge of guarding the palace. On the thirtieth day of the month, the feeble emperor lost consciousness. Seizing the opportunity, Wang Rong instructed his guards to block Prince Yulin (Xiao Zhaoye; 473–494), the other contender for the throne, from entering the palace and attempted to enthrone the Prince of Jingling by an edict that he had prepared. The mission was quickly aborted after the emperor was revived, and Prince Yulin and his supporter Xiao Luan (later Emperor Ming; r. 494–498) took control. After Prince Yulin ascended the throne, Wang Rong was put to death.[10]

Even more revealing than the incident itself are the comments of various observers at the time. One such comment was attributed to two students at the imperial academy by the names of Yu Xi and Qiu Guobin.[11] According to the *Nan shi*, they had privately exchanged notes and said that: "The Prince of Jingling is weak in ability, Attendant Gentleman Wang [Wang Rong] had no judgment, [and thus] their failure was already in sight."[12] In fact, they had figuratively said that "their failure was already before one's eyes" (*bai zai yanzhong yi*). Wang Rong's problem, in other words, was not seeing what was already in sight. According to the rest of his story, he had sighed and declared after his mission failed: "The master had impeded me."[13] He was apparently disappointed that the Prince of Jingling had simply submitted to Prince Yulin and Xiao Luan. He must have been even more disappointed when the prince was "too stricken with worry and fear" to come to his rescue after he was jailed.[14]

Wang Rong might have eventually seen the prince and maybe the "him" as well that others had already had in sight, but it was too late. The consequences of his attempted coup were immeasurable: Wei Zhun, also a student at the imperial academy, had supported his plan and was found dead, "his entire body blue," after being interrogated; the Prince of Jingling himself died the next year, reportedly from illness, at thirty-five *sui*; members of the prince's coterie had dispersed—Shen Yue, for one, left the capital for an assignment in Dongyang (in modern Zhejiang).[15] Xie Tiao appeared to have been spared, as he was serving Prince Sui in Jingzhou at the time, but some years later he found himself caught up in another court struggle and like Wang Rong was executed.

Of all the figures associated with the Yongming era, Xiao Yan emerged the most "victorious." Like Wang Rong, he was instructed by the Prince of Jingling to guard the palace after Emperor Wu fell ill. He apparently refused to involve himself in Wang Rong's plot, based on his observation that "establishing the throne is an extraordinary matter and it takes an extraordinary person to succeed. Wang Rong does not have the ability to assist the throne and we will witness his failure."[16] He decided to let Wang Rong's failure take its own course. Ironically, when Xiao Yan ascended the throne in 502, aided by Shen Yue and Fan Yun, an earlier premonition by Wang Rong about him was proven true: "The one to rule over all under Heaven will be him."[17] Though he did not live to see it, Xiao Yan's enthronement was already in Wang Rong's sight.

What is there to behold, then, when one faces a *wutong* tree? Shen Yue's poem will take us to another story from a much earlier time.

On the Wutong　　　　　　　　　　　　　　詠梧桐

As autumn returns, all at once its leaves have fallen;	秋還遽已落
When the day breaks in spring, it has yet to sprout.	春曉猶未荑
Although its tiny leaves are unworthy,	微葉雖可賤
In a single clipping one of them might become an imperial scepter.[18]	一剪或成珪

The story that his last line alludes to is from the *Shiji* (The Grand Scribe's Record): the young King Cheng of Zhou (trad. r. 1115–1091 B.C.E.) once gave a *wutong* leaf to his younger brother Shuyu, and, pretending that it was a scepter (*gui*), told him: "I enfeoff you with this scepter!"; later, the minister Shi Yi requested the king to select a day for establishing Shuyu in his fief, and King Cheng replied, "I only gave it to him in play," to which Shi Yi responded, "The Son of Heaven says nothing in play. Thus his words are recorded by the historian, enacted in ritual, set to music and sung." As a result, Shuyu was enfeoffed in the state of Tang.[19] The real question is, what is Shen Yue inferring by his allusion to the story? Xie Tiao alludes to the same story in his "You Dongtang yong tong" 遊東堂詠桐 (Wandering in the East Hall: On the Wutong):

It has no blooms, and yet it has no fruits—	無華復無實
What is there to send the one far away?	何以贈離居
Trim it into a scepter or a tablet:	裁為圭與瑞
It's sufficient to command the region of *Shen*.[20]	足可命參墟

By describing a precious tree as useless and then suddenly revealing its potential, Shen Yue and Xie Tiao have made observation—that is, the ability to see what is before the eyes—the focus of their poems. The *Shiji* story weighs in on the complicated nature of ruling: an innocent pretense can cause a misperception, which in turn requires serious intervention to be readjusted. Shi Yi played a crucial role: he was the one to notice the potential discrepancy between "what a king should be" and "what the king is," and it was his words that had compelled the king to turn play into seriousness. While Shi Yi, the sober-minded observer of the child play, can be credited for steering King Cheng's rule onto the right course, Sima Qian (ca. 145–ca. 87 B.C.E.), an observer of history, played a similar role for future kings and emperors. To bring the story full circle, Sima Qian added a prologue when he told the story: before Shuyu was born, his mother received a premonition from "heaven" that she would conceive a son who would be enfeoffed in Tang.[21] By "connecting all the dots," Sima Qian showed that the course of a king's rule, guided by heavenly will in mysterious ways, was not random at all. Amid word play and subtle signs, the ability to sharply observe and wisely interpret was the singular force that kept the king's rule and history itself on track. Herein lies Shen Yue's and Xie Tiao's real interest. By making a poem on the *wutong* tree into one that accentuates the loaded meaning of a single *wutong* leaf, they befit themselves as keen at observation and interpretation. That they are well versed in history and good at using allusions is without question; what is unusual is how they make the story out to be about the leaf. As Shi Yi and Siman Qian had fully demonstrated, the readjustment of perception—and hence of meaning and value—was done by acute observation of words, acts, and heavenly signs; our courtier-poets encapsulated that process in a single leaf.

In a court culture loaded with subtle signs, nothing was too trivial. At issue is not the triviality of things, but, rather, the ability to unravel the meaning behind the seemingly trivial. It is in that sense that the "physical smallness" of the things that the Yongming poets wrote about becomes significant. In fact, it is not "physical smallness" per se, but the likelihood of being overlooked or misconstrued that truly characterizes the things in their *yongwu shi*. Consider these examples: Shen Yue was once instructed "by imperial command" to write about the "singing cicadas"; Xie Tiao was challenged to "compose about an object seen from one's seat" at a social gathering; and Wang Rong was, of all things, fascinated with dodder (*nüluo*). Their court environment was such that meaning was hidden and value negotiable. The courtier had to observe intently, not missing the signs within his sight. When he did that, a leaf incongruent with the world's procession was revealed as the very symbol of its ordering; and as he brought its full potential to light, he brought to light his own potential as well. Emperor Wu of Qi once compared Shen Yue and Wang Rong to Liu Xizong (419–495), a "favored courtier" (*xingchen*), in an unfavorable way: "Those learned scholars are no good at managing the state at all; they only know how to read many books! One Liu Xizong is sufficient for managing the state. Hundreds of others like Shen Yue and Wang Rong—what use do they have?"[22] Like a leaf, their use value could be called into question easily, and they needed to convince all by displaying it.

"Resemblance in Form"

Seeing subtle signs has another level of meaning in the Yongming poets' *yongwu shi*: it is literally about seeing itself. Earlier studies have discussed the "descriptive mode" or "detailed realism" in their *yongwu shi*, associating it with the descriptive aesthetic of *xingsi* ("resemblance in form") as exemplified by Xie Lingyun's landscape poetry.[23] Heralded by the earlier expression of the concept *tiwu* ("modeling things"), *xingsi* would be given full articulation by Qi-Liang critics such as Liu Xie (ca. 465–532).[24] The Yongming poets would also interpret it in a new way.

The central issue is how one sees resemblance. In the Tang miscellany *Youyang zazu* (A Miscellany of Youyang), a story involving Yu Xin, the Liang courtier-poet who went north, raises this issue.

> Yu Xin told the Northern Wei envoy Wei Jin, "When I was in Ye [in modern Hebei], I ate a lot of grapes, which were amazingly flavorful." Chen Zhao said, "How would you describe their form?" Xu Junfang replied, "They bear resemblance to soft dates." Yu Xin then said, "Sir, you really did not know how to 'model things'—why didn't you say they resemble green lychees?"[25]

The image of "soft" dates obviously did not do justice to Yu Xin's memory;[26] that of "green" lychees, by contrast, has the effect of livening up the "amazing" grapes before the mind's eye.[27] The challenge of "modeling things," the anecdote suggests, is to not lay out semblance for one to see, but to inspire the *experience* of seeing semblance. This is how Liu Xie articulates the concept of *xingsi* ("resemblance in form"):

> In recent times, literary compositions are valued for "resemblance in forms." . . . Therefore, when artful language shapes the forms of things, it is like a seal being pressed into the seal paste; even without carving and shaving, the most refined details are skillfully depicted. Thus, one views the language and sees appearance, reads the words and knows the moment.[28]

The seal paste is flat before being pressed on—pressing *brings out* the seal's form; that is "artful language" (*qiaoyan*) at work. It is a process of transformation, for the poet as well as his audience. One "sees appearance" and "knows the moment" through "viewing the language" and "reading the words"; without the process, there is neither appearance nor knowing. The poet's vision can make a difference in whether or not things appear. Shen Yue captures that active process of *xingsi* in a comment he reportedly made:

> After Shen Yue built a storied study at his residence in the suburbs, Wang Yun composed ten *yongwu shi* on grasses and plants for it and wrote them on its walls. He simply wrote out the lines and words without adding a title to each poem. Shen Yue told someone: "These poems make the things that they are directed at present their forms (*zhi wu cheng xing*); they have no need for any titles."[29]

That is the most definitive characterization of Yongming style *yongwu*: poetry (*shi*), when directed at a thing, makes it *present its form*. In other words, things do not merely seem real—they *become* real through their *yongwu shi*.

Seeing as Happening

The Yongming poets faced various challenges in depicting things. Once, while attending the emperor, presumably upon a social occasion at the court, Shen Yue was given this topic: a drizzle. This is his response:

Courtyard Rain: Responding to an Imperial Command	庭雨應詔
Emerging from the sky, how can it be painted?	出空寧可圖
Entering into the courtyard, it is doubly difficult to put into verse.	入庭倍難賦
It is neither smoke nor cloud;	非煙複非雲
Like silk threads, and yet like fog.	如絲複如霧
Finely drizzling, just about to pour down;	靃霂裁欲垂
Its mistiness too light, it cannot come forth.	霏微不能注
Though it lacks the substance of a thousand in gold,	雖無千金質
It has provided amusement for a single morning.[30]	聊為一辰趣

He was not assigned the topic simply because it happened to be raining. His first two lines sum it up: drizzle is extremely difficult to portray, whether using colors or words. Moreover, this is a drizzle that has "entered the courtyard"—right there, before the eyes, making its existence and presence impossible to deny. It is helpful to reconsider the view that Shen Yue is engaging in a "negative litany" in the sense of "rejecting one image after another for the rain" here.[31] The key, I believe, is to see that Shen Yue is in fact depicting the drizzle as it exactly *is*. His gift was precisely the ability to capture the form (or forms) of a thing shifting from one state to another. Other examples by him and Xie Tiao include these couplets:

Shen Yue, "On Azure Moss"   詠青苔

Lines 3–4

Their tiny roots seem ready to break away;   微根如欲斷
Yet their light tendrils appear to join even closer.[32]   輕絲似更聯

Shen Yue, "On the Snow: By Imperial Command"   詠雪應令

Lines 3–4

The night's snow gathered and then dispersed;   夜雪合且離
The wind at dawn, so startling, has calmed down again.[33]   曉風驚復息

Xie Tiao, "On the Wind"   詠風

Lines 3–4:

The drooping willows, hanging low, rise up again;   垂楊低復舉
The young duckweeds gather and then spread out.[34]   新萍合且離

In these couplets, things evolve from one form into another, as if an event that is currently happening. Shen Yue's "courtyard rain" gives that impression—happening before the eyes, it continues to take and change form. Having met the challenge of depicting the rain, Shen Yue merely points out that the rain has provided "amusement" for one morning. His light-hearted remark reflects the court environment in another light: a playful curiosity about how to see.

Light-heartedness is not the tone in Xie Tiao's poetry. Even in *yongwu shi*, he often sounds melancholic. That, however, does not make him a less curious observer of the physical world. For example, he notices the plant that "no one is willing to look at" and he looks inside its "low bushes":

On the Rambler Rose   詠薔薇

How can its low branches hold up the leaves?   低枝詎勝葉
But the mild fragrance, luckily, comes through by itself.   輕香幸自通
Those sending new buds are only beginning to gather
    up in purple,   發萼初攢紫

While the ones that remain from earlier blooms still
    have a rosy red. 餘采尚霏紅
As the new flowers face the pallid sun, 新花對白日
The old sheaths fly away with the moving wind. 故蕊逐行風
Unevenly formed, they do not all shine together— 參差不俱曜
So who is willing to seek out these low bushes?[35] 誰肯盼微叢

Still common today, the *qiangwei* (rambler rose) is known for its light
fragrance, tiny thorns, and small flower petals ranging from deep pink to
white. Xie Tiao "defends" the plant by revealing the various detailed happenings within its bushes. Like a "stage," new buds and old sheaths come
and go, all at the same time. When he looks at bamboo, he again notices
"the old sheaths":

On Bamboos 詠竹

Before my front window is a grove of bamboo; 前窗一叢竹
Green and azure—I alone call them a wonder. 青翠獨言奇
Twigs on the south side cross the leaves on the north; 南條交北葉
New shoots mix with old branches. 新筍雜故枝
The moonlight, then sparse, now already clustered; 月光杶已密
When the wind comes, they rise and then fall again. 風來起復垂
The blue finches fly among them unobstructed; 青扈飛不礙
And the "yellow beaks" can peep on each other. 黃口得相窺
I only regret that the sheaths fly off with the wind, 但恨從風籜
For now the roots and branches are forever separate.[36] 根枝長別離

His view of the bamboo is also an unfolding of the various happenings
within it. Even though his initial attempt was to share the "wonder" of his
bamboo grove, by the time his eyes caught "the sheaths that fly off with
the wind," he slid back into a melancholic tone. If the bamboo had "paid
a price" for their growth, Xie Tiao paid his too—for seeing the minute
happenings.

    A point worth highlighting about the Yongming way of seeing a small
thing is that it gives the impression of lingering and "penetrating." This is
a stark contrast to the earlier *yongwu* tradition, which had a way of forcing
the view on a small thing outward. To see the difference, we will compare
a "He shi" (Poem on the Lotus) by Zhang Hua (232–300) and a poem on

the same topic by Shen Yue. The *he* (lotus), of course, is well remembered in Chinese poetry for this spectacular sight: its blooming flowers, casting their reflection upon the water, "brighten up the pond."

Zhang Hua, "Poem on the Lotus"   荷詩

The lotuses grow out of the green spring,	荷生綠泉中
Their emerald leaves as evenly formed as protractors.	碧葉齊如規
As the winding wind disperses the flowing mist,	迴風蕩流霧
Their pearl-like dew chases the drooping twigs.	珠水逐條垂
They illuminate this golden pond,	照灼此金塘
Just as their resplendence brightens my lord's jade pool.	藻曜君玉池
They have no worry that the world's admiration for them might end—	不愁世賞絕
They only fear that your great brilliance might shift elsewhere.[37]	但畏盛明移

We find the image to look for in the *he* in line 5—"They illuminate this golden pond." Incidentally, this line also tells us the context of Zhang Hua's encounter with the lotuses: it is their blooming season, which naturally calls for an outing to the garden to "admire" (*shang*) them. Before the lotus pond, Zhang Hua's vision moves "outward": it begins with the lotuses and then moves to the surrounding area—"drooping twigs" suggests a willow tree or other similar type of tree by the pond—and finally catches the entire view of the "illuminated pond." Shen Yue's lotuses, by contrast, are missing the spectacular sight:

On New Lotuses: By Imperial Command   詠新荷應詔詩

Do not say that these grass-like plants are unworthy—	勿言草卉賤
They are lucky enough to reside in the Heavenly Pool.	幸宅天池中
Their fine roots barely emerge from the ripples,	微根纔出浪
And their short branches do not yet wave in the wind.	短幹未搖風
Who would know that inside their inch-hearts	寧知寸心裏
Is stored not only purple but also red?[38]	畜紫復含紅

These lotuses have not even bloomed yet. Obviously, the challenge for Shen Yue was to make an apology for the young lotuses' presence in the "Heavenly Pool," a clear reference to the imperial compound. He begins by affirming the lotuses' "unsightly" appearance—having grown only slightly above the water's surface, they have nothing but "fine roots" and "short branches" to offer anyone who even cares to look at them. His apology then comes in a rhetorical question about "knowing." What is inside the small lotuses' "inch-hearts" is a hidden sight; it is not his sight though, but what he *knows* that allows Shen Yue to "see through" the tiny plants. By directing his mind's eye (and our eyes) inside something even smaller than what the eyes can actually see, he arrives at a "view" so simple—almost childlike—that it has the quality of truth. The tiny lotuses, in transformation, are worth anticipation.

Both Zhang Hua and Shen Yue were speaking as loyal and able assistants to the throne. In the last few lines of his poem, Zhang Hua's sight moves even farther away—in his mind's eye he sees his lord's (the emperor's or the crown prince's) "jade pool," wherein he might or might not, like the lotuses there, continue to enjoy the "admiration" of the lord himself. His fleeting view of the lotuses appropriately reflects the state of his distracted mind: the courtier is dutiful, dedicated, and yet insecure. When the blooming lotuses are replaced by "unsightly" ones in Shen Yue's poem, the courtier reveals a new energy that is playful and refreshing. Wang Rong's eyes refresh the *nüluo* (dodder) in a similar way:

On the Dodder	詠女蘿
Spreading everywhere—that's the dodder;	羃羅女蘿草
Profusely growing, it hangs from the pine tree's branches.	蔓衍旁松枝
As it absorbs the mist, it becomes yellow and green;	含煙黃且綠
Relying on the wind, it curls and again uncurls.[39]	因風卷復垂

Like drizzle, the *nüluo* is without form: it wraps around a tree with threadlike tendrils and grows in profusion.[40] By lingering on it, Wang Rong sees it undergo a transformation: of yellow and green, it curls and uncurls in the wind. In contrast to Zhang Hua, who expressed his wish to be appreciated by his imperial patron through his fleeting view, the Yongming poets did that by displaying their way of seeing with curiosity, freshness, and acuteness.

Seeing as Illusion

The issue of seeing is no doubt complex. Faced with a thing, does one defend its worth, or doubt it as unreal? Xie Tiao's vision of a plant enfolding both new buds and old sheaths has a larger meaning: it is the cycle of life and death. He presents this vision in a Buddhist poem:

A Lecture and Exposition on an Autumn Night　　　秋夜講解
Lines 3–10
Sinking deeper and deeper, the restless soul tossed in cycle;[41]　　沉沉倒營魄
While Suffering and the Aggregates bind the grieving heart.　　苦蔭蹙愁腸
Zithers and harps sound wonderfully to no avail;　　琴瑟徒爛熳
Beautiful faces fill the hall in emptiness.　　姱容空滿堂
Springtime color suddenly passes within a few days,　　春顏遽幾日
But autumn grave mounds in the end stretch on and on.　　秋壟終茫茫
Who can rescue those sinking and drowning?　　孰云濟沉溺
By way of the Vows, I entrust myself to Buddha's
　　　"ferrying and bridging."[42]　　假願託津梁

Xie questions human life based on the concepts of "Suffering" (*ku*; Skt. *duḥkha*), the condition of being trapped in the endless cycle of "rebirth" (Skt. *saṃsāra*), and "Aggregates" (*yin*; Skt. *skandha*), the five personality components that constitute the illusion of self.[43] In other words, his melancholic tone is more than a reflection of his personality or his circumstances as has been often suggested;[44] it underscores his inquiry into the phenomena of the physical world, human life included, from a Buddhist perspective. From this perspective, the world is in constant flux, having no permanence and no real form in and of itself; and the purpose of seeing, if any, is to gain insight into the transient nature of the world and of human life. His fellow poets' vision of a thing in constant transformation informs the same Buddhist perspective. As they sought further, the issue of seeing became more complex, but also eventually returned to worth and value.

Wang Rong's eyes are seeking after a moving object in this poem:

On the Pear Tree's Flowers above the Pond　　　詠池上梨花

Tossed down the steps, they conceal the tiny grasses;　　翻階沒細草
Gathered on the water, they separate the loose duckweed.　　集水間疏萍
In fragrant spring, they glimmer like drifting snowflakes;　　芳春照流雪
Deep into the night, they reflect a thousand stars.[45]　　深夕映繁星

In spite of the title, Wang Rong's eyes are not set on the pear tree's flowers, but their fallen petals. Trailing them from day through night, his unfaltering attention has a meditative quality, as if he is concentrating on the drifting petals only in his mind. The time element in his poem was certainly not overlooked by Liu Hui (458–502), also a noted member of the Prince of Jingling's literary coterie.[46] Responding to Wang Rong's poem, Liu Hui promptly picks up from where his fellow poet left off:

Responding to "On the Pear Tree's Flowers above the Pond"　和詠池上梨花

In the dewy courtyard, as the day ends, they flutter and pile up;	露庭晚翻積
In the windy boudoir, many enter by night.	風閨夜入多
Circling and gathering, they seem like butterflies in confusion;	縈聚似亂蝶
She holds up the candle: they take the form of conjoined moths.[47]	拂燭狀聯蛾

Wang Rong already sees two different views of the petals: "drifting snowflakes" by the day and "a thousand stars" by the night. Liu Hui also presents two views, which are seen through the woman in her boudoir: in two moments separated only by her act of "holding up the candle," she sees them consecutively as "butterflies in confusion" and "conjoined moths." The immediacy of the transformation presses the issue of seeing itself. The tiny petals have indeed "presented their forms," in fact, they have "come alive"—but that only begs the question of what is real.

When Shen Yue's eyes turn to a woman, we cannot be certain if she is real either, particularly in the example below, when he sees the woman through his "recollection."

Six Recollections　六憶

I remember when she ate:	憶食時
Before the plates, her expression kept changing.	臨盤動容色
She was going to sit, but yet was too shy to sit;	欲坐復羞坐
Then she was going to eat, but yet was too shy to eat.	欲食復羞食
She held the food in her mouth, as if not hungry;	含哺如不饑
She picked up the bowl, as if lacking in strength.	擎甌似無力

I remember when she came to bed:	憶眠時
While others slept, she insisted on staying awake.	人眠彊未眠
Removing her gauzy dress, she needed no encouragement;	解羅不待勸

Nearing the pillows, she had to be led by hand.　　　　就枕更須牽
Yet again, fearful to let her companion see her—　　　復恐傍人見
All coyness and shyness before the candlelight.[48]　　嬌羞在燭前

There is no denying the sensual and sexual pleasure in Shen Yue's "recollection." The twists and turns of the woman's body and the changing moods and expressions on her face all give great pleasure to her beholder. However, her constant "transformation" betrays her as unreal—she is the multiple forms that appear in Shen Yue's mind as he tries to grasp her "real" form. Even before the candlelight, "she" is still trying to evade his gaze. What comes after is left to our imagination, but in the poem, the flickering candlelight illuminates no more than her coyness and shyness.

Even non-living things can be seen "transforming." This is perhaps the most intriguing revelation of Yongming style *yongwu*, which further problematizes the issue of seeing. Strictly speaking, the two poems below do not depict court ladies as much as they do their apparel, and Shen Yue is particularly specific about where his focus is in the first example: the embroidery along the collar of a woman's blouse.

On Embroidery along the Collar　　　　　　　　　領邊繡

Her delicate hands are making something new and
　　wonderful,　　　　　　　　　　　　　　　　纖手製新奇
As they mend and sew lovely patterns.　　　　　　刺作可憐儀
Through winding silk fly swallowtails;　　　　　　縈絲飛鳳子
On knotted threads sit flowers.　　　　　　　　　結縷坐花兒
Without sound, they seem to move and whir;　　　不聲如動吹
There is no wind, but their stalks wave gently by
　　themselves.　　　　　　　　　　　　　　　　無風自裏枝
"If the bright colors on us have not yet faded,　　麗色儻未歇
We will for the moment hold her cloudlike locks as
　　they fall."[49]　　　　　　　　　　　　　　　聊承雲鬢垂

He becomes transfixed by the embroidered patterns. In one moment, he sees "winding silk" and "knotted threads," and in the next he sees "flying swallowtails" and "seated flowers." Before his eyes, the "birds" and "flowers" gain motion of their own and, at last, speak. Like the flower petals in Liu Hui's poem, these embroidered patterns have come alive.[50] As the boundary between the "real" and the "unreal" blurs, we cannot help but wonder if Shen Yue's "illusion" is a moment of being carried away by intoxicating sensuousness, or a moment of grasping the Buddhist thesis, "seeing is illusion."[51] In spite of his playful tone, he expresses the sober awareness that the colors on the embroidery *will fade*. In other words, there is no assumption that what one sees or wishes for is permanent.

In his other poem, often relegated to the category of Palace style poems, Shen Yue writes about a pair of women's sandals:

The Sandals beneath Her Feet   腳下履

On the scarlet staircase: ascending, rustling between
    hurried steps;   丹墀上颯沓

In the Jade Hall: descending, approaching with rhythmic
    taps.   玉殿下趨蹡

A backward turn and her pearl pendants dangle;   逆轉珠佩響

A forward motion and her embroidered jacket sends forth
    a fragrance.   先表繡袿香

Her skirt front flaps open, approaching the dancing mats; 裾開臨舞席

Her sleeves flutter while encircling the singing hall.   袖拂繞歌堂

"What makes us sigh is the heartless maid—   所歡忘懷妾

She abandons us once she enters the gauzy bed."[52]   見委入羅床

Here, he traces the sandals' route through the day via a sequence of movements—ascending, descending, a backward turn, a forward motion, approaching, circling. The interesting result is the impression not of one observing, but of one *being*. For the short moment that one may forget it is actually the woman who is moving and that the poet is observing her—or, rather, her feet—the poem itself has been transformed into an illusion.

It is true that the Yongming poets' *yongwu shi* invariably ends like this: "the human element sets, and the depicted object is endowed with some sort of human emotion."[53] To be more specific, the human element and emotion always involve the question of one's worth and its appreciation by one's sovereign. Before his prince and emperor, the courtier had to defend, display, and reveal the thing for its worth. What was truly unique about the court milieu of the Yongming era was that sovereigns and courtiers collectively turned their eyes toward the subtle, the unnoticed, and even the invisible. While they found worth, even use value, there, they also saw the world in altered perception, where it all became more real and yet more illusory. At the start of this chapter, I asked: Why, one might wonder, did the encounter with a single thing, presented in few lines and easy language, seem to captivate these courtier-poets? The *Chengshi lun*, in trying to encourage its practitioners to keep on cultivating *śamatha* (*ding* or *zhi*; "a state of deep concentration"), uses this metaphor: if a bottle keeps on spinning without stopping, it will find its pivot point.[54] In their active act of seeing, constantly grasping the thing before their eyes, the Yongming courtier-poets were like a spinning bottle, trying to find a pivot point on which to center themselves. And that metaphor transcends a pure Buddhist context. In a court environment in which the pursuit of religion was invariably mixed in with political and other concerns, their grasping eyes were at the same time trying to pivot on the socio-political platform of their day.

FOUR

In the Garden

The "garden" (*yuan*) in early medieval literature can vary from an outdoor area with shrubs, trees, and other vegetation to the entire compound of a large estate. Tao Yuanming (Tao Qian; 365–427), the famous "field and garden poet" (*tianyuan shiren*), often used *yuan* to refer to his vegetable gardens,[1] whereas Shen Yue called his "three thousand *mu*" (roughly 430 acres) suburban estate a *jiaoyuan* ("suburban garden").[2] While the notion of the garden may have differed depending on the poets' imagination, the *yuan* was portrayed more and more in the Southern Dynasties as a personal space that one *returned to* (*gui* or *huan*), signaling a retreat from public life and a turning inward toward "one's true nature."[3]

The *yuan* figures more prominently in Yongming literature than in the literature of earlier periods. Coming after Tao Yuanming and Xie Lingyun, the garden idealism in Yongming literature clearly reflects their influence. But neither the willing and private farmer-poet that impresses us in Tao Yuanming's poetry nor the individualistic and often strong-willed aristocrat that stands out in Xie Lingyun's poetry is the dominant persona in Yongming literature. Rather, the central figure is the courtier-poet actively involved in the culture and politics in the capital but also restricted by that involvement. As such, the idea of a private space or a private life is particularly elusive in Yongming literature. But it is through the elusiveness of the idea of *yuan* as a private space that we see up close the personal struggles, the aesthetic acuteness, and the spiritual pursuits of the Yongming courtier-poets.

Rejecting the Ostentatious Garden

Against the popular belief about the "sumptuousness" of their material culture, it is perhaps surprising to see that the Yongming poets' portrayal of gardens is in fact a critique of "the ostentatious garden," which is represented by the imperial hunting parks and pleasure gardens splendidly depicted in the *fu* of the Han dynasty and the elaborate private garden estates of earlier times, such as the Golden Valley Garden (Jingu yuan; in modern Henan) of Shi Chong (249–300).[4] This new vision of the garden was first articulated by Xie Lingyun, who declares in his celebrated "*Fu* on Dwelling in the Mountains" ("Shanju fu") that what he writes about is not "the grandeur of capitals, palaces, lodges, excursions, hunts, sights and sounds."[5] In his "*Fu* on Dwelling in the Suburbs," Shen Yue, too, rejects the culture of "clustered terraces" and "splendid harems" among the "noble officials" of the past.[6] But unlike Xie Lingyun, who, in "Shanju fu," clearly shuns the glamour of the capital and focuses his attention on the local landscape of his Shining family estate in the Zhejiang area, Shen Yue's rejection of "the ostentatious garden" is not a clear attempt to disengage himself from the capital or the central court. In fact, the garden culture in Yongming literature poses the interesting but also vexing question of how one might avoid the glamour and power of the capital city *while* maintaining a deep connection to it.

In his "*Fu* on Dwelling in the Suburbs," there is no question that Shen Yue is drawing a distinction between his own garden estate and an example of "the ostentatious garden" from his own time. This is how he describes the garden estate of Crown Prince Wenhui, whom he once served, in one section of his *fu*:

Amongst tall woodlands were added cassia trees;	脩林則表以桂樹
Rows of grasses were topped by fragrant orchids.	列草則冠以芳芝
Wind-blown balconies with layered-flying-eaves;	風臺累翼
Moonlit pavilions with tiered-beams.	月榭重栭

A thousand capitals rose up magnificently,	千櫨捷嶪
A hundred columns supporting them.	百栱相持
Black carriage shafts drove through the woods;	皁轅林駕
Magnolia oars played on the rivers.[7]	蘭枻水嬉

Through these lines, Shen Yue highlights the grand and elaborate architecture in Wenhui's garden estate. His depiction can be put into better perspective by the vivid account of Wenhui's obsession with ornate objects and elaborate construction in the *Nan Qi shu*. According to the history,

> the halls and chambers inside Crown Prince Wenhui's palace were filled with delicate carvings and exquisite patterns, exceeding even the emperor's palace. He also built the Mystic Orchard Garden, along with the Northern Moat by the palace tower, and more. Within the garden, there were towers, lodges, pagodas, and houses; and unusual rocks were piled up, displaying the most wondrous forms of mountains and rivers. The prince was worried that the emperor could see these from his palace, so he lined up rows of tall bamboos by his palace gate and set up high fences inside; he also built movable walls several hundred *jian* in length, to which he added a mechanical contrivance, which allowed them to be put up quickly when more concealment was needed and to be removed easily by hand should they need to be dismantled.[8]

The *Nan Qi shu* also recounts that after the prince's death, Emperor Wu, in an outburst of anger about his extravagance, ordered all his "playthings" destroyed;[9] according to another version of the story, the emperor eventually had the prince's garden estate sold off.[10] Wenhui's premature death was caused by poor health, and was unrelated to his obsession for ornate objects and elaborate construction. But in Shen Yue's mind, Wenhui's "posthumous" loss of his garden estate is the same as all destructions in history, as he sighs in his *fu*:

After three years it was an affair of the past;	踰三齡而事往
Suddenly, two-dozen years have passed, leading to today.	忽二紀以歷茲
That all is destroyed, completely wiped out,	咸夷漫以蕩滌
Is no different whether in the past or at present.[11]	非古今之異時

How to protect oneself from that destruction, both in life and in posterity, is a subtle but profound concern underlying the depiction of gardens in Yongming literature. As Wenhui's story hints, the most formidable source of one's downfall is none other than the watchful eyes of the emperor. Shen Yue's rejection of "the ostentatious garden," one might conclude, was a form of self-preservation. Instead of tall bamboos, high fences, and movable walls, Shen Yue turned to ideas from the *Laozi* for his self-preservation:

Do not hanker after power in cities and towns;	不慕權於城市
Why solicit fame in the slaughterhouse and the marketplace?	豈邀名於屠肆
I chant the "intangible-inaudible" as I seek out a house,	詠希微以考室
Feeling fortunate just to be sheltered from wind and frost.[12]	幸風霜之可庇

Obviously, Shen Yue has a passage from the *Laozi* in mind: "The great sound is inaudible, the great image is formless" (*dayin xisheng, daxiang wuxing*). An annotation to the *Laozi* says: "What is not heard when listened to is called 'inaudible'; what is not grasped when one reaches for it is called 'intangible'" (*ting zhi buwen ming yue xi, bo zhi bude ming yue wei*).[13] Using these ideas and expressions to represent his private residence, Shen Yue portrays the idea of a house "stripped down" to its bare function: protection from "wind and frost." The form of his new garden, however, is much more complex than that.

Between the Human and Wilderness

According to Xie Lingyun, there are four types of "dwellings," each defined by its location:

> The ancient way of dwelling in nests and residing in caves is called "cavern perching" (*yanqi*); beams and houses erected by the mountains are called "mountain dwellings" (*shanju*); residences in woods and wilderness are called "hill and garden [dwellings]" (*qiuyuan*); living in the suburbs is called "by the city" (*chengbang*). These four types [of dwellings] are different, and each of them can be identified accordingly.[14]

All four are presumably worthy in their own way, even though Xie Lingyun obviously holds "mountain dwellings" in the highest regard.[15] By contrast, the most representative type of "dwelling" in Yongming literature is the fourth on Xie Lingyun's list: in the suburbs. Shen Yue's Eastern Garden (Dongyuan), as well as the Prince of Jingling's Western Villa—the two garden estates most often conjured up in Yongming literature—were both located in the suburbs.[16] In his "Jiaoju fu," Shen Yue describes how he has come to reside there:

I am a person of narrow intent,	伊吾人之褊志
And have no great ambition for designing the world	無經世之大方
I long to reside in the forest, furling my wings;	思依林而羽戢
And I wish to flow with the water, hiding my scales.	願託水而鱗藏
Indeed, I have no yearning for beautiful or magnificent buildings;	固無情於輪奐
Nor do I desire broad avenues or wide streets.	非有欲於康莊
I combed through the vast emptiness of the eastern suburb,	披東郊之寥廓
And entered its boundless desertion covered in tangled underbrush.[17]	入蓬藋之荒茫

Consistent with the ideas that he has cited from the *Laozi*, Shen Yue becomes "inaudible-intangible" (*xiwei*). The "eastern suburb" is not merely a location; it is also a symbol for his retirement from office, indicating not only his physical but also mental departure from the city. In a later part of the same *fu*, again describing his selection of the suburb to build his garden estate, Shen Yue nonetheless contradicts his earlier statement:

I rejected the sunbirds and picked the city;	排陽鳥而命邑
By its river and mountain built the foundations.	方河山而啟基
I still guide the Crown Prince in the Three Goodness;[18]	翼儲光於三善
And head the royal duties among the hundred officials.[19]	長王職於百司

His retirement is not a complete withdrawal after all. He "rejects the sunbirds," the symbol of recluses, and even suggests that his preference for the suburb is based on its closeness to the capital, Jiankang. Known to have been built on the slopes of Zhongshan, Shen Yue's Dongtian garden estate was just northeast of the city proper.[20] Its convenient location certainly allowed Shen Yue to make frequent trips to the central court, and he appears to have done just that periodically during his retirement.[21] That Shen Yue should rationalize his choice of the suburb in contradictory terms within the same *fu* reveals his attempt to maintain flexibility in interacting with the central court.

It is perhaps Yu Gaozhi (441–491) who, in a letter portraying the Prince of Jingling and his suburban life, best captures the nuances of this location:

> The prince sought a residence in the suburbs, where the rivers and hills wind all around. When he shows himself (*xian*), he does not boast about his merits; and when he makes himself obscure (*hui*), he leaves no trace. Moving with ease between the human and wilderness (*congrong hu ren ye zhijian*), he achieves the best of both worlds.[22]

The context of Yu Gaozhi's letter makes it clear that he is mostly referring to Jingling's Buddhist activities at the estate.[23] Residing at the Western Villa, located on Chicken Cage Mountain (Jilong shan), just northwest of Jiankang, the prince seemed to have it both ways: he maintained a certain detachment from the central court and its politics in order to focus on his Buddhist pursuits, but he also promoted Buddhism through active engagement with leading monks of the day and cultural elites in the capital at large as well.[24] In fact, Jingling's active engagement was not limited to the realm of Buddhism. As the historian Xiao Zixian pointed out, the prince "extends his welcome to retainers and guests, and all the men with talent and learning in the world socialize and gather at his estate."[25] Commenting on the prince's success, Xiao Zixian offered another interesting observation: the prince, he noted, "resides at a place that invites few suspicions" (*ju buyi zhi di*).[26] The word *di* ("place") in this comment is both literal and metaphorical. Second in line of succession to the throne, Jingling occupied a "place" that naturally invited suspicion. But he was able to shift himself to "a place that invites few suspicions" through his intimate relationship with Crown Prince Wenhui, the emperor's trust for him, and his image as a devout Buddhist who had no interest in fame and power.[27] But this *di* is also the suburbs—by physically distancing himself from the central palace, the prince not only signaled his lack of interest in the throne, but also avoided his competitors at the court and the watchful eyes of the emperor.

Whether for a prince such as Jingling, or for a high-ranking courtier such as Shen Yue, the best way to position oneself was probably to retain one's flexibility. To use the language in Yu Gaozhi's letter, there were times when those at court "showed themselves" (*xian*) and there were times when they "obscured themselves" (*hui*). But could a garden "between the human and wilderness" really allow its owner to have it both ways? This is what history tells us about the fate of the two garden owners: the Prince of Jingling died prematurely after a failed palace coup led by Wang Rong to enthrone him; Shen Yue died "in fear" after an unpleasant audience with Emperor Wu of Liang.[28] We do not know what happened to their garden estates after their death, but the memories of them in poetry continue to struggle between the two spaces: that of the human and that of wilderness.

The Naturalistic Garden

Even though their ideal garden was always founded in the wild (*huang* or *ye*), the Yongming poets were in agreement that humans cannot reside in wilderness *as it is*. Residing in wilderness as it is—like "dwelling in nests and residing in caves," the first type of dwelling on Xie Lingyun's list—was seen as a stage in human history that had passed for good. Navigating their way back to the wilderness, the Yongming poets had no doubt that they first had to tame it. In terms of aesthetics, the result was a new, naturalistic garden.

Shen Yue's effort at "taming nature" is reflected in a section in his "*Fu* on Dwelling in the Suburbs." Presented in more than twenty lines, the effort appears to be speedy and efficient.

Thereupon,	爾乃
By the bare wilderness—	傍窮野
Against the deserted suburb—	抵荒郊
I braided the frosty sedges,	編霜菼
And thatched the cold reeds.	葺寒茅
I structured a home where perching and chirping birds would gather;	構棲噪之所集
Built fields and pathways, crisscrossing them.	築町疃之所交
Because they invaded the eaves, the trees were cut down;	因犯檐而刊樹
When they blocked the foundation, the bird nests were trimmed back.	由妨基而剪巢
I dredged filth and dregs from the sandbars and the streams;	決漳洿之汀濴
Filled holes and leaks in the brick walls of the wells;	塞井甃之淪坳
Potted fragrant hedgethorn along the north canal;	藝芳枳於北渠
Planted lithe willows by the south bank;	樹脩楊於南浦
Moved jar-shaped windows to the orchid rooms;	遷甕牖於蘭室
Evened out the shoulder-high walls to match the florid fences;	同肩牆於華堵

Wove year-long thistle to form a gate;　　　　織宿楚以成門
And made doors out of the outer frames.　　　籍外扉而為戶
Having used the courtyard foliage for a shade,　既取陰於庭樾
I further lined up the fragrant pear trees to make a hedge.　又因籬於芳杜
I opened up the storied-chambers to gaze afar;　開閣室以遠臨
Threw wide the lofty verandas for sideward views.　闢高軒而旁覿
Ponds and islets gradually filled with dripping from
　　　the eaves;　　　　　　　　　　　　　　漸沼沚於霤垂
Beneath the hall, field-paths and roads wound all
　　　around.[29]　　　　　　　　　　　　　　周塍陌於堂下

The typical *fu* style of these lines creates a deep impression: step by step the overgrowth is tamed and design after design is made to promote human convenience. But, in stark contrast to his depiction of Wenhui's garden, Shen Yue keeps nature in sight at all times in his depiction here. Line 6, for example, tells us that his home is structured such that "birds would gather"; and lines 8 and 9 express the notion that nature is cut back *only* when it interferes with human life. His attempt is to negotiate with, rather than destroy, nature.

Indeed, the result of Shen Yue's human-centric approach is a garden that is not at all natural. After all is done, wilderness is shaped into a space occupied by man-made structures: chambers, windows, doors, halls, verandas, eaves, courtyards, fences, gates, field-paths, roads, and more. More significant than the artificiality of the construction, however, is the representation of spatial experience in Shen Yue's lines. After the various structures have been put in place, for example, a path leading from the inside to the outside is clearly formed; in other words, these structures are the human's means—the poet's—of framing a space. Scholars including Kang-i Sun Chang and Xiaoshan Yang have noted the occasional use of artificial frames in Xie Lingyun's and Xie Tiao's poems;[30] I will further note that the practice is in fact more prevalent and significant in Yongming poetry than we had previously realized. A window is not just a window, and a door is not just a door—they are a representation of human perception in and of space, or, more specifically, a representation of perceptive eyes. In the poem below, for example, Xie Tiao gives the impression that his study was built "lofty" for the specific purpose of aiding his vision.

Gazing at Ease from My Lofty Study in the Xuancheng
Commandery: In Reply to Legal Counsel Lü　郡內高齋閑望答呂法曹

Lines 1–6

Structured such that it rises higher and higher—	結構何迢遞
My panoramic view stretches far and deep.	曠望極高深
Within the window frame, the distant ridges are in lines;	窗中列遠岫
Beyond the balconies, the lofty forest bends down.	庭際俯喬林
As the sun rises, birds in a flock disperse in every direction;	日出眾鳥散
When the mountains darken, a lone gibbon cries out.[31]	山暝孤猿吟

Served by the height of the building, Xie Tiao enjoys the "panoramic view."
The frame of the window focuses his sense of distance and alignment; the
balcony accentuates his sense of height. If not for his "lofty study," he would
be unable to see all at once the birds dispersing "in different directions" or
to hear so acutely the cry of "a lone gibbon." The loftiness of his study allows him another panoramic view in a different poem:

Reviewing Matters in My Lofty Study　高齋視事

Lines 1–4

Remaining snow reflects the green mountain;	餘雪映青山
Chilly fog opens up to the day's sun.	寒霧開白日
Slowly, faintly, riverside villages appear;	曖曖江村見
Lushly, profusely, coastal trees emerge.[32]	離離海樹出

What is being accentuated in this instance is a slowly emerging view: as the
fog disperses in the rising sun, trees and villages on the farthest edges of the
water come into sight bit by bit. In another poem, titled "Setting Up My
Residence" ("Zhizhai"), Xie Tiao turns the simple act of "opening doors and
windows" into a revealing moment of seeing in great detail.

I push open the doors to face the autumn wind;	闢館臨秋風
Throw wide the windows and gaze at the wintry dawn.	敞窗望寒旭
Wind shatters the lotuses in the pond;	風碎池中荷
Frost cuts the knotgrasses of "South of the River."[33]	霜翦江南菉

Xie Tiao's "crossing over" the threshold of interior and exterior is done
solely by vision. Viewing from the inside, protected from wind and frost,
he focuses on details—it is not the lotuses, but their reflections in the water

that are being shattered by the wind; and the patterns of cracks formed by the frost make it appear as if it is "cutting" the knotgrasses.[34]

Even more importantly, the Yongming poets' distinctive use of framing reflects not only their acute sense of how human perception works in space but also their keen observation of nature. Xie Tiao's poem about "setting up a north-facing window" best demonstrates this point. In earlier literature, the north-facing window, being the coolest place in a house, is commonly depicted as the best place for taking a nap on a warm summer afternoon. Tao Yuanming put it this way: "I have once said that if, in the fifth or sixth month, I could lie down beneath the north-facing window, by chance catching a cool breeze for one brief moment, then I would call myself [Fu] xi, the Emperor on the High."[35] Xie Tiao's north-facing window, however, is not for catching a nap or a breeze, but *the view*.

Setting Up a North-facing Window Recently:　新治北窗和何從事
Harmonizing with Retainer He

Lines 3–10

I open the window, anticipating a clear and panoramic
　　view;　　　　　　　　　　　　　　　　　　　　闢牖期清曠
Rolling up the curtains, I await the beautiful sight.　　開簾候風景
How grand it is! The sun casts its light on the streams,　泱泱日照溪
As round clouds emerge from the peaks.　　　　　　　團團雲出嶺
High above, the magnolia rafters are steep;　　　　　岧嶢蘭橑峻
Joined together, the stone paths are straight.　　　　駢闐石路整
North of the pool, trees are afloat;　　　　　　　　池北樹如浮
Beyond the bamboo groves, the mountains loom
　　like shadows.[36]　　　　　　　　　　　　　　竹外山猶影

Having framed his gaze with the north-facing window, Xie Tiao waits for the sun to cast its rays in the "right" direction. When that happens, as it does in the poem, the best view comes into sight. The words *qi* ("expect") and *hou* ("await") highlight his anticipation of this visual experience. Even though he cannot control the sun, Xie Tiao observes and then predicts its emergence, and frames his view based on that prediction. The trees are already "afloat," and the dark shades of the mountains rise up in the background, threatening to absorb all the shapes and forms that human eyes—with the help of light—have come to recognize as "beauty." Xie Tiao's north-facing window is the symbol of a pair of eyes that do not merely see beauty—they see the momentariness of beauty.

Not only architectural structures are built as such; flowers, trees, and grasses are planted based on prediction too. In his *fu*, as he catalogues the plants that he grows in his garden, Shen Yue also tells us how he *expects* them to turn out:

I want them to spread out in dense growth,	欲令紛披蓊鬱
Sprouting green and harboring red;	吐綠攢朱
Lacing the windows, brightening the doors;	羅窗映戶
Receiving raindrops, holding up the corners;	接霤承隅
Opening their vermilion petals to shine all around;	開丹房以四照
Extending their jade-green leaves to all nine avenues;	舒翠葉而九衢
Drawing crimson blooms from their purple stalks;	抽紅英於紫蔕
Holding plain white buds on their green calyxes.[37]	銜素蕊於青跗

In an interesting twist in perspective, he even anticipates the plants "peeping into" his window:

Tooth of wild goose, tongue of elaphure,	雁齒麋舌
Oxlip and wild boar's head,[38]	牛脣彘首
Spreading profusely by the sunny bank of the south pool,	布濩南池之陽
Glittering brightly to the rear of the north terrace.	爛漫北樓之後
Some shade the islets and cover the ground;	或幕渚而芘地
Some encircle the frames and peep into the windows.[39]	或縈窗而窺牖

It was a unique form of human control—one based on prediction and anticipation of the course of nature—that fundamentally shaped the garden aesthetic of the Yongming era.

Vacating the Garden

If it is a matter of the state of mind, the place does not matter—or does it? Tao Yuanming chanted these famous lines:

I build my hut within the human realm,	結廬在人境
Yet there is no noise from carriages and horses.[40]	而無車馬喧
May I ask how, sir, are you able to do this?	問君何能爾
When the mind is far, the place is naturally remote.[41]	心遠地自偏

These lines reflect the basic premise of the philosophy of Zhuangzi (late fourth century B.C.E.): it is one's state of mind, rather than one's physical being, that is most vital in sustaining a "natural" (*ziran*) way of life. But, if the state of the mind is what truly matters, why then the need to "return to the garden" (*gui yuan*)? In Tao Yuanming's "Field and Garden Poetry" (*tianyuan shi*), we already see that the relationship between garden and mind is not static but interactive and dynamic. While the garden can "enlighten" the mind, the mind can also shape the garden; in the ideal state, the garden and the mind become one, when words are "forgotten" (*wang*) and the desire to act dissolves away. Even when the influence of Tao Yuanming is evident, in the Yongming poets' works the mind interacts with the garden in a distinctively different manner.

In the context of their Buddhist outlook, the Yongming poets seek to transcend the garden. This is exactly Wang Rong's aspiration in his poem about *youyuan* ("roaming the garden"). The word *you* may suggest a kind of spontaneity or randomness, but Wang Rong's *you* is very focused.

Roaming the Villa Garden after Listening to a Lecture at the Monastery of Residing-in-Mysticism: Writing in Seven Rhymes at the Command of the Director of Instruction. 棲玄寺聽講畢遊邸園七韻應司徒教

When the Way presides, the Deeds will go far from here;	道勝業茲遠
When the mind is unoccupied, the place can be vacant.	心閒地能隟
The cassia rafters are still aromatic, being newly chiseled;	桂橑鬱初裁
The orchid platform is level, extending outward.	蘭墀坦將闢
The empty eaves face toward a long isle;	虛檐對長嶼
And the lofty balconies overlook a wide lake.	高軒臨廣液
The fragrant grasses are lined up in rows;	芳草列成行
And the beautiful trees mingle, as if piled together.	嘉樹紛如積
Flowing breezes turn along the winding path;	流風轉還逕
Light mists rise above the tall rocks.	清煙泛喬石
The sun swells, and the mountains become radiant;	日汨山照紅
In the pines' reflection, the water gleams brilliantly.	松映水華碧
Let it roam—appreciation outside the human realm!	暢哉人外賞
Gradually, gradually, my longing fades like the west-setting sun.[42]	遲遲眷西夕

Wang Rong apparently wrote the poem after attending a Buddhist lecture, as the impact of the lecture on him still lingers.[43] For Wang Rong, the "Way" (Dao) is not Zhuangzi's *ziran*, but Buddhist enlightenment; and "deeds" (*ye*) are *karma*, "the unrelenting record of meritorious or demeritorious acts, words, and thoughts, which determine a person's progress toward, or regression from, Enlightenment."[44] Wang Rong's Buddhist tone, however, does not preclude him from echoing Tao Yuanming's very Zhuangzi-like line—"When the mind is far, the place is naturally remote." We assume Tao Yuanming's place is *not* remote to begin with, and the same assumption can be made about Wang Rong's locale: the garden is not "vacant" (*xi*). And his "roaming" is a mental process of "vacating" the garden, not by simply forsaking it, but by contemplating its forms in a systematic manner. The platform is "about to extend outward," the eaves "face toward a long isle," the balconies "look over a wide lake"—in Wang Rong's eyes, all the appurtances of the monastery are oriented outward, in the direction of nature. And so he moves on toward nature, heeding the "guidance" of the monastery: the "fragrant grasses" are "lined up in rows," the breezes flow along "a winding path," and the pines reflect in the water, causing it to "gleam brilliantly." As it turns out, the nature he sees is as organized as the monastery. Wang Rong is, after all, surveying a garden estate—a human imitation of nature. In the context of this space, the phrase "appreciation outside the human realm" (*renwai shang*) in the last couplet is particularly ironical. But the irony is only ours. For Wang Rong, the effect of his "systematic roaming" is that

Gradually, gradually, my longing fades like the west-
    setting sun.   遲遲眷西夕

Richard B. Mather sees a "natural association with death and rebirth in the Western Paradise of Amitābha Buddha" in this line.[45] When all longings have faded, one transcends the cycle of death and rebirth and reaches Nirvāna. Wang Rong's poem reveals a gradualist's approach to achieving Nirvāna: his mind slowly "vacates" the garden by moving *through* it piece by piece, in a focused, meticulous, and orderly fashion; here, the systematic and diminutive analysis of the Chengshi school's training seems to have come to fruition. In contrast to Tao Yuanming, Wang Rong has as his ultimate aim transcending and not becoming one with the garden. Recast through a Buddhist perspective, the garden is but a path along the mind's journey.

Wang Rong's contemplative view of the garden finds resonance in a poem by Xie Tiao. Written "in the middle garden," this poem is linked to (*lian*) those of others, forming a series.

In the Middle Garden of Merit Officer Ji 紀功曹中園

Retainer He: 何從事:

The orchid courtyard embraces the distant breezes;	蘭庭迎遠風
The fragrant trees join the cloudy cliffs.	芳林接雲嶠
As their slanted leaves move with the mild whirlwind,	傾葉順清飆
Their lengthy stalks await the high-soaring cranes.	脩莖佇高鶴

Palace Gentleman Wu: 吳郎:

On and on, the evening clouds return;	連綿夕雲歸
Murkier and murkier, the sun is about to descend.	晻曖日將落
Not an inch of time can be made to stay,	寸陰不可留
So, on the orchid platform, why stop drinking?[46]	蘭堭豈停酌

The Grand Warden [Xie Tiao]: 府君:

Vermillion cherry blossoms still gleam on the trees;	丹櫻猶照樹
Green bamboo skins are now shedding their sheaths.	綠筠方解籜
Forever intent on "double forgetting"—[47]	永志能兩忘
Through instant appreciation, we part with the hills and the valleys.[48]	即賞謝丘壑

The first two poems tell us where the poets are viewing from: on the "orchid platform" in the "orchid courtyard." Retainer He begins "on a high note" by associating the view of the garden with distant, lofty, almost other-worldly images, giving the impression that he is looking upward, "roaming" far beyond the garden itself. Palace Gentleman Wu uses the "evening clouds" to provide a link to the first poem, but his view of the garden "descends" after that, as he follows "the sun that is about to descend." His concern also turns toward the mundane: he is reminded that time—the force against human existence—is upon them. And his "solution" reminds us of the tone of an earlier kind of poetry:

Light and darkness change places in a flooding course,	浩浩陰陽移
our span of years is like morning dew.	年命如朝露

Man's life is as swift as a sojourn,	人生忽如寄
old age, not so firm as metal and stone.	壽無金石固
. . .	
The best thing is to drink good ale	不如飲美酒
and to dress in silks fine and pale.[49]	被服紈與素

Xie Tiao's response to Palace Gentleman Wu is worth noting in two respects. First, his view "descends" even farther—in fact, it has come so close that he can see the small cherry blossoms that remain on the trees and the sheaths that the bamboo branches have just shed. As an interesting contrast to Wang Rong's "outward" view, Xie Tiao's and his friend's view moves downward and inward, from "beyond" to "right here," immediately in front of the eyes. And, second, as discussed in Chapter Three, Xie Tiao was a sensitive observer of "old sheaths." As he does in other poems, he juxtaposes the image of "old sheaths" with a contrasting one here ("Vermillion cherry blossoms still gleam on the trees")—again, he sees both the signs of life and death. When they "cancel" each other out, one reaches the state of *liangwang* ("double forgetting"). Even though the phrase *liangwang*—and his dualistic approach of juxtaposing life and death—recall such terms as *zuowang* ("sitting in forgetfulness") and *jianwang* in the *Zhuangzi*,[50] there is no doubt that Xie Tiao is referring to the Buddhist concept *śūnyatā*, like Shen Yue's usage of *jianwang* in his Buddhist essay, "On the Non-Extinction of the Spirit."[51] The idea of *wang* ("forgetting") in Yongming poetry, in other words, is not "to be one with the Grand Whole" (*tong yu Datong*), as expressed in the *Zhuangzi*, but a Buddhist state of absolute and complete void.[52] Even though his viewing of the garden moves in a different direction from Wang Rong's, his conclusion nonetheless resonates with Wang's. In Wang Rong's poem, that Buddhist state is "the fading of all longings," and in Xie Tiao's, it is to *part with* (*xie*, not *tong*, "to be one with") "the hills and the valleys." In Xie Tiao's poem, the garden functions once again as a space for contemplative viewing in which the ultimate aim is for the mind to "vacate" the garden. In this state of mind, the mundane issue about time's passing, raised by Palace Gentleman Wu, is no longer relevant; and past generations' attitude of "don't stop drinking" is deemed invalid.

Xie Tiao calls what is a contemplative observation of the garden *jishang*, "instant appreciation." The adverb *ji* indicates both an element of time and of space: right now and right here. It is given specific emphasis in Chinese

Buddhist discourse about the perception of form, as reflected in such terms as *jise* ("instant form") and *jiwu* ("instant thing").[53] Even though they agreed with the basic concept that all forms or things were only the temporary congregation of *yin* and *yuan* and hence not real, Southern Dynasties Buddhists—as noted in Chapter Two—tended to hold a more flexible position in regard to how the idea might be understood at the levels of the Mundane Truth and the Ultimate Truth. If *se* (Skt. *rūpa*, "form") can be "real" at a certain "mundane" level, then the need to "destruct" it is unquestionable. But earlier, Sengzhao (384–414) had already advocated a more direct approach:

> By "instant form," it is clear that form is not form in itself; hence, though called form it is not form. Those who speak of form should only take it as instant form and that is it—there is no such thing as having to wait to form the form before it is form![54]

Even though Xie Tiao lapses into the kind of dualistic or relativistic view that Sengzhao criticizes, his idea of "instant appreciation" shows the characteristics of the latter's thesis. He "views" and "parts with" the forms *in the same instance*. Here, Xie Tiao shows an unusual awareness of how his mind is perceiving an instance and in an instant—right now and right here. As such, his mind can move on, "parting with" all that it encounters on its path. In both Wang Rong's "outward" view and Xie Tiao's "inward" view, the garden becomes a space through which the mind "roams" and then "vacates."

The Garden Conflicted

As we have seen, the Yongming poets' garden is shaped by various forces, including pragmatic, aesthetic, and religious. In this garden, the courtier-poet attempted to balance his relationship with the central court, rejected the ostentatious, created an idealized nature, and practiced his Buddhist faith. While these forces come together in shaping the garden, they also act against each other. When we consider the conflict that they bring into the courtier-poet's vision of his garden, we see a more profound and more realistic image of him. Because the Yongming poets did not attempt to find consistency in their depiction of the garden or construct only a singular form of it, they revealed their personal struggles, private sentiments, and deepest anxieties in a fuller way. In the case of Shen Yue, the conflict arose from his desire to be distant from but also close to the central court; it also emerged from his simultaneous pursuit of spiritual progress and aesthetic fulfillment.

Aspiring to let all his attachments and desires fade away, he allows his Buddhist faith to reverberate throughout his "*Fu* on Dwelling in the Suburbs":

Dispel external things, be rid of them altogether;	排外物以齊遣
It is I alone who will make or break attachments.	獨為累之在余
To calm my heart and banish all attachments,	欲息心以遣累
I must turn away from humans and then I can be free.	必違人而後豁
I lodge my will in the Pure Land,	棲余志於淨國
And return my heart to the *bodhi* field.[55]	歸余心於道場

The Pure Land is the Western Paradise of Amitābha Buddha, where "fallen blossoms from the jeweled trees accumulated to a depth of four inches thick on the ground and are blown away by a heavenly wind every few hours."[56] That is the only vision of "a garden" to be beheld—but, due to "attachments to external things," what Shen Yue sees is his own garden, changing ever so beautifully through the four seasons.

The evening trees open their flowers;	晚樹開花
The early blossoms shed their spikes.	初英落蕊
At times they are in different groves, separated into vermilion and green;	或異林而分丹青
Suddenly, as the wind comes, they are mixed together in red and violet.	乍因風而雜紅紫
The purple lotus sprouts at night;	紫蓮夜發
The red water lily unfurls at dawn.	紅荷曉舒
While a light breeze gently blows,	輕風微動
Their fragrance enfolds me.	芬芳襲余
The wind rustles and patters through the garden trees;	風騷屑於園樹
The moon casts flickering shadows of the pool bamboos.	月籠連於池竹
Long boughs spread out from the cassia by the eaves;	蔓長柯於簷桂
Yellow flowers come forth from the chrysanthemums in the courtyard.	發黃華於庭菊
Ice hangs on the ditches and encircles the embankments;	冰懸垎而帶坻
Snow hovers over the pine trees and covers the wilds.	雪縈松而被野

| Ducks fly in flocks and do not disperse; | 鴨屯飛而不散 |
| Wild geese, soaring high, are ready to descend. | 雁高翔而欲下 |

All these are seasonal things to be cherished;	并時物之可懷
Though coming from outside, they are not unreal.	雖外來而非假
Indeed, my feeling and nature are stored within them;	實情性之所留滯
I am the one who will them, unable to let them go.[57]	亦志之而不能捨也。

From the Buddhist perspective, these seasonal things—no matter how beautiful they are in our eyes—are not real. But the garden owner, having built them all, cannot view them as unreal. For him, "vacating" the garden is a very personal and difficult struggle, in spite of the promise of the real garden. Here, near the close of his *fu*, Shen Yue faces his attachment to worldly beauty with complete honesty.

In another poem where he writes about the variety and luxuriance of the vegetation in his garden, Shen Yue suddenly reveals a different kind of impulse.

Shen Yue, "Strolling Through the Garden"	沈約, 行園
Cold melons have just been laid out on the ridges,	寒瓜方臥壠
And fall wild rice, too, has filled up the banks.	秋菰亦滿陂
The purple eggplants, all mixed up, are especially colorful;	紫茄紛爛熳
The green taro, dense now, has uneven leaves.	綠芋鬱參差
New cabbages are approaching "being grabbed by the handful";	初菘向堪把
Seasonal leeks grow more and more luxuriant by the day.	時韭日離離
The tall pear trees bear abundant fruits—	高梨有繁實
In what way is it inferior to the "Branches of Ten Thousand Years"?	何減萬年枝
Even the deserted ditch has gathered some wild geese—	荒渠集野鴈
So why the need for Kunming Pool?[58]	安用昆明池

Evoking the memory of the ostentatious garden by his mention of an exotic tree ("Branches of Ten Thousand Years") and a famous lake ("Kunming Pool"), Shen Yue makes the point that his is a different kind of garden.[59] Indeed, it is buzzing with the life and colors of ordinary fruits and vegetables. But his busy "stroll" reveals a material need: with every step, he takes in another sight of a sure harvest; even "the deserted ditch" has "borne fruits" now that it has "gathered some wild geese." In his own garden, he is self-sufficient, blessed with abundance, and assured. And it is in that material sense that the garden is, in Xie Tiao's words, "a place to rest the heart" (*qixindi*). He responds to Shen Yue in the following poem.

Harmonizing with Libationer Shen's　　　　和沈祭酒行園
"Strolling Through the Garden"

The clear Qinhuai River is "east of the Lengthy Thicket,"	清淮左長薄
Where a deserted path hides away the lofty hut.	荒徑隱高蓬
Returning tides rise at dawn and at dusk;	回潮旦夕上
Cold canals flow through left and right.	寒渠左右通
Frosty pathways, in multitude, crisscross in webs;	霜畦紛綺錯
Fall field-dividers are becoming dense from profuse undergrowth.	秋町鬱蒙茸
Ring-round pears, hanging down, have deepened their color;	環梨縣已紫
Pearl-like pomegranates, about to break off, are just showing red.	珠榴折且紅
You have found a place to rest your heart—	君有棲心地
And my happiness is the same as yours.	伊我歡既同
Why the need to reside by the Sweet Spring,	何用甘泉側
Where the jade trees overlook the green onions?[60]	玉樹望青蔥

Is the desertion described in the third couplet due simply to the end of the farming season or a lack of care? The sight of colorful fruit trees in Xie Tiao's poem, though an obvious "harmonizing" with Shen Yue's poem, could not be more sudden and unexpected. Has Xie Tiao been looking for colorful fruits in his own garden or did Shen Yue's colorful garden appear in his mind's eye? Whichever is the case, his vision invariably incorporates signs of life and signs of decline. His line congratulating Shen Yue—"You have found a place to rest your heart"—underscores a different kind of materialism. A garden wherein one can "rest his heart" is not a garden in the abstract, but one that literally "feeds." The field paths and irrigation system, alluded to in Xiao Tiao's poem, were all a part of a supply mechanism that would ensure the garden's self-sufficiency.[61] Does Xie Tiao feel that he, too, has found a garden to "rest his heart"? His poem gives no clear answer, but it certainly makes the abundance in Shen Yue's garden seem extravagant by comparison.

If the sight of fruits and vegetables offers assurance to the garden owner, what happens when all is gone? The end of the year, especially when the day is closing, is not the time to stroll through the garden.

Shen Yue, "Spending the Night in the Eastern Garden" 沈約, 宿東園

The path where the Prince of Chensi pitted fighting cocks,	陳王鬥雞道
The road where Pan Anren gathered firewood—	安仁采樵路
How is this Eastern Suburb any different from those of the past?	東郊豈異昔
It can at least let me ease my steps.	聊可閒余步
The wild trails already are winding this and that way;	野徑既盤紆
And the deserted footpaths, too, are crossing each other.	荒阡亦交互
The hibiscus hedges are sparse, but again dense;	槿籬疏復密
The twig fences, some new, and some old.	荊扉新且故
From treetops come the howls of windy gales;	樹頂鳴風飆
On grassroots, frost and dew are thickening.	草根積霜露
A startled deer runs off, not stopping for a moment;	驚麏去不息
The migrating birds, every now and then, look at each other.	征鳥時相顧
On the hut's beam, a sorrowful owl screeches;	茅棟嘯愁鴟
And along the level ridge, a shivering hare runs.	平岡走寒兔
While evening shadows enwrap the layered mounds,	夕陰帶層阜
The drawn-out mists extend like white silk.	長煙引輕素
Time that flies by suddenly overwhelms me—	飛光忽我遒
Is it just the year that's ending?	豈止歲云暮
If only I could be granted an elixir from the West Mountain,	若蒙西山藥
Then in my declining years I may still make it [to the end].[62]	頹齡倘能度

With the farming season now over, Shen Yue simplifies the function of the garden to this: "ease my steps" (*xian yubu*). But his stroll this time has the same intensity as before. Here, with every step also comes a new sight, only that all he sees now is a series of disorder and desertion and, ultimately, of things ending. Wilderness has come back to reclaim the garden. Walking among deserted paths, thick frost, and wild animals, Shen Yue's "unease" cannot be more obvious. When the garden goes into a state of "rest," it neither "rests his heart" nor "eases his steps." And that reflects the fundamental struggle of his attempt to carve out an existence for himself between the human and wilderness. Coming face to face with wilderness, he suddenly sees that he is helpless before its force; as he recalls the "eastern suburbs" of the past and their poets, he sees himself and his own garden being absorbed into time and history, taken over by wilderness. Even an elixir from the Western Mountain may only help him "make it" (*du*).

When the Candle Goes Out

Tao Yuanming has most successfully personified one who "returns to the garden." Like a bird returning to its old woods and a fish to its former pool, he takes leave of the "dusty snares" (*chenwang*) into which he has "fallen by mistake for thirty years"; and he returns to the "gardens and fields," where he truly belongs.[63] It is a heroic homecoming. A sense of relief, like a burden lifted from one's shoulders, comes through Tao Yuanming's lines:

I have been trapped for long inside a bird cage;	久在樊籠裏
Now, once again, I can return to nature.[64]	復得返自然

Life after the "return" might not be as romantic as it appears.[65] But Tao Yuanming's garden idealism conveys the idea that it is about making a choice and the "return" is a choice made. In spite of their faint echo of Tao Yuanming, the Yongming poets' "return" is never a choice in the real sense of the word. The final poem of this chapter is one of Xie Tiao's. Here, a withdrawn, exhausted, and dispirited Xie Tiao, "professing sickness," returns to his garden.

Professing Sickness, I Return to My Garden: Informing My Relatives and Associates	移病還園示親屬
Tired of schemes, exhausted of worldly affairs—	疲策倦人世
I turn back my nature to reside among secluded hedges.	歛性就幽蓬
Setting aside the zither, I stand looking at the chilly moon;	停琴佇涼月
Extinguishing the candles, I listen to the returning geese.	滅燭聽歸鴻
Cool mists become clear as dusk falls;	涼薰乘暮晰
Autumn beam-light, against the night's sky, is hollow.	秋華臨夜空
The leaves hang low, so I know the dew is dense;	葉低知露密
Mountain peaks are blocked, and I realize the clouds are thick.[66]	崖斷識雲重

Upon his return, Xie Tiao finds no relief, only a cessation of activities. He "sets aside the zither" and "extinguishes the candles," for at this moment he wants no human construct to stand between him and his senses. When the candle goes out, the senses become more acute: the eyes adjust, the ears sharpen. Not to mention this is Xie Tiao: he does not have to touch it to know that "the dew is dense" or to see them to know that "the clouds are thick." In his dejected and yet acute state, the garden is minimized to these: the sound of "returning geese," "chilly and hollow" moonlight, cool mists, leaves, dew, and the blocked-out view of clouds and mountains. At this moment, he no longer tries to accentuate the form of the garden.

A deep mystic permeates the next half of Xie Tiao's poem:

Breaking a lotus to patch up my cold sleeves;	折荷葺寒袂
Opening the mirror, I see my declining face.	開鏡眄衰容
The lake, darkening, stirs up pure vapors;	海暮騰清氣
The river, reaching the pass, conceals the residing breath.	河關秘棲沖
Misty asarum, at this time, has not yet stop growing.	煙衡時未歇
While polypores and orchids are, one after another, withering away.[67]	芝蘭去相從

These rather cryptic images are clearly inspired by the *Chuci* (Songs of Chu): the first line originates from "Encountering Sorrows" ("Lisao"): "I made a coat of lotus and water-chestnut leaves. / And gathered lotus leaves to make myself a skirt";[68] the third line recalls the spiritual journey described in the "Nine Songs" ("Jiuge"): "Flying aloft, he soars serenely, / Riding the pure vapour, guiding *yin* and *yang*";[69] and "asarum," "polypores," "orchids"—symbols of the integrity of a loyal minister—are recurring images throughout the anthology. Earlier studies have interpreted these lines as Xie Tiao's declaration of his intention to go into reclusion.[70] But Qu Yuan, the main persona of the *Chuci*, is no recluse; he is an unjustly maligned courtier forced into exile.[71] Xie Tiao is taking on that persona in this poem. A sense of impending end—that there is no way out—prevails through his "return." We have no idea where this end will lead, but signs of life and death emerge again in his finale.

The choice to "return to the garden" is perhaps a false premise for understanding the courtier-poets of Qi-Liang times. Their "return to the garden" does not signal a choice, but rather a *temporary* retreat from life at the court or a *moment* of inward turning toward "one's true nature." Situated between the human and the wilderness, this garden is an in-between space, where man-made constructs and nature are negotiated, both material life and religious life are pursued, and political considerations and personal fulfillment are weighted side by side. As elusive as their moments in the garden may seem to be, they not only reveal the personal struggles of the courtier, but, even more refreshingly, a self-acknowledgment and honest accounting of these struggles.

Leaving the Capital City

> The courtiers in the land "South of the [Yangzi] River,"
> who had crossed the river following the "mid-term
> restoration" of the Jin, originally traveled there only as
> émigrés (*jilü*).[1] Yet until now, despite having been there
> for eight or nine generations, none of them has culti-
> vated any farmland; they all rely on official compensa-
> tion and salaries to feed themselves.[2]

The epigraph is by Yan Zhitui (531–ca. 591), himself a ninth-generation descendent of a "courtier in the land 'South of the [Yangzi] River.'"[3] An ad-
vocate of rigorous family education and strict parenting, Yan Zhitui was
writing to warn his own children of "feeling privileged and becoming com-
placent" (*youxian*).[4] Read in the broader context of the Southern Dynasties,
his statement testifies to an important shift in the mindset of the courtiers
and other elites of the time, particularly those of northern émigré origins. It
points to, among other things, a fading of the émigré mentality among the
descendents of the northern émigrés in the Jin. In other words, they no longer felt like northerners residing only temporarily in the south. Even so, the
state of "temporarily residing in a foreign place"—what Yan Zhitui called
jilü—had never disappeared from their experience, and the Yongming poets
would write about it often in their poems. To be sure, for them the vision
of "returning" to the north—if it was there at all—was vague. Nevertheless,
their poems on *jilü* immediately touch upon the most human issue about
belonging and displacement, often in a complex and ironical way.

"Where the Master Is From, No One Knows"

A case in point is Xie Kun (d. 324), an ancestor of Xie Tiao of five generations earlier. According to a 1965 report of an archaeological excavation, the
items found in Xie Kun's grave, which was located near Nanjing (the modern site of Jiankang), include a funerary inscription that reads in part:

> The former administrator of Yuzhang of Jin, Xie Kun, *zi* Youyu, of Yangxia
> in Chen Commandery died on the twenty-eighth day of the eleventh month
> of the Taining reign period [January 10, 324] and was temporarily buried at
> Shizi gang in Jiankang district.[5]

As William G. Crowell points out, the reason Xie was only "temporarily
buried" (*jiazang*) was in "the hope of later reburying him in the north."[6] But
there his grave remained—in the south—until our time. Something else
has also remained, through his funerary inscription as well as his biography
in the *Jin shu*, for more than a millennium: his identification as "a man of
Yangxia in the Commandery of Chen" (*Chenguo Yangxia ren ye*).[7] Yangxia in
Chen Commandery, in modern day Henan, was of course in the north. The
fact that, as a practical matter, the identification meant that he could enjoy
the social, economic, and political privileges awarded to northern émigrés
under the Eastern Jin's system is beside the point.[8] The state of his burial—
that it was meant to be only temporary—speaks to a profoundly human
issue: where one believes he or she truly belongs. In *Cannery Row* by John
Steinbeck (1902–1968), the Chinese grocer Lee Chong, "a soft man with the
bones of his grandfather," resolves the issue for his grandfather in a touch-
ingly macabre scene:

> For Lee Chong dug into the grave on China Point and found the yellow
> bones, the skull with gray ropy hair still sticking to it. And Lee carefully
> packed the bones, femurs, and tibias really straight, skull in the middle, with
> pelvis and clavicle surrounding it and ribs curving on either side. Then Lee
> Chong sent his boxed and brittle grandfather over the western sea to lie at
> last in ground made holy by his ancestors.[9]

The issue, then, is about *xiang* or *guxiang* ("hometown," "native place") and
of how the condition of *jilü* evokes the emotions and imaginings surrounding the idea of one's hometown, and, in some cases, provokes a vivid enact-
ment in an attempt to reach it.

Simply put, *jilü* is the state of being away from one's *guxiang*. As portrayed in Chinese literature, *jilü*—regardless of the circumstance under which it happens—always causes emotional distress, as the memory of *guxiang* lingers on and the longing for it intensifies. Not forgetting one's *guxiang* and longing for it are certainly considered virtuous sentiments in the Chinese cultural tradition. As Laozi said: "When passing through one's *guxiang*, he would descend from his carriage—is he not implying that he does not forget his past?"[10] Shen Yue would see the same sentiment in the northern émigrés of the Eastern Jin, whom he described as "those lodging in a drift" (*liuyu*):

> After the Rong and the Di violated the inner land, the Jin moved east, and the refugees of the middle plain spread out beyond the [Yangzi] River; while the territories encompassing these prefectures—You, Bing, Ji, Yong, Yan, Yu, Qing, and Xu—were lost to the rebels. Many, on their own, supporting their elders and their feet bound, pledged their loyalty and lodged themselves in the Jing and Yue; and among the hundred commanderies and thousand cities, those lodging in a drift made up all the households. While the common folk listened for the "Wild Geese Song," the learned men bore thoughts of cherishing their origins—they all established their own towns and districts, in the hope of restoring their old communities.[11]

By "establishing their own towns and districts" and "restoring their old communities," Shen Yue is referring to a unique phenomenon. The northern émigrés of the Eastern Jin had renamed the places in the south in which they had come to reside with the names of their hometowns in the north. As a result, "in the town of Wei there was the Han district, and in the county of Qi there were natives of Zhao."[12] This was not a practice left only to individuals; it became a part of Eastern Jin's administrative restructuring. In 335, for example, Langye, a northern commandery in modern-day Shandong, was "lodged" (*qiaozhi*) under the jurisdiction of Jiangcheng (in modern Jiangsu) and called South Langye Commandery (Nan Langye Jun); and since there was a Linyi County—Wang Rong's ancestral hometown— in Langye Commandery in the north, a county of the same name was also "lodged" under South Langye Commandery.[13] That raises an interesting question: when a person is said to be "a man of Linyi in Langye" (*Langye Linyi ren ye*), which is exactly how Wang Rong is identified in his biography in the *Nan Qi shu*, is he a man of northern or southern Langye?[14] The situation was further complicated by the policy called "residence determination" (*tuduan*); first implemented in the Eastern Jin between 326 and 334, it meant that "a person who was a native of one area but who was actually residing in another was to be made a legal resident of the latter place."[15] Under this policy, a person's official native classification could change. In the *Chen shu*, for example, Emperor Wu (Chen Baxian; r. 557–559) is identified as "a man of Xiaruo li in Changcheng of Wuxing [in modern Zhejiang]" (*Wuxing Changcheng Xiaruo li ren ye*), which means he was a southerner; however, that was only because his ancestors, having uprooted themselves from Yingchuan (in modern Henan) during the Jin and moved south, "made Changcheng their home" (*sui jia yan*) and "became men of Changcheng" under the "residence determination" of the Xianhe reign period (326–334).[16] Obviously, Emperor Wu's ancestors made a very different choice from Xie Tiao's ancestors.[17] The contrast highlights the fact that one's sense of belonging—that is, what place one would call *guxiang*—hinges not only on what one actually remembers but also on what one *chooses* to remember. The state of *jilü*—a drifting in longing for the *guxiang*—does not persist in an unchanged manner; instead, it shifts and evolves.

In the *Nan Qi shu*, Xie Tiao bears the same identification as his ancestor Xie Kun—"a man of Yangxia in the Commandery of Chen."[18] However, separated as the two Xies were by 140 years, the identification evolved into something distinctively different for Xie Tiao. He would experience the distress of *jilü* as well, but the memory that tormented him—at least in his poems—had little to do with the north.[19] The place that he called *guxiang* was where Xie Kun's grave laid in "a drift" and continued to remain so for more than a millennium. In light of that, one cannot help but recall how Tao Yuanming "subverted" the standard biographies' practice of identifying a person by his place of origin: in the "Biography of Master Five Willows," his "fictive autobiography,"[20] he begins by declaring, "Where the master is from, no one knows."[21]

The Elite Men of the Capital City

In a memorial attributed to him, Shen Yue offers this criticism: "The elite men of today all gather in the capital city, some of them hoarding its land and refusing to leave—are they not ignorant and unworthy?"[22] In this memorial, he again romanticizes a more open, equitable, and talent-driven time during the Han.[23] He admires how "the non-differentiation between elites and commoners" at the time had encouraged people to stay in their villages and towns (as opposed to "gathering at the capital city" in search of opportunities for official appointment); even those who held the highest positions, according to his observation, returned to their home districts after retirement.[24] It was a time when, he wrote, "one would not travel to the capital city, unless one became an appointed official."[25] However, given that he had retired to the suburbs of Jiankang rather than to his hometown in Wuxing, one could accuse Shen Yue of "hoarding land" in the capital city as well.[26]

Somewhat ironically, Xiao Zixian would describe Shen Yue and his fellow Yongming courtier-poets in the light of another "gathering" culture: "At the end of the Yongming reign period, the elite men of the capital city greatly enjoyed literary composition and discussion of arguments, and they would all gather (*cou*) at the Prince of Jingling's Western Villa."[27] Xiao Zixian identifies these men simply as "the elite men of the capital city" (*jingyi renshi*). As three of the Eight Friends known for their gathering at the Prince of Jingling's Western Villa, Shen Yue, Wang Rong, and Xie Tiao were certainly the most famous of these "elite men of the capital city."[28] *Jingyi* stands in contrast to *xiangli* or *xiangyi*, which refers to the villages or towns where ordinary people reside but also has the loaded meaning of "hometown" or "native place" as in *guxiang*. To be in the *jingyi*, as implied in Shen Yue's memorial, is to be away from one's *guxiang*—in that case, can one exist as both a *jingyi renshi* and a man of his *guxiang*?

Xie Tiao was one such man, for he had grown up in the Jiankang area.[29] In other words, the line between *jingyi* and *guxiang* is not always clear. Even though he had originally come from Wuxing, Shen Yue was not always clear on the separation between *jingyi* and *guxiang* either. The blurring of the two was perhaps caused by the culture of "gathering in the capital city" among elite men. And, more often than not, it was when they were leaving Jiankang, as they set out into *jilü*, that the Yongming poets' vision of the capital city became most acute and yet most complicated.

The Capital City, My Hometown

Situated along the Yangzi River, Jiankang was protected by gated walls; waterways ran through it and mountains stretched along its borders.[30] Most significantly, it was "the world's most populous city" at the time, with a booming commercial trade and beautiful palaces and other elaborate constructions.[31] In Xie Tiao's poetic view, Jiankang usually sits at the center.

Climbing Three-Peaks Mountain at Dusk,
Gazing Back toward the Capital City　　　　晚登三山還望京邑

On Ba River's shores, Wang Can gazed toward
　　Chang'an;[32]　　　　　　　　　　　　　灞涘望長安

From the North Bank of the He, Pan Yue saw the
　　capital, Luoyang.[33]　　　　　　　　　河陽視京縣

The bright sunlight dazzles the flying-rafters;　白日麗飛甍

High and low, all is in sight.　　　　　　　參差皆可見

The rosy clouds that remain disperse outward, forming
　　a brocade;　　　　　　　　　　　　　餘霞散成綺

The limpid Jiang is calm, like a piece of white silk.　澄江靜如練

Chirping birds cover the springtime isles;　　喧鳥覆春洲

Mixed flowers fill the fragrant grassland.　　雜英滿芳甸

Once gone, I shall be away for a long time;　　去矣方滯淫

In longing, laughter and banquets will be forsaken.　懷哉罷歡宴

The day for reunion—I wonder with disappointment
　　whether it will ever come,　　　　　　　佳期悵何許

And tears run down my cheek like flowing sleet.　淚下如流霰

All sentient beings know to gaze toward their
　　hometown—　　　　　　　　　　　　有情知望鄉

So who can keep his glossy hair from turning gray?[34]　誰能鬒不變

The "Three-Peaks Mountain" in Xie Tiao's poem was situated by the Yangzi, about 15 miles southwest of Jiankang.[35] Here, he uses two earlier poets' visions as a prelude to his own. Once, when he gazes back at Chang'an (in modern Xi'an), all Wang Can sees is the destruction, separation, and death that have befallen the city; and as he flees south toward Jing (in modern Hubei), he becomes engulfed by grief and cries out: "The barbaric land in Jing is not my hometown!"[36] However, Pan Yue's gaze toward Luoyang (in modern Henan) expresses a different sentiment. Serving in a backwater town at the time, he hopes that a path leading back to Luoyang, the capital, might open up for him.[37] By juxtaposing the visions of Wang Can and Pan Yue, Xie Tiao implies that he sees "the capital city" *as well as* "my hometown" through his gaze at Jiankang. For him, the location is both personal and political. Synthesizing the two visions into one, he sees a Jiankang enclosed by nature. "The flying-rafters," brilliantly lit by the sunlight, are presumably those atop the palaces of the imperial city. Then come its outer expanses: the colorful sky, a tranquil Yangzi, isles full of birds, and grasslands filled with flowers. The view could not be more beautiful, but we understand what really preoccupies Xie Tiao: the "dusk," noted in the title, is threatening that it will all be "gone" (*qu*).

Based on Xie Tiao's visual mapping of Jiankang, leaving the capital city meant that he would exit the shelter of its "flying rafters" and enter into the expanse of nature. At the point of departure, that prospect invariably offered little assurance to the Yongming poets, for the sight and thought of nature were the antithesis of all things familiar. The Shitou Fortress, a point of departure in one of Xie Tiao's poems, was only a few miles west of Jiankang, and the Beacon-Fire Loft was apparently even closer to the capital city, so close that from it Xie Tiao could see the palace grounds.[38]

**About to Set Out from the Shitou Fortress,
I Ascend the Beacon-Fire Loft** 　　　　　將發石頭上烽火樓

Pacing back and forth, I pine for the capital city;	徘徊戀京邑
With uncertain steps, I climb the storied tower.	躑躅躔曾阿
As I gain height, the courtyards and palaces appear closer;	陵高墀闕近
When I look farther, the winds and clouds are many.	眺迥風雲多
The Jing and the Wu are separated by mountain peaks;	荊吳阻山岫
And the Jiang and Sea merge their surging waves.	江海合瀾波
To make the homebound flight I am without feathers and wings—	歸飛無羽翼
What am I to do about this separation?[39]	其如離別何

Simple as it is, the word *jin* ("close") depicts not only Xie Tiao's physical sense of closeness, but, more revealingly, his emotional closeness to the "courtyards and palaces." The "winds and clouds" in the distance, by contrast, only seem to him unpredictable and threatening; and the "surging waves" that he visualizes only make "the limpid Jiang" in the previous poem seem like the calm before a storm.

Xie Tiao was not always comfortable with the palaces. Confiding in Wang Deyuan (d. 497), a fellow courtier who was posted to Jin'an Commandery (in Fujian), he expresses clear grievances about his life there.

In Reply to Wang Deyuan, Grand Warden of Jin'an 　酬王晉安德元

Rustling in the wind, the branches are stripped bare early;	梢梢枝早勁
Dripping on and on, the dew is late to dry up.	塗塗露晚晞
In the south, as the oranges and pomelos ripen—	南中榮橘柚

How would you know the swans and geese have flown away?	寧知鴻鴈飛
Brushing aside the fog, I pay morning-audience at the Azure Hall;	拂霧朝青閣
And, as day turns to dusk, sit in the Vermillion Chamber.	日旰坐彤闈
I gaze, disappointed, at the single path obstructed;	悵望一途阻
Some minor, some major—a hundred worries follow.	參差百慮依
Spring grasses are by autumn even greener,	春草秋更綠
Yet your lord has not returned to the west.	公子未西歸
Who can stay long in Capital Luo?	誰能久京洛
Its black dust stains white clothing.[40]	緇塵染素衣

His last two lines echo the Western Jin courtier-poet Lu Ji, who laments in a poem:

Taking leave of home, I went on a long-distance journey;	辭家遠行遊
Far and remote, three thousand *li* away.	悠悠三千里
In Luo, the capital city, there is much wind and dust;	京洛多風塵
White clothing will be turned to black.[41]	素衣化為緇

For both Lu Ji and Gu Yanxian, the former's fellow southern genteel man on whose behalf his poem was written, Luoyang, the Western Jin capital, was not "home"; "home" was in the Zhejiang area in the south, where the climate was milder and more pleasant. Lu Ji always depicted his travels to Luoyang through the antithesis between "home" and "the capital city," thereby presenting it as a hardship, both emotionally and physically.[42] As he recasts Lu Ji's "dusty" Luoyang as Jiankang, Xie Tiao suspends his attachment to his "hometown." In this instance, neither the "Azure Hall" nor the "Vermillion Chamber" evokes any feeling of intimacy or familiarity—they are rather the symbols of the restrictive and lifeless existence of a courtier. In this state, he even feels envy for his fellow courtiers farther south, where there are "ripening oranges and pomelos" rather than "branches stripped bare" and "dripping dew."

Xie Tiao would portray his (non-)existence as a courtier again in a different poem:

Watching over myself, I often bend low, walking in small steps;	敕躬每跼蹐
And I look up for favor, only to tremble and shake with fear.[43]	瞻恩惟震蕩

Once again, he echoes Lu Ji, who presents this self-portrait in a poem:

A Poem Written in the Eastern Palace   東宮作詩

Traveling into a foreign land, far have I gone as I wander
    in officialdom;   羈旅遠遊宦
Becoming dependent, I have come to reside by the
    glamorous one.   託身承華側
Holding a sword, I follow behind the bronze carriage;   撫劍遵銅輦
Straightening out my capstrings, I bow in absolute respect. 振纓盡祇肅
    . . .

As I think of joy none seems enticing;   思樂樂難誘
Speak of returning, yet the thoughts of it will not pacify. 曰歸歸未克
What am to do with the worries and bitterness,   憂苦欲何為
Which twine and extend in my heart and mind?   纏綿胸與臆
Lifting my eyes to the birds soaring in the sky,   仰瞻陵霄鳥
I envy them for their homebound wings.[44]   羨爾歸飛翼

Lu Ji was one of the most renowned courtier-poets of the Western Jin; in
his poetry, however, he is a wayfarer "roaming in a foreign land," "wandering in officialdom." His feeling of alienation in the palaces, as in this poem,
only intensifies his longing for home. But for Xie Tiao, there is no way of
channeling his similar sense of alienation into an impulse to "return home."
The "homebound wings" are only for those who have a clear sense of where
home is.

"I'm Tired of the Long Road"

According to their biographies, Xie Tiao and Shen Yue had been away from
the capital city for extended periods in two kinds of situations: to take up a
new post elsewhere on their own, or to follow a prince to his new post elsewhere.[45] These experiences were very memorable to them, as evinced by the
fact that they documented them meticulously, as if writing a travelogue. In
particular, they remembered the journey *out of* the capital city most vividly.

    In the *Wenxin diaolong*, Liu Xie calls the couplet below by Wang Zan "a
song of grievance about roaming in a foreign land" (*jilü zhi yuanqu*).[46]

As the north wind stirs the autumn grass,   朔風動秋草
The horse at the frontier longs for home.[47]   邊馬有歸心

The grievance (*yuan*) here is of an earlier tradition: a soldier at the frontier—when the north wind blows, it not only chills his bones, but also his heart, as the prospect of returning home eludes him. In Yongming poetry, it is no longer the unsparingly one-directional wind that stirs up grief in the traveler. Going away, as it turns out, is not a simple forward motion.

When Xie Tiao is on the road, his sense of forward motion is always restrained by a backward one.

Going to Xuancheng Commandery, Leaving Xinlin Port, Proceeding toward Banqiao 之宣城郡出新林浦向板橋

Lines 1–4

Along the Yangzi River, the southwest route never ends;	江路西南永
While the homebound current rushes on toward the northeast.	歸流東北鶩
On the horizon, I recognize a returning boat;	天際識歸舟
Through the clouds, I make out the riverside trees.[48]	雲中辨江樹

Traveling by boat along the Yangzi, Xie Tiao is making his way to Xuancheng (in modern Anhui), less than 75 miles southwest of Jiankang, to take up the post of Grand Warden (Taishou). "Xinlin Port" and "Banqiao," both located along the Yangzi, make up the first part of his journey.[49] While moving along the "southwest route," Xie Tiao is keenly aware of the "northeast current," which runs toward the ocean, in the "returning" direction leading back to Jiankang. As his boat moves out into the open river, he looks backward, spotting "a returning boat" on the horizon and craning his neck to see the shore. In another poem, he uses time as a counterpoint for his journey out of the capital city.

Setting Out at Night on the Capital Road 京路夜發

Lines 1–8

Amid great disorder, I pack the night baggage;	擾擾整夜裝
In much haste, order the long-distance carriages.	肅肅戒徂兩
Stars at dawn are just beginning to look scarce,	曉星正寥落
And the morning hue has not yet brightened.	晨光復泱漭
Still damp from remaining dew dripping down in drops—	猶霑餘露團
Barely catching sight of dawn clouds rising—	稍見朝霞上
My hometown is already vague and remote,	故鄉邈已夐
As the mountains and rivers extend and broaden.[50]	山川脩且廣

The subtle changes in the sky, light, and air make time appear slow-moving; and that second-by-second movement in time—which reminds us of Shen Yue's analysis of *nian*—is a clear contrast to the sense of rush and swiftness of the departure.[51] By the time Xie Tiao has a chance to gaze back, the sight of "hometown" has already diminished; and he finds himself in the large expanse of natural landscape. Through his unique ability to create tension among motion, sight, and time, Xie Tiao produced a new kind of travel poetry particularly rich, intricate, and complex in sense perception and emotion. The last two lines in the segment cited above again echo Lu Ji:

Traveling to Luo: Two Poems Written on the Road (No. 2)   赴洛道中二首

Lines 1–6

Roaming far, I have crossed mountains and rivers—	遠遊越山川
Mountains and rivers that extend and broaden.	山川脩且廣
I hasten my whip as I climb the high mounds;	振策陟崇丘
And loosen the reins to follow along the level thickets.	安轡遵平莽
Retiring in the evening, I wrap my own shadows in sleep;	夕息抱影寐
Setting out in the morning, I bear thoughts of home as I advance.[52]	朝徂銜思往

Unlike Lu Ji, who uses the juxtaposition of two time frames—"evening" versus "morning"—Xie Tiao depicts one seemingly brief but continuous time frame, that is, the dawn moments during which he takes to the road. As a result, his experience has a vivid, intense, and "real-time" feel not found in Lu Ji's poem.

Shen Yue's poems about leaving Jiankang give a similar impression of a "real time" experience. In the poem below, he is on his way to Dongyang Commandery (in modern Zhejiang), south of Jiankang, where he would take up the post of Grand Warden.[53] Tracing his travel through Zhufang (near modern Zhenjiang), located downstream on the Yangzi, northeast of Jiankang, he presents his journey out of the capital city in the form of a moving landscape.[54]

Traveling to Assume My Post: Via the Roads of Zhufang   循役朱方道路

Lines 1–12

With a divided silk-tally, I take leave of the Emperor's capital;[55]	分繻出帝京

My package ready, I follow the assignment of the late
    Crown Prince.[56]   升裝奉皇穆
Penetrating the wilderness, moving closer to the open sea;   洞野屬滄溟
Passing through conjoined suburbs, against the river
    current.   聯郊溯河服
The sun reflects upon the Azure Mound Isle,   日映青丘島
And dust stirs up on the Handan land.[57]   塵起邯鄲陸
As the Yangzi River shifts, the forested shore diminishes; 江移林岸微
Where the valleys deepen, the misty peaks overlap.   巖深煙岫複
The year's severity has destroyed the grasses along the
    stony steps;   歲嚴摧磴草
The chill at noon spreads over the lofty trees.   午寒散嶠木
Hovering over treetops, evening gusts whirl;   縈蔚夕飆卷
Lingering on, dusky clouds hang still.[58]   蹉跎晚雲伏

Marked by one landscape scene after another, Shen Yue's depiction creates the vivid impression of "moving away." The progression in time—highlighted by the "reflecting sun" in line 5, "the chill at noon" in line 10, and "the dusky clouds" in line 12—enhances a sense of continuous forward motion. At the same time, as Xie Tiao does in his travel poems, he also creates a sense of counter-motion: "*passing through* the conjoined suburbs" is contrasted to "*going against* the river current"; and the downward casting of sunlight is met by the "stirring up" of dust. The tension in the countering motions implicitly conveys his reluctance to leave. In reality, however, he has to keep moving on. The fourth couplet is one of Shen Yue's best known and is worth a closer look.

As the Yangzi River shifts, the forested shore diminishes; 江移林岸微
Where the valleys deepen, the misty peaks overlap.   巖深煙岫複

What is really shifting is Shen Yue's boat, and, along with it, his view. The impression that the river is "shifting" and the valleys "deepening" reminds us of Shen Yue's Palace style poem about a pair of women sandals—it is the woman, and not the sandals themselves, who is actually moving.[59] "Illusion" is wherever and whatever the eyes see—the altered vision informed by the Buddhist perception had come to be deeply embedded in Yongming poetics, often surfacing at the most unexpected moments. Keenly aware that he and his vision are shifting along with the moving boat, Shen Yue nevertheless cannot call off his journey: as he said, he is "following the assignment of the late Crown Prince."[60] But, as the "dusky clouds hang still," his hesitation to proceed suddenly becomes explicit.

After making the "transit" from the capital city into natural landscape, the Yongming poets often turn to self-reflection. Shen Yue feels the need to explain his hesitation:

Lines 13–18

The "rosy cloud ambition" is not easy to pursue,[61]	霞志非易從
And my "decorated body" indeed is hard to marshal about.[62]	旌軀信難牧
How can I yearn for the phoenix tree at Zi Palace,	豈慕淄宮梧
Having just parted with the bamboos at Hare Park?	方辭兔園竹
My traveling thoughts—how can they be expressed?	羈心亦何言
The lost path—I hope it can be retrieved.[63]	迷蹤庶能復

"Zi Palace," probably "a Daoist paradise,"[64] matches the phrase "rosy cloud ambition" in that it is also a reference to a life of reclusion. "Hare Park," also known as "Bamboo Park" (Zhu yuan), was built by Liang Xiaowang of the Han, who entertained his guests and gathered his retainers there;[65] it refers, by contrast, to the life at court and, in that sense, matches the earlier mention of "my decorated body." In Yongming poetry, leaving the capital city is a "transit" not only in a geographical sense; it can also imply that one is leaving behind his courtier life and going into reclusion. Perhaps reassuring himself, perhaps making it known to his fellow courtiers, Shen Yue suddenly feels obliged to declare that he is *not* going into reclusion and hopes to retrieve "the lost path," probably a reference to his political setback at the time.[66] Admitting that going into reclusion is not easy for a "pampered" courtier, Shen Yue speaks with his usual tone of honesty and self-mockery. By contrast, still on his way to Xuancheng, Xie Tiao is already imagining a life in "hiding" (*yin*):

Lines 5–12

Traveling thoughts tire me out, as the boat sways from side to side;	旅思倦搖搖
Solitary roaming—I already done much in the past.	孤游昔已屢
I take joy in the feeling of procuring a salary,	既懽懷祿情

Yet I am attuned to the wonder of Glaucous Isles.[67] 復協滄洲趣

From now on noise and dust are blocked out; 囂塵自茲隔

That which fulfills my heart is found herein. 賞心於此遇

Though without the black panther's beauty, 雖無玄豹姿

I shall at last hide within the South Mountain mists.[68] 終隱南山霧

Xie Tiao's longing for Jiankang seems to have dissipated, but propelling his vision of a new life in "hiding" is not his rejection of "hometown," but of "the capital city" as a place filled with "noise and dust." It is the "misty rain," according to the story alluded to here, that the black panther is avoiding, for it could harm its beautiful fur.[69] Anyone familiar with Xie Tiao's or his fellow Yongming poets' stories knows that the "noise and dust" of the capital city could indeed do more than destroy one's beauty. In another instance on the road, Xie Tiao fails to find the way to "return home":

Soon official documents and reports will pile up before
  me, 文奏方盈前

And, missing my dear ones, I will forsake all the delights
  in my heart. 懷人去心賞

Watching over myself, I often bend low, walking in small
  steps; 敕躬每跼蹐

And I look up for favor, only to tremble and shake with
  fear. 瞻恩惟震蕩

I have moved on, but I'm tired of the long road; 行矣倦路長

Yet I have no way of unhitching the harness and returning
  home.[70] 無由稅歸鞅

Neither the life ahead of him, which he imagines in the first couplet cited here, nor his life as a courtier in the capital city, described in the second couplet, seems comforting. As he moves on, the thought of "returning home" catches up with him in the middle of the road. Once, as he was leaving by another "imperial command," Xie Tiao wrote a farewell letter to his patron Prince Sui; in it he mentions *gui* ("return") three times, but each time it is unclear if he means returning to his prince-patron or retiring from office and returning to his "true nature." Only this is clear: he wishes to end a life "on the forked road, where one stands looking to the east and to the west" (*qilu dongxi*).[71]

"You, Sir, A Man of the City and Palaces"

| Gazing toward hometown, we all shed tears— | 望鄉皆下淚 |
| Not only I alone feel the grief. | 非我獨傷情 |

The "we" in the two lines above are He Xun (d. 518) and his "fellow expatriates" (*tongji*).[72] By highlighting their united gaze, he underscores their affinity for Jiankang and one another; a sense of shared identity and common purpose is conveyed through his lines. Within this community of expatriates, the courtier-poet learns to adjust, adapt, and negotiate his identity. Below we will see this process play out in Xie Tiao's poems.

Xie Tiao had probably gone the farthest away from Jiankang when he traveled to Jiangling, the administrative seat of Jingzhou, as a member of staff in Prince Sui's entourage. Writing to his fellow expatriates, he cannot hide his unhappy mood during the lingering winter:

Exilic Feelings at the End of Winter: Presented to Consulting Aide Xiao, Administrator for Cultivated Fields Yu, and Two Attendants-in-Ordinary, Liu and Jiang 冬緒羈懷示蕭諮議虞田曹劉江二常侍

Lines 1–10

I left the capital thinking of "hill and garden";[73]	去國懷丘園
Having come this far, I'm still attached to the city and palaces.	入遠滯城闕
By the chilly lamp, disquieted by nightly dreams;	寒燈耿宵夢
Before the clear mirror, grieving over the morning hair.	清鏡悲曉髮
Grasses in the wind do not accumulate frost;	風草不留霜
Ice and pond are one in the second lunar month.[74]	冰池共如月
It is quiet and lonely by this idled curtain,	寂寞此閑帷
Where zither and wine jar are left facing each other.	琴樽任所對
Thoughts of being a guest gradually lengthen and entwine,	客念坐嬋媛
As the year's blooms slowly grow luxuriant.[75]	年華稍苒蔱

Xie Tiao speaks as a man of "the city and palaces" who now finds himself a "guest" (*ke*) in a western town. He notices that the wind is stronger, for the grasses "do not accumulate frost"—this is unlike the winter closer to home, where the crack-patterns formed by the frost on the grasses make it appear as if "Frost cuts the knotgrasses of 'South of the River.'"[76] His "thoughts of being a guest" extend ever so gradually that every spring spent and every autumn passed in a foreign land needs to be counted:[77]

| Once listened was the spring warblers' song; | 一聽春鶯喧 |
| Twice seen was the autumnal rainbow's fading. | 再視秋虹沒 |

As he confides in his fellow staff, his complaint about not being used to life in Jiangling can be overheard.

In a different poem about a night gathering that takes place upon the visit of "a guest from hometown," Xie Tiao unhesitantly switches his voice to that of a host.

Gathering at Night with Fellow Expatriates   同羈夜集

Our thoughts for each other accumulated while separated by hot and cold climates;	積念隔炎涼
And our fast-paced words only began this evening.	驤言始今夕
Already facing cups of thick wine,	已對濁樽酒
We have, in addition, a guest from our hometown.	復此故鄉客
Frosty moonlight has only started down the stony steps;	霜月始流砌
Cold-weather crickets have for some time now chirped in the cracks.	寒蛸早吟隙
Luckily, through you, we make excursions to the glories of the capital;	幸藉京華遊
And, in this frontier town, celebrate with this fine banquet.	邊城讌良席
As wood-gatherers, those of us here have come together;	樵採咸共同
On straw or on sedge, we can all lean on each other.	荊莎聊可藉
We are just worried about you, Sir, a man of the city and palaces—	恐君城闕人
How can you stay long among pines and cypresses?[78]	安能久松柏

The courtiers-turned-wood-gatherers, already used to sitting on just straw or sedge mats, now worry about the hometown guest instead, for he is the only "man of the city and palaces" on this night. Xie Tiao's role reversal is indeed "playful."[79] That he and his fellow "wood-gatherers" have any reason to worry, however, only betrays their own sense of alienation. The question he asks at the end recalls, in an ironic way, another question he asks in a different poem: "Who can stay long in Capital Luo? / Its black dust stains white clothing."[80] One suspects his two questions are both directed at himself. Writing to a fellow expatriate who has been assigned to Qixing, 60 miles north of Jiangling and deeper into the northern frontier,[81] Xie Tiao would give another twist to his question:

You will be revered for your "double-eared" merits,	子蕭兩岐功
While I stay on in my "three-winters" post.[82]	我滯三冬職
Who knows longing for Capital Luo?	誰知京洛念
We are as if residing by Mount Kunlun.[83]	彷彿昆山側

Still in Jiangling himself, Xie Tiao apparently feels the need to cheer his fellow expatriate. Attempting to sound upbeat, he now compares the western region to the Kunlun Mountains, the domain of the Goddess Xiwang Mu (Queen Mother of the West), where one should find his longing for the capital city simply forgotten. Life as an expatriate requires constant adjustment; doing that in poems presented to his fellow expatriates, Xie Tiao negotiates his identity and his relationship with Jiankang not on his own and not only for himself, but in a collective manner and on behalf of a community of courtiers in exile.

The Returning Road

It may be difficult to leave the capital city, but returning is not easy either. In a poem about returning to Jiankang, Xie Tiao addresses his fellow courtiers still in Jiangling, revealing an ambiguous vision of "hometown" and mixed emotions.

Going Down to the Capital on a Temporary Assignment, Starting Out at Night from Xinlin and Arriving at the Capital City: Presenting to Colleagues at the Western Administrative Office   暫使下都夜發新林至京邑贈西府同僚

The great Yangzi flows on day and night;	大江流日夜
The traveler's heart grieves without end.	客心悲未央
I only thought the passes and the hills were near,	徒念關山近
But finally realized the returning road would be long.	終知返路長
The "autumnal river" glistens brilliantly;	秋河曙耿耿
The cold isle by night grows greener.	寒渚夜蒼蒼
I crane my neck to see the capital's buildings:	引領見京室
Palaces and city walls now face each other.	宮雉正相望

The "golden waves" light up the Ostrich Tower;	金波麗鳷鵲
Jade Rope hangs down over Jianzhang Palace.[84]	玉繩低建章
Speeding up my carriage outside the Tripod Gate,	驅車鼎門外
I see in my mind the sun rising from King Zhao's Mound.	思見昭丘陽
Even swift rays of sun cannot connect us,	馳暉不可接
Let alone when separated by two [home]towns.	何況隔兩鄉
In wind and mist there is a path for the birds,	風煙有鳥路
But the Jiang and the Han are cut off without a bridge.	江漢限無梁
I always fear the hawks and falcons may launch an attack,	常恐鷹隼擊
Or that the seasonal chrysanthemums may wither under severe frost.	時菊委嚴霜
But send my words to those spreading nets and snares:	寄言罻羅者
I have soared high in the broad and empty sky![85]	寥廓已高翔

In line 4, the "returning road" (*fanlu*) leads not to Jiankang but to Jiangling; in line 14, the two *xiang* ("[home]towns")—Jiankang and Jingling—come to the poet's mind at once. Xie Tiao's ambiguous vision and mixed feelings are further revealed in lines 7 to 12: here, as the palaces of Jiankang come into sight, causing Xie Tiao to speed up his carriage in an urge to reach it, the vision of "the sun rising from King Zhao's Mound," a monument in the western region, suddenly appears in his mind.[86] When dawn comes in the east, where Jiankang is located, the sun will move westward toward Jiangling, eventually reaching King Zhao's Mound—however, "Even swift rays of sun cannot connect us." These flashes in his mind's eye reveal Xie Tiao's uncertainty about the direction of his "return" and the location of his "hometown." Though aimed at boosting his own confidence in the face of the danger at the court, his message at the end only intensifies his sense of crisis. Instead of "soaring high in the broad and empty sky," the Qi-Liang courtier often finds himself having to struggle intensely with his existence and identity. As the antithesis between "hometown" and "the capital city" blurs, no easy answer can be found to the question of where or what "hometown" really is. As Xie Tiao's uncertainty on the return road and his double vision of "hometown" show, there may be more than one "hometown" or perhaps no "hometown" at all. For Xie Tiao and his fellow courtier-poets, the moment that comes closest to being "at home" is when they are with men like themselves, whether in Jiangling or Jiankang, in whom they would confide poem after poem.

That brings us to the question of whether *xiang* or *guxiang* is a specific place or even a place at all. In a memorial calling for "residence determination" in 389, Fan Ning (339–401) writes:

> In the past when the central plain was lost and fell into chaos, the people came to reside in a drift "South of the River." Since they still bore the hope of returning [to the north] one day, the government allowed them to register their households under their places of origin. Much time has passed since then, and people have settled down in their new life. Their grave mounds and the cypresses beside them are lined up in rows. In name they are not their hometowns, but in reality these lands are where they have settled. It is now time to rectify our territories by adjusting the household registration through "residence determination." . . . It is the case that even though all people originally came from their own clans, they migrated to other places in later generations, so why should it be different in our time?[87]

But government policies cannot resolve the most personal issue. When Liu Yu, later Emperor Wu of Song, proposed another "residence determination" in 413, he would touch upon the emotional aspect of the issue:

> It is a human sentiment to dwell on things being unchanged and hence difficult to make people consider a new beginning. What is meant by the saying "his parents' hometown is what a person considers his native place" is that he was born there and will die there; it is the place that he loves and respects.[88]

According to Liu Yu, one loves and respects his "hometown" simply because he is physically there—he was born there and will die there. Does physical attachment naturally lead to emotional attachment? Will physical presence "default" to emotional presence? If the answers to these questions are positive, then the meaning of *guxiang* is simple: the place where one resides.

Other than Xie Kun's, the graves of Wang Rong's ancestors, also near Nanjing, have been excavated, giving more physical evidence that, as Fan Ning observed, the northern émigrés had "in reality" settled down in the land of the south.[89] The fact that they had never ventured from the south, however, did not make Xie Tiao and his fellow courtiers any more certain or any less perplexed when it came to the question of "hometown." In recorded history, their native identity—in the case of Xie Tiao and Wang Rong—is tied to a northern land on which they had never set foot; "in reality," as Fan Ning would have it, they were "settled" in the south. By Liu Yu's measure, they should have felt love and respect for the place where they were born and later died. But the perplexity and uncertainty evoked by the trope of "hometown" in their poetry probably reflect their existence more accurately. When Yan Zhitui, whose statement about *jilü* ("residing in a foreign place temporarily") is cited at the start of this chapter, came to write about his own life as an émigré, history had moved into a different phase. Jiankang was lost in the Liang and regained in the Chen, only to be completely wiped out in the end. Amid all these events, Yan Zhitui had fled to the north and begun his life serving in the northern court as a southerner, but one question still tormented him: "I am now roaming in a foreign land, my body like the floating clouds, and I do not know where the hometown that will be my burial ground is."[90] Given the history behind Yan Zhitui's displacement, his question about "hometown" is not only relevant for himself, but also has grave significance for an entire state. By comparison, Xie Tiao and his fellow courtiers' struggle to find their place in Jiankang may seem overly indulgent. Their part of history, however, was as unsparing: Wang Rong was only twenty-seven *sui* when he was thrown into prison and "granted death"; and Xie Tiao was thirty-six *sui* when the same fate befell him.[91] Yan Zhitui had lived to experience the destruction of Jiankang, but, before that, Wang Rong and Xie Tiao had met their own ends *in* Jiankang. Their stories lead to this conclusion: one could certainly be "displaced" in one's own hometown.

In and Out of the Landscape

If one tries to sum up the Qi-Liang courtier, poetry, and landscape based on a common impression, the result might be a statement like this:

> Shen Yue's poems are like one who travels the mountains in embroidered clothing, which is caught in thorny brambles every so often.

The person who made this statement is Mou Yuanxiang (1760–1811), the author of *Xiaoxie caotang za lun shi* (Miscellaneous Comments on Poetry from the Thatched Hall by the Small Stream).[1] His statement is impressive in that, by drawing an image of an awkward Shen Yue in the mountains, it combines the three objects just mentioned, commenting on the person as much as it does his poetry. Given the large number of landscape poems produced by Shen Yue and his fellow courtier-poets, it is worth asking: Were Shen Yue and his fellow courtiers really incapable of mountain travel?

It is true that the encounter with the natural landscape is often something "chanced upon" in Yongming poetry. The courtier-poets seek out beautiful landscapes only as a "detour" during an official trip or as an opportunity presented by a posting away from the capital city. That said, their encounter with the natural landscape is nothing but engaging and refreshing. Given that the landscape is often portrayed as an antithesis to officialdom in earlier poetry, their landscape poems present the unique question of what the landscape really means to a courtier-poet. Coming after Xie Lingyun, the landscape poetics of the Yongming poets also offers a much-needed opportunity for understanding the responses to the former's influence within the century following his death. Entering the natural landscape can be as simple as leaving the capital city, or it can be as complicated as being on the verge of leaving everything behind. As much lovers of landscapes as many of their predecessors and contemporaries, the Yongming poets have entered and exited the landscape many times; as they go in and out of the landscape, we will observe if they have indeed "obtained" (*de*) the beauty they seek.

To Bring Back the Mountains and Rivers

When Chen Da, Chen Emperor Wu's ancestor in the Jin, went to what is now the Zhejiang area to assume his post as a prefect, he "took delight in its mountains and rivers" and decided to make his home there.[2] That, however, is only one way to "obtain" a landscape. The Chinese word for landscape is *shanshui*, which implies a balanced form: mountains *and* rivers. *Shanshui* is not nature as it is or by itself, but nature as beheld by humans. In that sense, a degree of human involvement is already inherent in the idea of *shanshui*. For one to be "constructing mountains and rivers" (*ying shanshui*), therefore, is not at all unimaginable. Kong Zhigui (447–501), a fellow courtier whom Shen Yue once pressed a charge against, and who later made the charges for Wang Rong's death sentence, had done just that. His *Nan Qi shu* biography mentions that he "indulged in constructing 'mountains and rivers' at his residence."[3] Exactly how he did that is unfortunately not described, but one would assume it involved designing with rocks, as in the case of Prince Wenhui, who collected many unusual rocks in his garden to "display the most wondrous forms of mountains and rivers."[4] Rather than making one's home in *shanshui*, one can instead bring home *shanshui*. But what is the difference?

The real question is whether one can recognize the difference or not. Wang Rong wrote a poem that goes like this:

On the slanting peaks, the surrounding trails are tortuous;	斜峰繞徑曲
And the soaring rocks circle the mountains, joining them.	聳石帶山連
The flowers that remain stroke the playing birds;	花餘拂戲鳥
While the trees, being dense, hide the chirping cicadas.	樹密隱鳴蟬

While this is by no means his best poem, the title puts it in perspective for us: "Making a Palindromic Poem in the Back Garden" ("Houyuan zuo huiwenshi").[5] The key word here is *zuo* ("to make"). The "back garden" is a "made" space and it is entirely possible that the so-described "slanting peaks," "tortuous trails," "soaring rocks," and "joined mountains" are in fact the view of several unusual rocks there.[6] The poem itself is also more "made" than usual: it is a *huiwen shi* meant to be read from the first to the last words and then in reverse, and, in this case, that is facilitated by not only its syntactical structures but also its tone patterns.[7] Visually, the poem gives the impression that the view is moving from a large landscape to things closer and then vice versa. Given that the poem is twice removed from actual mountains and rivers—it is a "made" poem about "made" *shanshui*—one can certainly question how much is "obtained" in the end. While "fake mountains and fake rivers" (*jiashan jiashui*) would come into vogue in the Tang and Song, in Wang Rong's time, the more common object of obsession was *real* mountains and rivers.[8]

During the Southern Dynasties, to claim that one loved landscapes and had seen them was popular, if not fashionable. Xie Lingyun, the first great master of landscape poetry, who had compiled a *Record of Traveling in Famous Mountains* (*You mingshan zhi*), comes to mind.[9] But his contemporary Zong Bing (375–443) also had taken the famous mountains that he had visited as seriously. Instead of writing about them, Zong Bing "obtained" them by painting. "Whichever mountain he has set foot on, he would paint it in his room."[10] To him, painting a landscape is a form of representation that is relatively direct:

Those principles that have been lost in mid-antiquity or earlier can be sought after by thoughts after a thousand years; ideas that are so subtle that they exist beyond language and images can be acquired in the mind within books and scrolls. How even more true this is for one who has roamed through them and gazed at them to form them with form and color them with color.[11]

But in spite of the directness of "forming with form and coloring with color," he realizes that there is the issue of distance and seeing:

> Given how big Mount Kunlun is and how small the pupils are, one cannot see its shape if one's eyes are only a few inches away. If one steps back several *li*, then one can encompass its shape within one's inch-large pupils. This is because as one moves farther away, what one sees becomes smaller. Now, if I spread out a piece of white silk to trace it from a distance, Lang Peak of Kunlun can be encompassed within [a few] square inches. Three inches drawn vertically stand for the thousand *ren* in height;[12] several more stretched horizontally model the hundred *li* in width. Because of this the viewers of painted landscapes are concerned with similitude only and would not let their diminutive forms affect the semblance; this is a natural tendency. As such, the gracefulness of Mount Song and Mount Hua and the spirit of the dark valleys can all be obtained within one painting.[13]

Unlike Wang Rong, Zong Bing does not arouse the suspicion that he is playing a trick on the eyes. It was his ailing health, according to the *Song shu*, that had motivated him to paint; he once said, "As old age and illness catch up with me, I'm afraid I will not get to see all the famous mountains."[14] And, for him, the painted landscape could indeed replace the real one, as he describes in his preface:

> Thereupon, I reside in idleness and regulate my breathing, at times lifting a wine cup, at times playing the zither. Then, I roll out the painting, face it quietly, and, while seated, delve into the wilderness on all four sides. I am not obstructed by the shrubs in nature and come alone to the field with no human trace. Mountain peaks are steep and erect, and the forests in the clouds are deep and far. While the saints and the worthies, though matchless in later generations, are hereupon reflected, ten thousand delights are all combined in the spirit thought. What more should I hope to accomplish? I shall let my spirit roam and that's all. And where but in this will it roam.[15]

We hear an echo of his conclusion in Wang Rong, who, after surveying the view outside a Buddhist monastery in Jingling's garden estate, exclaims: "Let it roam—appreciation outside the human realm!" (*Chang zai ren wai shang*).[16] If a painting can replace an actual landscape, a constructed garden can certainly exist "outside the human realm." In the same spirit, a rock can become a mountain. As the representation of the landscape took center stage in Southern Dynasties arts, being there in the landscape was only one part of the aesthetic, the other part—the more important one—was about *as if* one were there.

The Balancing Act

Looking at a landscape is different from looking at a single thing or an enclosed space. If one were to be meticulous, the feeling could be overwhelming. In the *Shishuo xinyu* (A New Account of Tales of the World), Wang Zijing (344–386), referring to the landscape in Shanyin (in modern Zhejiang), makes a wonderful comment: "The beauty of the mountains and rivers there is such that it does not give one a moment of leisure in handling it" (*shanshui zhi mei, shi ren yingjie buxia*).[17] If seeing them is difficult to handle, how much more so would it be to try to create their semblance?

Zong Bing's landscape aesthetic is about evoking *lei* ("similitude") or *si* ("semblance"). As discussed in Chapter Three, a similar idea—*xingsi* ("resemblance in form")—had also come to dominate the period's descriptive and visual poetics. As the leader of this poetics, Xie Lingyun is famous for using a specific method of "scanning the landscape."[18] The best way to describe his method is "balanced": a water scene is followed by a mountain scene, which in turn is followed by another water scene, and so on.[19] This balanced form was a significant achievement, for it allowed him to outline the broad contours of a landscape and depict its details as well. The impression of Xie Lingyun as a viewer of the landscape, as such, is of one looking in all directions but also observing intently. In other words, he had proven himself more than capable of handling the challenge of landscape beauty. By the time of the Yongming poets, Xie Lingyun would remain very influential, but his method of scanning would now seem to bring forth no more than the normative form of the landscape.

In a poem simply called "Roaming the Mountains" ("You shan"), Xie Tiao pays tribute to the older Xie.[20] The title is worthy of attention because it is unlike those of most landscape poems, which are usually more specific, providing information from the names of sites to the time of the visit or the travel route. And, as it turns out, the poem is not about a specific experience in the mountains, but contemplating about "roaming the mountains" in a generalized way. Most believe that Xie Tiao wrote the poem when he was in Xuancheng (in modern Anhui), where he held the post of Grand Warden from 495 to 497.[21] But, other than calling it "a town of mountains and rivers," the poem has nothing to do with Xuancheng or the landscape there.

Xie Tiao begins with an introspective tone, which obviously is triggered by his being posted away from the capital city:

Cared for by the state, I am bereft of limbs;	託養因支離
Residing in leisure, I have become a tired and crippled horse.	乘閑遂疲蹇
To speak out or to keep silent—I have not found the answer;	語默良未尋
Gain or loss, who can tell the difference?	得喪云誰辨
Luckily, I have come to this town of mountains and rivers;	幸蒞山水都
And, what's more, the cold winter is still far away.	復值清冬緬

By comparing himself to "one bereft of limbs" and "a tired and crippled horse," he shows that he is perfectly capable of self-deprecatory humor.[22] His sense of having suffered a political setback and uncertainty about his future, however, become obvious in the second couplet. After this opening, he channels his energy into an account of a "proto-roaming" in the landscape.

To stand overlooking from a cliff, one has to climb a thousand *ren*;	凌崖必千仞
To trace the source of a creek, one is prepared to take ten thousand turns.	尋谿將萬轉
Not only do sturdy crags soar up in rugged forms,	堅崿既崚嶒
Creeks that wind back also turn and twist.	迴流復宛澶
Dark and obscure, cloudy caves deepen;	杳杳雲竇深
Splattering loudly, water over rocks becomes shallow.	淵淵石溜淺
Look sideward: the *biao* and *lao* bamboos are luxuriant;	傍眺鬱篻簩
Turn around to gaze: the *nanmu* and elms have grown thick.	還望深柟梗
The uncombed river banks are covered with wood-sorrel and sedge;	荒隩被葳莎
The spilt-opened mountain walls are wrapped in moss and lichen.	崩壁帶苔蘚

Flying squirrels and long-tailed gibbons screech along the
    layered cliffs;　　　　　　　　　　　　　　　　鼯狖叫層嵁
Seagulls and wild ducks play by the sandy bars.　　　鷗鳧戲沙衍

Through the adverbs *bi* ("must") and *jiang* ("about to"), which he uses
in the first two lines of this passage, Xie Tiao indicates to us that he is
depicting how one *should* roam the mountains, not how he had actually
done it. His suggestion is clearly adopted from Xie Lingyun: every couplet,
except for the one in the middle (the fourth couplet above), contains a
line that depicts a mountain scene and another that depicts a water scene.
This balanced landscape is literally framed by the alternating upward and
downward motions of one's head, with a mid-way variation (in the middle
couplet) of "looking sideward" and "turning around to gaze." Cynthia L.
Chennault has asked a very apt question: "Is 'Roaming the Mountain' a
poem which merely reflects the pervasive influence of Lingyun's style on
later poets, or is it a poem *about* the style of Lingyun?"[23] If it is about the
style of Xie Lingyun, what is Xie Tiao saying about it? It is interesting to
note that even though Xie Lingyun is known for his meticulous cataloguing
of the local plants in the Zhejiang area,[24] Xie Tiao would instead cluster
the names of plants—*biaolao, nanpian, zhensha*—that evoke the memory
of much earlier *fu*.[25] In a subtle way, he is associating Xie Lingyun with an
earlier descriptive tradition, not only in regards to his preference for difficult diction and his tendency to be "excessively long" (*rongchang*), but, even
more importantly, to his conclusion about what is to be "obtained" from
the landscape.

    In appearance, Xie Tiao's conclusion to his "proto-roaming" is very simi-
lar to Xie Lingyun's, for it also involves a philosophical and/or religious
reckoning of the engagement with landscapes.

Whatever incites my appreciation I can only view it myself,　觸賞聊自觀
While the moment's delight has already unfolded.　　　　　即趣咸已展
As they go past my eyes, I treasure what I meet;　　　　　　經目惜所遇
Upon the path ahead, I rejoice at what I'm about to come
    across.　　　　　　　　　　　　　　　　　　　　前路欣方踐
Do not say that the fragrant grasses are withering away,　　無言蕙草歇
For, lingering by the wall, one may still smell their
    sweetness.　　　　　　　　　　　　　　　　　　　留垣芳可搴

Shangzi, at the time, had not yet "returned," 尚子時未歸
While Master Bing considered his own dismissal.[26] 邴生思自免
Forever intent on what has long been admired— 永志昔所欽
Marvelous sites, among which I may now choose. 勝跡今能選
Send words to sojourners with an appreciative heart: 寄言賞心客
To obtain your own true nature is the best. 得性良為善

His final two lines recall Xie Lingyun's conclusion in "Building Fences along the Rapids in the Tree Garden South of the Field" ("Tiannan shuyuan jiliu zhiyuan"):

The appreciative heart is not to be forgotten; 賞心不可忘
Through marvelous goodness one can hope to become
    one [with the Grand Whole].[27] 妙善冀能同

If Xie Lingyun's vision, as suggested by the couplet above, is indeed focused on the Grand Whole or the Dao, then one can see the more pervasive meaning of his balanced landscape. It is normative in that it manifests the Grand Whole or the Dao. By contrast, as we have seen in their poems on the garden (Chapter Four), the Yongming poets' vision cannot be sufficiently explained by such a *Zhuangzi*-like concept. Even though he also sees philosophical and/or religious meaning in the landscape, Xie Tiao's attempt is to emphasize the specificity and individuality in one's experience of it. In a different poem, the older Xie sees "oneness" in himself and the two recluses of the past: "Having completed the marriages of my children, I'm just like Shangzi; / And, having wandered slightly in officialdom, I'm similar to Master Bing."[28] But what Xie Tiao does in his couplet about the same two recluses is bring attention to the time *before* they went into reclusion: Shangzi was waiting for all his children to be married, and Master Bing was considering "his own dismissal." The process involves very personal considerations and it is not the same for everyone. And, likewise, "Whatever incites my appreciation, I can only view it myself." For Xie Tiao, the viewer of the landscape is a *ke* ("sojourner") not in the sense that he wants to keep moving on to see the Grand Whole at more and newer sites, but in that there is no Grand Whole to encompass all. His landscape aesthetic, as a result, is about increasing specificity and individual-ness; and what he obtains is something more personal and individualized: his "true nature." We shall have the opportunity to discuss Xie Tiao's conclusion again at the end of this chapter.

Exchanging a Rapids

Forces in nature can best attest to the idea that the phenomenal world is inconstant and impermanent. When the human eye meets such forces, it may either comprehend them with clarity or be overwhelmed and confused by them. The "Jibuji" (Heaped-Rocks Rapids), located on the upper Yangzi about 65 miles west of Jiujiang (in Jiangxi), apparently posed one such challenge to its viewers.[29] When Liu Hui, another noted member of the Prince of Jingling's literary coterie, had the chance to view it, he re-created his experience in a poem titled "Entering the Lute Gorge, Gazing at Heaped-Rocks Rapids" ("Ru Pipaxia wang Jibuji shi"). This is what he saw:

Lines 5–14

Emitting multi-colored lights, like rainbows intertwining with their reflections;	照爛虹蜺雜
Swirling together, brocades and embroideries are formed.	交錯錦繡陳
They are ruffled like swallow tails,	差池若燕羽
And jagged like dragon scales.	崱屴似龍鱗
Previous sights, now gone, are unlike those before;	卻瞻了非向
Yet views ahead have become new once again.	前觀已復新
They rush up to mid-slope, blocking the scenery at the top;	翠微上虧景
And fall down toward the sedge grasses, brushing by the ford.	青莎下拂津
Rough and abrupt like a thing carved,	巉嚴如刻削
They can be gazed at, but may not be approached.[30]	可望不可親

Two lines—"Previous sights, now gone, are unlike those before; / Yet views ahead have become new once again"—perfectly express an awareness of the ever-changing nature of what one sees. And they recall how Xie Tiao sees:

Whatever incites my appreciation I can only view it myself,	觸賞聊自觀
While the moment's delight has already unfolded.	即趣咸已展
As they go pass my eyes, I treasure what I meet;	經目惜所遇
Upon the path ahead, I rejoice at what I'm about to come across.[31]	前路欣方踐

In other words, every sight is specific to the moment and hence disappears with the moment as well. Framed as an experience in time, Liu Hui's poem calls forth a different view of the rapids with and *within* every line, like a movie played in slow motion. Just as a movie can replay past moments in the present, his poem re-creates his experience of gazing at the Heaped-Rocks Rapids as if it is happening in real time.

Based on the response of Xie Tiao, the recipient of his poem, Liu Hui obviously had succeeded in arousing a vivid imagination of the rapids. In his poem "harmonizing" with Liu Hui's, Xie Tiao tells him:

Lines 7–10

While on sick leave, I saw your new composition;	移疾覯新篇
I put on my coat, roused by the delight of faraway thoughts.	披衣起淵瓵
With deep longing, I reminisce about my past footsteps—	惆悵懷昔踐
It is as if I have obtained a unique viewing.[32]	彷彿得殊觀

In Xie Tiao's experience, reading Liu Hui's poem about the rapids is as vivid as "obtaining a unique viewing." By "past footsteps," he means his own experience visiting the site in the past.[33] Having re-experienced the rapids through Liu Hui's poem, Xie Tiao depicts his own "gaze" at them:

In red and in purple, they are brilliantly variegated,	頳紫共彬駮
As clouds and their brocades mix in irregular forms.	雲錦相凌亂
Like shooting stars, they race up but not yet reach the top;	奔星上未窮
And like roaring thunder, plunge down to about half-way.	驚雷下將半
Their returning tides wash away the collapsing trees;	回潮漬崩樹
And, swirling and rolling down, smash against the banks.	輪困軋傾岸
Some *xiao* bamboos by the cliffs have fallen to one side;	巖篠或傍翻
And the *jun* bamboos on the rocks have lost their long branches.	石箘無脩幹
Crisp and clear, the glittering shore is beautiful;	澄澄明浦媚
Blowing on and on, the refreshing breeze spreads all over.	衍衍清風爛

Like Liu Hui, Xie Tiao presents a series of visual images that are continuous: they allow us to follow the rapids *while* they move in fierce motion. His poem reminds us again of the issue of representation. Even though inspired by a reading experience and re-created from memories, Xie Tiao's poem has the same vivid effect and instantaneous quality that we find in Liu Hui's poem. This exchange between the two poets best reflects how a landscape poem was composed and received during Qi-Liang times—the fundamental idea at both ends was the same, that is, to approach a landscape poem as a specific experience. The two poets have created two viewings of the same site: while Liu Hui's focus is on the "texture" of the rapids ("Rough and abrupt like a thing carved"), Xie Tiao is drawn to their speed and force ("Like shooting stars, they race up but not yet reach the top; / And like roaring thunder, plunge down to about half-way"). As an interaction between one's perception and time, no single view of a landscape is permanent or static. No landscape, in other words, has only one view.

Moving in the Landscape

If not in balanced alternation, how does one move in the landscape? Just as they frame the space in a garden with doors and windows, the Yongming poets would mark a landscape with individual elements—a mountain, a river, a creek, a gorge. But, ultimately, it is through their eyes and their movement in it that they would come to "grasp" a landscape. The challenge for them was to move in a manner that would give movement to the landscape.

How one moves—whether by foot, by carriage, or by boat—makes for a different experience in the landscape. In "Setting Out Early from Mount Ding" ("Zao fa Ding shan"), Shen Yue fully relates how he sees to the specific means by which he is traveling. This is the "wondrous mountain" (*qishan*) before his eyes:

Its peaks are erected beyond the varicolored rainbow;	標峰綵虹外
Its ridges set amid the white clouds.	置嶺白雲間
The inclined cliffs suddenly slanted, suddenly straight;	傾壁忽斜豎
The unscalable summit again arced, again round.[34]	絕頂復孤圓
Returning to the sea, the river flows on and on;	歸海流漫漫
Spilling over the banks, the water splashes and splatters.	出浦水濺濺
Wild crabapples, fully opened, have not yet fallen;	野棠開未落
Mountain cherries are budding, ready to bloom.[35]	山櫻發欲然

He begins by framing the height of the mountain: "beyond the varicolored rainbow," "amid the white clouds." What follows is the mountain in changing views, which makes us realize Shen Yue is looking up at Mount Ding from a boat that is at sail. As in some of his other poems, there is the "illusion" that the thing itself—the mountain in this case—is moving or changing. It helps to know that Mount Ding, southwest of modern Hangzhou, overlooks the Zhe River "as it begins to broaden into the estuary."[36] As his boat moves farther away from the mountain and toward the open river (presumably the Zhe River), Shen Yue's eyes follow the water and turn to the wild plants growing along the shore. Even there, he keeps a sense of motion in his depiction. The river water is moving with force and even the "wild crabapples" and "mountain cherries" are "moving" quietly—the adverbs *wei* ("not yet") and *yu* ("about to") suggest that they are constantly undergoing a transformation rather than remaining static. In this example, Shen Yue uses the sail on a boat to frame his perspective and takes us along a "moving" landscape at Mount Ding.

In his preface, Zong Bing alludes to the use of vertical and horizontal brush strokes in painting a mountain. In poetry, creating lines and contours is central to the depiction of mountains as well. It is important to realize that a mountain has more contours than the vertical line of its height. Xie Tiao obviously realizes this as he roams on Mount Jingting, north of the city of Xuancheng, where he was serving as Grand Warden.

Thrusting upward, it blocks the bright sun;	上干蔽白日
And, falling down, it trails along a winding stream.	下屬帶迴溪
Crisscrossing vines now sparse, now thick;	交藤荒且蔓
Crooked branches sway up, and pitch down again.[37]	樛枝聳復低

He draws the upward and downward limits of the mountain to situate his roaming in the space within, where he finds "crisscrossing vines" and "crooked branches." In the space of only four lines, Xie Tiao has shown that a mountain is capable of different forms, lines, and contours. To these, he further adds animal sounds, which, in this poem, serve as a reminder of the passing of time.

A lone crane just cried out in the morning,	獨鶴方朝唳
And hungry squirrels are chirping away this evening.	饑鼯此夜啼
The racing clouds have spread and thickened;	泄雲已漫漫
The night rain, too, is turning chillier and chillier.	夕雨亦淒淒

He set out in the morning and went on until "this evening," when the clouds are thick and the rain feels colder by the minute. Ending his roaming at a moment made specific by the changes in time and weather, he increases the particularity of his experience, while revealing the haunting beauty of Mount Jingting with added vividness.

Capturing a specific moment, as Xie Tiao does in the poem above, can most easily evoke the sense of real-time experience. Shen Yue renews this point when he depicts his experience at the Xuanchang lou (Loft of Mystic Exultation), located in modern Jinhua, in two different ways.[38] First is the view *of* the loft:

The precipitous peaks are joined along the northern mountains,	危峰帶北阜
And a towering summit thrusts out above the southern hills.	高頂出南岑
Between them is a wind-facing loft;	中有陵風榭
It looks back toward the southern river bank.	迴望川之陰
The shore is rugged from many rising and receding tides;	岸險每增減
And the current is calm, running shallow and then deep.	湍平互淺深
The water flows out from three tributaries;	水流本三派
The loft, being tall, commands all four directions.[39]	臺高乃四臨

Here, it appears as if Shen Yue is orienting himself (and us) to the landscape surrounding the Xuanchang lou as he ascends the loft. His lines read like an informative travel guide, whose purpose is to prepare the traveler for the real experience. After he singles himself out as the traveler—"On it there is a wanderer separated from the crowd; / His heart yearns to return home"—he sees this:

As the descending light reflects the lengthy shore,	落暉映長浦
A luminous view lights up the middle isles.	煥景燭中潯
The clouds rise up; the peaks suddenly turn dark;	雲生嶺乍黑
As the sun falls low, the streams become half-shaded.	日下溪半陰

Unlike the generalized view in the first half of the poem, this is a specific view caught by the eyes of the wanderer on the loft. As the sun descends and the clouds shift, the view he sees changes dramatically from illumination to darkness.[40] As Xie Tiao wrote, "Whatever incites my appreciation I can only view it myself." It is not one's knowledge about a mountain range or a river system, but the view one sees with one's own eyes at a specific moment, which truly defines a landscape.

In Yongming poetry, the specificity of a moment is often created through the changes in light and shadow or the movement of clouds and mist. Shen Yue "grasps" all of them in the four lines just cited. Though these moments are extremely brief and especially so when seen inside a landscape, they represent the Yongming poets at their best and separate them most distinctively from their predecessors such as Xie Lingyun. Below is another such moment:

Glittering sunrays move above the water,	日華川上動
While lights in the wind float across the grassland.[41]	風光草際浮

This is not the only time that Xie Tiao has written about an image of floating light. While light can illuminate, glisten, or "float," when it disappears, the effect can be equally provocative. In a poem about the "Eight Retainers Mountain" ("Bagong shan"), Xie Tiao uses its coming into view and then disappearance from view to evoke the memories of its history:

Lush and lavish, trees of all forms rise above it;	阡眠起雜樹
Dense and shady, tall bamboos give it cover.	檀欒蔭脩竹
When the sun is hidden, the streams are confused for hollows;	日隱澗疑空
And when the clouds gather, the peaks seem as if multiplied.	雲聚岫如複
As they appear and disappear, I see glimpses of their battle towers and walls;	出沒眺樓雉
Now far, now near, my springtime eyes follow them.[42]	遠近送春目

Although it was his own clansman Xie Xuan (343–388) who had fought in the Battle of the Fei River there in 383, Xie Tiao's springtime eyes were not keen on wars. In the clouds and shadows, the ghost of the past appears and disappears, haunting his intent eyes. Without the sun to illuminate them, the streams turn into long stretches of dark hollows, causing "confusion." This image of dark hollows, like what we "see" when the lamp is suddenly turned off at night or when we shut our eyes in a dark room, recalls the other *kong*, the Buddhist nothingness or emptiness. The unambiguous use of *kong* as *śūnyatā* in Qi-Liang poetry can be traced to a poem by Prince Sui, whom Xie Tiao was very close to:

Passing the Tomb of Liu Huan   經劉瓛墓下
Lines 7–10

The early pines make the tomb birds sound mournful;	初松切墓鳥
The new willows hasten the wind at dawn.	新楊催曉風

The gate in the underbrush leads toward a dense thicket,　　榛關向蕪密

As the nether path gradually fuses into emptiness.[43]　　泉途轉銷空

In a deeply Buddhist period, it is hard not to see Prince Sui's solemn association of death with *śūnyatā* in Xie Tiao's glimpses into the past. There will be another image of *kong* in a different poem by Xie Tiao, but there, *kong* appears with light.

The moment of his visit is encapsulated by the title of his poem: "About to Travel to Xiang River, I First Seek Out Fish-hook Creek" ("Jiang you Xiangshui, xun Gouxi").[44] And this is how and what Xie Tiao sees at that moment:

Gurgling gently, it forms long stretches of shallow flow;　　瑟汨瀉長淀

Then, splashing and sloshing, it rushes toward the forked

　　streams.　　潨湲赴兩歧

Above, light duckweed profuse and dense;　　輕蘋上靡靡

Below, various rocks strewn and distinct.　　雜石下離離

Cold grasses gleam through separated flowers,　　寒草分花映

And playful sturgeons dart in and out of the empty spaces.　　戲鮪乘空移

Stirred by the late autumn moon,　　興以暮秋月

Clear frost falls from the bare branches.　　清霜落素枝

His eyes exhaust all the spaces on and within the creek. After surveying its long stretch of water, he looks at the duckweed above and the rocks beneath, and then proceeds to "close up" the remaining spaces: first, there are the grasses that "gleam through" from amongst the flowers, and then there are the sturgeons that "dart in and out of the empty spaces." But it is not a "closing up," since the line just referred to gives the illusion that

[. . .] playful sturgeons dart in and out *in emptiness.*

In the late autumn moonlight, the creek is as clear as an empty mirror, just as the rapids are in the only surviving poem from Liu Zhen, Liu Hui's younger brother:

When the misty peak darkens, it appears like daylight;　　煙峯晦如晝

And when the cold water is clear, it is as if empty.[45]　　寒水清若空

In the end, just as Xie Tiao's gaze moves up toward the source of light, it suddenly falls back down onto the creek again, following the frost that "falls from the bare branches." This unexpected movement increases the fluidity of his penetrating gaze. As the title reminds us, Xie Tiao is taking a detour from his travels; now that his viewing is done, he presumably is ready to move on.

Exiting the Landscape

Those who enter the landscape never intended to stay there for good. This is what Chen Da said when he made his home in Zhejiang during the Eastern Jin: "Given the beautiful mountains and rivers in this place, a monarch shall in no time rise up from here. Two hundred years from now, my sons and grandsons will definitely enjoy such good luck."[46] Indeed, if not for his descendant Emperor Wu of Chen, born about two hundred and forty years after the founding of the Eastern Jin, we might not have any record of Chen Da's story. The purpose of entering the landscape, as the story seems to suggest, is so that one eventually comes out better. What does it mean, then, if one were to "forget about returning" (*wang gui*), an idea often expressed by or about lovers of the landscape? Xie Lingyun, for example, alludes to this idea in his well-known poem, "Shibi jingshe huan hu zhong zuo" (A Poem Composed while Returning to the Lake from the Stone Wall Study):

From dusk to dawn, the weather keeps changing;	昏旦變氣候
While the mountains and rivers emit glittering lights.	山水含清暉
As glittering lights can be enchanting,	清暉能娛人
The wanderer, happy there, forgets about returning.[47]	游子憺忘歸

This wanderer is a recast of the "beholder" (*guanzhe*) in the *Chuci* song "Dongjun" (The Lord of the East): "How enchanting are the sounds and sights! The beholder, happy there, forgets about returning."[48] What follows in "Dongjun" and in Xie Lingyun's poem is the same: "The Lord of the East" sets on the "gloomy night journey back to the east";[49] as for Xie Lingyun, he was composing the poem on his "returning" route after all. In this final section, our question returns to what is "obtained" from the landscape.

Like earlier poetry, Yongming poetry is filled with expressions of the wish to prolong or even make permanent the stay in the landscape. And, as in earlier traditions, these expressions can be interpreted as thoughts about either retiring from office or becoming a recluse. The two situations, at least in poetry, are simply treated as analogies of each other. Since their landscape poems always foreground the occasion of being posted away from the capital, their appreciation of landscape beauty is often a comment on the life of a courtier. For example, after taking a detour to see the Xin'an River while on his way to Dongyang, Shen Yue concludes that:

It immerses me, blocking out the noise and the dregs—	紛吾隔囂滓
What's the need to rinse my robe and cap in it?[50]	寧假濯衣巾
I wish to use its gurgling water	願以漉淚水
To dampen the dust on your capstrings![51]	霑君纓上塵

Here, he invariably returns to his identity as one who wears an "[official] capstring"; the difference, as he sees it, is that he has been "purified" at the moment, while his "friends and associates in the capital," to whom he is sending the poem, are still covered in "dust." Even more representative of the Yongming poets' attitude, however, is a self-restraint or a self-reminder in the face of landscape beauty. In one instance, after wandering on Mount Jingting from morning until evening, Xie Tiao is tempted to "mount the cinnabar stairs," which supposedly lead to "heaven and transcendence":

My life's journey, though with many turns and obstacles,	我行雖紆組
Has, at the same time, allowed me to seek out secluded trails.	兼得尋幽蹊
I surely have not traced their sources to the very end—	緣源殊未極
But my returning path is blurred as if I'm lost.	歸徑窅如迷
If I should desire to pursue extraordinary wonders,	要欲追奇趣
At this very spot is where I shall mount the cinnabar stairs!	即此陵丹梯
When the imperial favor finally comes to end,	皇恩竟已矣
This reasoning, I hope, will not lead to misgivings.[52]	茲理庶無睽

In this instance, Xie Tiao has gone far—one more step will put him on a different life path. The "extraordinary wonder" is vividly alluring to him, but the thought of "imperial favor" eventually pulls him back, causing him to curb his desire and halt from stepping further. This leads us to two related points. First, as discussed earlier, the pursuit of reclusion—if that can be understood as a complete devotion to cultivating spiritual growth or, in a religious sense, pursuing enlightenment—is a personal and individualized process in Xie Tiao's mind. In his poem about a "proto-roaming" in the mountains, he is reminded that even past recluses, such as Shangzi and Master Bing, needed time to resolve a practical matter or simply to consider before they could make that final decision. Second, it is worth noting that in a 493 edict in which Emperor Wu of Qi announces his death will, he specifically instructs his court and successor that, while they should faithfully pray to and make offerings to the "jade statues of the various Buddhas" (*yuxiang zhu Fo*) in the palace, no one—whether those in or outside the court—should be allowed to "leave home" (*chujia*; Skt. *āraṇyaka*) to become a priest, a monk, or a nun, build pagodas or temples, or turn a residence into a monastery.[53] While there might not have been any such state laws or imperial orders that could affect Xie Tiao's or any other courtiers' poems, Emperor Wu's edict provides at least one context for Xie Tiao's reference to "imperial favor." For a courtier, even while deeply engaging the landscape, maintaining a level of "rationality" and even caution would seem necessary.

The Yongming poets' sense of restraint or "rationality" in the face of a beautiful landscape not only leads to a refreshing tone of honesty that we find in other types of poems by them as well, but also reveals a different possibility as to how a landscape might be appreciated. Having seen the changing views of Mount Ding from a boat, Shen Yue writes:

Forgetting about returning, I now belong with orchids and asarum;	忘歸屬蘭杜
But relishing salary, I still live among fragrant herbs.	懷祿寄芳荃
I long to cull the triple-blooming polypores;	眷言採三秀
Lingering on, I gaze after the Nine Immortals.[54]	徘徊望九仙

He "forgets about returning" in one moment, only to remember his "relished salary" in the next. And, as he continues to gaze at the world of the immortals, his boat simply sails on, taking him farther and farther away from Mount Ding. While he might appear irresolute, it is worth reminding ourselves that Shen Yue probably had no intention of staying there for good in the first place. This is Xie Tiao after stealing a moment by Fish-hook Creek:

Amongst fish and birds I'm now at play;	魚鳥余方翫
As for the capstring, you have tied them yourself.	纓綏君自縻
Coming here has allowed my cherished thoughts to roam free—	及茲暢懷抱
Mountains and rivers have always been like that![55]	山川長若斯

As Mather points out, Xie Tiao is addressing his *alter ego* in the second line.[56] The interesting point is that he recognizes it is *himself* who has "tied the capstrings." That, however, does not take away his joy for the moment;

on the contrary, he takes stock of such a moment, particularly as it stands in contrast to the longevity of the mountains and rivers. In a poem that "harmonizes" with those of two acquaintances, Xie Tiao makes his point even more directly:

On the Return Route, Overlooking the Isle	還塗臨渚
The Grand Warden, harmonizing from afar:	府君遙和:
The transparent water brightens outside the fields;	白水田外明
A single mountain peak rises above the pines.	孤嶺松上出
The moment's delight, being great, may be made to linger;	即趣佳可淹
But this lingering is not a stepping down from office.[57]	淹留非下秩

His abrupt declaration at the end—as if reassuring his fellow courtiers or even himself—may seem to reveal his concern about his image as a courtier on duty.[58] But, read in a different way, it may in fact reveal his understanding about how the appreciation for "the moment's delight" can go hand-in-hand with his being in office. In other words, there is no contradiction between the engagement with the natural landscape and the engagement with officialdom. And that is the most compelling insight found in the landscape poetry of the Yongming era.

It is, in other words, about the memories of the moment. In the last poem cited from Xie Tiao, one might note that he is harmonizing with his acquaintances "from afar." Just as the time when he harmonized with Liu Hui's poem about a rapids, he is probably not "overlooking the isle" *on site* in this poem. But no one is. Even the painter Zong Bing, who probably came closest to "forgetting about returning," had to "paint them [i.e., the mountains that he had visited] in his room."[59] His method of capturing the semblance of the mountains through brush strokes and colors on silk and later re-experiencing them by viewing the painted silk—what he called "roaming them while lying down" (*wo yi you zhi*)—is not unlike what Xie Tiao and his fellow courtiers did with landscape poems.[60] For them, Xie Lingyun's balanced landscape could no longer satisfy the requirement for the specificity of the moment; such specificity, when done properly, not only retained the memory of the moment for oneself but allowed it to be exchanged with others as well.

The pretext of specificity is individual observation—that is, with one's own eyes—which calls into question the assumption that there is an all-encompassing form for all to emulate or follow. Xie Lingyun once concluded that:

When worries dissolve in tranquility, external things are light on their own;	慮澹物自輕
And, as thoughts are on contentment, the Truth will naturally follow.	意愜理無違
Send words to sojourners who cultivate life:	寄言攝生客
Try reckoning with this principle![61]	試用此道推

As one may recall, what Xie Tiao called for was more personal and individualized:

Forever intent on what has long been admired—	永志昔所欽
Marvelous sites, among which I may now choose.	勝跡今能選
Send words to sojourners with an appreciative heart:	寄言賞心客
To obtain your own true nature is the best.	得性良為善

The life of a courtier came with little freedom to choose. This is the only utterance in Yongming poetry of the concept of choice. Memories were the one thing that courtiers could keep and bequeath to history. Given that the lives and works of the Yongming poets were all closely related to Xiao Ziliang, the Prince of Jingling, it is appropriate to end this chapter with his memories:

Preface to "Strolling in My Estate" 行宅詩序

My given nature is such that I am impartial and adrift, and my only love is the ease of being outside of things. In the past while on distant mission in Zhedong, I fully experienced the beauty of mountains and rivers. There was not a famous city or a magnificent site wherein I did not climb to the highest point or view to the fullest. Whether on a mountain plain or a stony path, every step brought a new feeling; as for the winding lakes and the most remote gullies, they were, more often than not, old acquaintances to me. I chant and sing about them, so that some of the feelings in my heart may be expressed.[62]

余稟性端疏，屬愛閑外。往歲羈役浙東，備歷江山之美，名都勝境，極盡登臨。山原石道，步步新情；迴池絕澗，往往舊識。以吟以詠，聊用述心。

Epilogue

Throughout this book, I have referred to the Yongming poets as courtier-poets. The Chinese terms *gongting wenren* ("court literati") and *gongting shi-ren* ("court poets") can sometimes have a negative connotation, as if these courtiers were not "real" poets, but wrote merely to please and entertain their court patrons. While certainly mindful of the need to please, entertain, and most importantly, win the favor of their patrons, the Yongming poets were also writing at a time when poetry was woven deep into a uniquely multifaceted and vibrant court culture. Writing as courtiers, they sought many things simultaneously: to display their talent, to negotiate their political and personal pursuits, to refine their arts. By fully considering their identity as courtiers, we do not see less of their poetry and poetics; instead, we hear their voices probing the most fundamental human issues, and witness their intricate artistry and refreshing sensibilities. Previously known mostly for a set of prosodic rules dryly labeled as *sisheng babing* ("the four tones and eight defects"), the Yongming poets as presented in this study are active participants at an important juncture in the history of Chinese court culture and the precursors of a new poetics that had a long-lasting effect.

One main line of study in this book has been to examine how Buddhism was integrated into the fabric of the Chinese courtier's life by the fifth and sixth centuries. My main concern is not how Buddhism was practiced or what Buddhist views were expressed per se, but rather how the Buddhist perspective came into play in the Chinese courtier's poetic representation of his way of life. Particularly relevant to the foregrounding of this discussion is a hybrid concept of personal worth. This concept is revealed in Shen Yue's discourse, where one finds a Confucian ideal of "individual talent" as well as a Buddhist vision of "the worthy one." While the two can easily lead to two separate lines of investigation—the courtier-poet as a Confucian and the courtier-poet as a Buddhist—what is more intriguing—and more realistic—is the mixing of both and their simultaneous presence in the courtier-poet. As evinced by many works analyzed in this book, the Yongming poets often revealed their vested interest in being recognized and promoted alongside their pursuit of Buddhist enlightenment. From that vantage point, a beautiful object such as a piece of embroidery simultaneously calls forth the courtier's "use value" and the ultimate emptiness of all things. In their depiction, the garden is a personal space for imitating nature, creating self-sufficiency, and cultivating the Buddhist vision, all of which, however, are premised on a temporary retreat from life at the court. To them, the capital city is both home and not home, evoking a sense of belonging and nostalgia at times but causing an uneasy feeling and a sense of urgency for spiritual enlightening at other times. Though the antithesis of officialdom, the natural landscape is enjoyed as an experience in spiritual renewal and treasured as memories of past footsteps in their poems. By tracing their Buddhist outlook amid other inclinations and within a wide range of issues, we see even more acutely how Buddhism had come to be embedded in the Yongming poets' self-representation and self-expression. The richness and hybridity of their poetic voices are thus highlighted.

Even more crucially, the Buddhist influence on their poetics is revealed in the way the Yongming poets *sensed* the world around them. As discussed, the particularly analytical and diminutive approach taught by the Chengshi school of Buddhist scholasticism could perhaps explain Shen Yue's unusual awareness of the intricate processes of the mind. His dissection of the stream of thought into individual *nian* ("thought-instants") was a defining moment in the Chinese perception of the mind and of time. The realization that followed was that only a mind devoid of chaos—a mind that *completes* one thought-instant after another—could lead to enlightenment. Subsequently,

Shen Yue and his fellow Yongming poets would emphasize a process of diminutive grasping in their poetics. Be it a chain of sounds, a minor object, a busy sight, or a constant motion, the Yongming poets always revealed it piece-by-piece, bit-after-bit, giving the impression that they were seeing and hearing in a continuous manner while maintaining clarity and precision. As a result, their poems are individualized experiences wherein the senses are highly focused and alert. Imbued with religious meaning, their new process of the senses had major implications for Chinese poetics.

Most significantly, the representation of sound, sight, space, and motion could now fully represent the poetic self. Rather than shifting the attention to the "surface" or "exterior" forms of poetry, the Yongming poets were calling attention to the perceptive mind behind their process of seeing and hearing. Not conceding that they were merely crafting the outer, they established themselves as a new kind of poetic and aesthetic subject. The traditional paradigm of *shi yan zhi* ("poetry expresses what is intently on the mind"), which presumes an inner-to-outer process in poetry, had not shifted; rather, the inner *zhi* could now be expressed through how one sees or hears, a process now seen as directly reflecting the processes of the mind.[1] Liu Xie, their likeminded critic, acknowledged this new notion of *zhi* most directly in a discussion about rhyme change: when comparing the practice of Jia Yi (200–168 B.C.E.) and Mei Cheng (d. 140 B.C.E.) of changing to a new rhyme after two rhyming lines to the practice of Liu Xin (d. 23) and Huan Tan (ca. 23 B.C.E.–C.E. 56) of not changing the rhyme even after a hundred lines, he attributed their difference to the fact that "they each had their own *zhi*."[2] On the Western Jin (265–316) writer Lu Yun (262–303), he commented: "When observing the way he placed his rhymes, I see that his *zhi* was the same as Mei Cheng's and Jia Yi's."[3] Liu Xie interpreted the rhyming pattern that a poet crafted as a representation of his *zhi*.[4] This poetics ushered in a new poetic and aesthetic consciousness that sought to express the inner state not only through what is said but also through *how* it is said. The presentation of an acute and refined sense of hearing and seeing now stood at the center of Chinese poetics.

To see the later transformation of the poetic and aesthetic subject established by the Yongming poets, let us look at a poem by Wang Wei (701–761), the Tang dynasty "poet-Buddha" (*shifo*):

Written while Crossing the Yellow River to Qinghe　　渡河到清河作

I sail a boat on the great river,　　泛舟大河里

Where swelling water stretches to the sky's end.　　積水窮天涯

The sky and waves suddenly split open:	天波忽開拆
In the district, thousands of homes.	郡邑千万家
Moving on, I see the city market,	行复見城市
Where there appears to be mulberry and hemp.	宛然有桑麻
I turn back to gaze toward my old hometown:	回瞻舊鄉國
Flooding water joins the clouds and mists.[5]	淼漫連云霞

The sensuous perception presented in this poem, drawing broader lines and vaguer contours, no doubt lacks the sense of diminutive grasping in Yongming poetry.[6] But Wang Wei's forward gaze toward the water and sky as his boat moves out in the Yellow River still recalls Xie Tiao, who gazes backward as his boat moves out in the Yangzi: "On the horizon, I recognize a returning boat; / Through the clouds, I make out the riverside trees."[7] That the continuous forward motion of his boat is created through his changing views also recalls one of Shen Yue's journeys out of Jiankang: "As the Yangzi River shifts, the forested shore diminishes; / Where the valleys deepen, the misty peaks overlap."[8] At the center of Wang Wei's poem is his sense subject—though presented through a less accentuated way of viewing, it nonetheless reflects a clear consciousness about how one sees and how that in and of itself is poetry. Incidentally, even though by Wang Wei's time, the prosodic movement in poetry was already heading in the direction of using the more simplified concept of "level (*ping*) versus deflected (*ze*) tones," this poem still retains traces of the more meticulous "four tones" prosody of Yongming poetry.[9] The tones of the final syllables in its eight lines, for example, form a highly crafted pattern: B/A/D/A/B/A/D/A.[10] Here, in a poem written by an eighth-century poet deeply influenced by the Chan Buddhism of his time, we still recognize the origin of his poetics in the Yongming poetics of sound and sight.

The Ming dynasty (1368–1644) critic Lu Shiyong (fl. 1633) rather sarcastically commented: "Shen Yue has sound without resonance, sight without brilliance."[11] The critical criterion on which Lu Shiyong based his judgment is called *shen* ("lively spirit") or *shenyun* ("lively spirit and reverberating resonance"), which seeks a poetic presence, whether imagistic, emotional, moral, or philosophical, that exists "beyond words."[12] However, the concept by which the Yongming poets guided their own poetics, displayed their talent, and sought enlightenment was *jing*, "refinement." The process of "refinement," by contrast, gravitates toward "words." It requires an audience to follow the alternation in tones and rhymes, the continuous shift in perspective, the details in a view, and the subtle changes in time and light. Through such a process of diminutive grasping, the reader of Yongming poetry partakes in a concentrated sensuous experience filled with subtle religious meanings and complex emotions. Clearly, we no longer hear the "four tones" or the many rhyming syllables that the Yongming poets heard; often enough, used to the speed of digital and electronic sight and sound, we also lack their minute awareness. The sensory world of Yongming poetry does not present itself naturally to our modern sensibility or to premodern critics in the canonical tradition. But in the difficulty of imagining the Yongming's sensory world we find an opportunity to better understand early medieval China and our own senses, if we are to meet the challenge of reading this poetry beyond the "mute semantic text."[13]

Reference Matter

Abbreviations

CLEAR	*Chinese Literature: Essays, Articles, Reviews*
HJAS	*Harvard Journal of Asiatic Studies*
JAOS	*Journal of the American Oriental Society*
JAS	*Journal of Asian Studies*
SBCK	*Sibu congkan*
SBBY	*Sibu beiyao*
Taishō	*Taishō shinshū daizōkyō,* edited by Takakusu Junjirō and Watanabe Kaikyoku
XQHWJ	*Xian Qin Han Wei Jin Nan Bei chao shi,* compiled by Lu Qinli

Notes

Prologue

1. *Shang shu zhengyi*, 8.196; cf. Legge, *The Chinese Classics*, 3:180.

2. Ban Gu, *Han shu*, 81.3342.

3. E.g. *Hanyu da cidian* and *Zhongwen da cidian*.

4. The idea that sensual pleasures have to be guided by ritual propriety and that "improper" sensual pleasures will have political, moral, and cultural consequences is an important one in early Chinese historiography, as evidenced by the *Zuo zhuan* and the *Guoyu* (see Schaberg, *A Patterned Past*, 223–34).

5. *Li ji zhengyi*, 53.1466; cf. Legge, *The Chinese Classics*, 1:433. The two *Shijing* poems cited are *Mao* 235 and 260 (Legge, *The Chinese Classics*, 4:431, 544).

6. Shen Deqian, *Shuoshi zuiyu*, 9a.

7. See Cai Zhongxiang, *Zhongguo wenxue lilun shi*, 4:452–54.

8. *Shuoshi zuiyu*, 9a.

9. Ibid., 9a–b.

10. Ibid., 8b.

11. Cao Pi, "*Dian lun* Lun wen," in Xiao Tong, *Wen xuan*, 52.2270–72.

12. See Zhao Erxun, *Qing shi gao*, 84.2528.

13. 南北朝所以不治，文采勝質厚也 · Ouyang Xiu, *Xin Tang shu*, 165.5067.

14. Lu Xun, "Shige zhi di," in *Jiwai ji shiyi*, 345.

15. Comments about the "decadence" of Southern Dynasties elite culture and literature can be found in popular works such as Wang Yao, *Zhonggu wenxueshi lun*, 286.

16. Chennault, "Odes on Objects and Patronage during the Southern Qi," 398.

Chapter One

1. Mather, *The Poet Shen Yüeh*, 14.

2. Mather, *Eternal Brilliance*.

3. Yao Silian, *Liang shu*, 49.690. Many later commentaries on the Yongming style, including those by modern scholars, can be traced to this comment in the *Liang shu*. Ami Yūji, for example, sees the Yongming poetic style as the beginning of a trend in ornateness and superfluity (*Chūgoku chūsei bungaku kenkyū*, 390–91).

4. 梁陳以來，艷薄斯極。沈休文又尚以聲律，將復古道，非我而誰歟? (Li Fang, *Taiping guangji*, 201.1511).

5. Tian, *Beacon Fire*, 211–59.

6. For a discussion of the prosodic patterns of Palace style poems, see Gui Qing, *Nanchao Gongti shi yanjiu*, 203–18.

7. The name *Lüshi* can be traced to Shen Quanqi (ca. 656–713) and Song Zhi-wen (d. 712); see Liu Xu, *Jiu Tang shu*, 190.5056.

8. Zhong Rong, *Shi pin jizhu*, 340.

9. Shen Qingzhi (386–457), also from Wuxing, was a commander during the Song and is said to "have hands that cannot write and eyes that cannot read" (Shen Yue, *Song shu*, 77.2003). For Shen Yue's family background, see Mather, *The Poet Shen Yüeh*, 7–14; Lin Jiali, *Shen Yue yanjiu*, 1–30. For Shen Yue's biography, see *Liang shu*, 13.232–43, and Li Yanshou, *Nan shi*, 57.1403–14.

10. A common saying in the early years of the Eastern Jin goes: "The Wangs and the [Si]mas share the power under Heaven" (*Nan shi*, 21.583). See Tian Yuqing, "Shi 'Wang yu Ma gong tianxia,'" in idem, *Dong Jin menfa zhengzhi*, 1–38. For Wang Rong's biography, see Xiao Zixian, *Nan Qi shu*, 47.817; *Nan shi*, 21.575–78. For the literary heritage of the Xie family, see Cheng Zhangcan, *Shizu yu Liuchao wenxue*, 51–88; Ding Fulin, *Dong Jin Nanchao de Xie shi wenxue jituan*. For the political rise of the Xie family during the Eastern Jin, see Tian, *Dong Jin menfa zhengzhi*, 199–231. For Xie Tiao's biography, see *Nan Qi shu*, 47.825–28; *Nan shi*, 19.532–35.

11. For the power structure and relationship among the northern émigré families such as the Wangs and the Xies from the Eastern Jin through early Song, see Tian, *Dong Jin menfa zhengzhi*. For a general review of the situation from the Song through the Chen, see Tang Changru, *Wei Jin Nan Bei chao Sui Tang shi san lun*, 159–64; Wang Zhongluo, *Wei Jin Nan Bei chao shi*, 131–32.

12. A southerner from a military family faced even more discrimination, as being a general or a commander was considered "vulgar" and would hurt one's social standing (Tian, *Dong Jin menfa zhengzhi*, 339); as Lin Jiali points out, Shen Yue made the pivotal effort of transforming the Shens of Wuxing from "a strong military family" into "a family of cultural elites" (*Shen Yue yanjiu*, 15–16).

13. Tian Yuqing, alluding to how his rise signaled a new socio-political structure, calls Liu Yu one of the two main "grave diggers" (*juemu ren*) of the old political system dominated by eminent northern émigré families (*Dong Jin menfa zhengzhi*, 292–329).

14. See Chen Yinque, *Wei Jin Nan Bei chao shi jiangyanlu*, 215–25.

15. *Nan shi*, 21.573–5; *Nan Qi shu*, 47.827.

16. *Song shu*, 94.2301–2.

17. Taigong is Lü Shang, who is also known as Jiang Shang. He was said to be poor and was fishing by the bank of the Wei River when King Wen of Zhou met him. Later he was credited with aiding King Wen and King Wu in defeating Shang and was revered as Master Shangfu. The legend has it that Fu Yue, a man of Shang, was a laborer who built walls; later he was discovered and appointed a minister.

18. Hu Guang, whose ancestors lived in reclusion after Wang Mang (r. 9–23)

usurped the throne, was appointed as a *xiaolian* ("Filial and Upright") and made his way up the ladder until he became a Grand Tutor (*Taifu*). Likewise, Huang Xian, who was the son of an "ox-curer," was appointed a *xiaolian* at first; even though he did not rise up in official ranks in the end, he impressed the elites whom he met in the capital, earning a name for himself.

19. *Song shu*, 94.2301–2.

20. 下品無高門，上品無賤族. Shen Yue was probably referring to a memorial that Liu Yi presented to Emperor Wu of Jin (in Fang Xuanling, *Jin shu*, 45.1273–77), in which he argues for the abolishment of the "Nine Ranks System."

21. *Song shu*, 94.2301–2.

22. Ibid., 94.2302.

23. Shen Yue was the author of a memorandum that argues for establishing an accurate registry to differentiate the commoners from the gentry (Du You, *Tongdian*, 3.59–61; Yan Kejun, *Quan Liang wen*, in *Quan shanggu sandai Qin Han sanguo Liuchao wen*, 27.3110ab). See Tian, *Beacon Fire*, 35–38; Mather, *The Poet Shen Yüeh*, 159–60.

24. In an edict from 509, Liang Wudi announced that those from humble ranks should be "tested for officialdom based on their talent" (*Liang shu*, 2.49). For the changes that Liang Wudi made to the recruitment system, see Tian, *Beacon Fire*, 39–52; particularly illuminating is her analysis of the difference between *hanmen* ("men of humble lineages") and *hanren* ("commoners").

25. *Liang shu*, 14.258.

26. Ibid.

27. In 438, Song Wendi (Liu Yilong; r. 424–453), who was known for his interest in "arts and literature" (*yiwen*), set up an academy for "literary learning," along with three other academies: for "Confucian studies" (*ru*), "mysterious learning" (*xuan*), and "historical learning" (*shi*); in 470, Mingdi (Liu Yu; r. 465–472) further established a department to oversee the administration of these academies, including that for "literary learning" (*Nan shi*, 75.1868; *Song shu*, 93.2394; Sima Guang, *Zizhi tongjian*, 132.4152). As noted by David R. Knechtges, there is no way of knowing what "literary learning" might have entailed in the Song educational system ("Culling the Weeds and Selecting Prime Blossoms," 216); the establishment of the academy was nevertheless consistent—as suggested by Knechtges—with the emergence of a more precise concept of "literary learning" and of literature in general during the period.

28. Luo Xinben, "Liang Jin Nanchao de xiucai, xiaolian chaju," 123. Albert E. Dien also notes "the value that came to be placed on the literary quality of the questions posed to the candidates, as evidenced by the presence of the genre of examination questions (*cewen*) in the *Wen xuan*" ("Civil Service Examinations," 105); in a study on a *cenwen* written by Wang Rong, Fujii Mamoru, too, notes that *cewen* was treated seriously as a literary genre after the recommendation system became problematic ("Ō Yū no 'Saku shusai bun' ni tsuite," 291–92).

29. See Tian, *Beacon Fire*, 77–110, 150–60.

30. *Liang shu*, 13.233.

31. *Nan Qi shu*, 47.823.

32. Ibid., 47.825.

33. *Nan shi*, 6.168. On the Eight Friends, see Ami, *Chūgoku chūsei bungaku kenkyū*, 57–116; Liu Yuejin, *Menfa shizu yu Yongming wenxue*, 27–70.

34. Lin, *Shen Yue yanjiu*, 400–435.

35. *Nan shi*, 59.1452.

36. Ibid., 59.1455.

37. *Liang shu*, 233–35. The details of Xiao Yan's ascension and Shen Yue and Fan Yun's involvement have been carefully reconstructed by Mather (*The Poet Shen Yüeh*, 126–29).

38. The "three eternities" (*san buxiu*) of the Confucian school are: *li de* ("establishing virtue"), *li gong* ("establishing merits"), and *li yan* ("establishing speech") (*Chunqiu Zuozhuan zhengyi*, 35.1003; Legge, *The Chinese Classics*, 5:507). The notion of "establishing speech" was absorbed into that of literary achievement, as expressed by Cao Pi, who called literature "a splendid affair that is eternal" (*buxiu zhi shengshi*) ("*Dian lun* Lun wen," in Xiao Tong, *Wen xuan*, 52.2270–72).

39. The most successful expeditions launched by the southern states against the north were probably those led by Liu Yu (later Song Wudi), who, at one point, was able to push the borders of the Eastern Jin to the Guanzhong region (in modern central Shanxi) and several provinces between the Huai and the Yellow Rivers. Towards the end of the Song, after suffering a number of military defeats by the Northern Wei, the state was forced to retreat southward, until its northern frontier was shifted to the region south of the Huai. The Qi did not actively campaign against the north. See Chen, *Wei Jin Nan Bei chao shi jiangyanlu*, 226–39.

40. *Nan Qi shu*, 47.821–2; *Nan shi*, 21.575–6. Wang Rong was twenty-seven *sui* in the eleventh year of the Yongming reign (493), but according to Chen Qingyuan, the incident took place in the tenth year of the Yongming reign, when Wang Rong was twenty-six *sui* ("Wang Rong nianpu," in Liu Yuejin and Fan Ziye, *Liuchao zuojia nianpu jiyao*, 490). Sima Xiangru's "Fengshan wen" is cited in the *Shiji* (117.3063–68) and was later collected in *Wen xuan* (48.2139–45).

41. This is the "Preface to Poems on the Qu River" ("Qushui shi xu"), composed at the instruction of Qi Wudi upon the celebration of the Rite of Purification (*xiyan*) in 491; the piece apparently won Wang Rong the praise of his contemporaries (*Nan Qi shu*, 47.821) and was later included in *Wen xuan* (46.2056–67).

42. Other poets in the south, such as Xie Lingyun, Shen Yue, and Ren Fang, were also known in the Northern Wei (Wei Shou, *Wei shu*, 12.313, 85.1876). Yu Xin was probably chosen by the Liang court to be an envoy to the north for his literary fame; most likely for the same reason, he was retained and even appointed to major positions in the Western Wei (535–556) after its army had invaded the Liang capital and killed Emperor Yuan (see Bear, "The Lyric Poetry of Yü Hsin," 213–14; Lu Tongqun, "Yu Xin nianpu," in *Liuchao zuojia nianpu jiyao*, 2:463–64). The northern elites' admiration of southern writers sometimes mirrored the literary rivalry among the latter: while the competition between Ren Fang and Shen Yue to be "the best poet" is well-documented (*Nan shi*, 59.1452, 1455), Xing Zicai and Wei Shou (507–572) of the Northern Qi (550–577) were said to have fought each other

at banquets because the former admired Shen Yue but not Ren Fang and the latter felt just the opposite (Yan Zhitui, *Yanshi jiaxun huizhu*, 60; Teng Ssu-yü, *Family Instructions for the Yen Clan*, 97).

43. *Nan Qi shu*, 52.908.

44. Like Xiao Zixian (*Nan Qi shu*, 52.907–9; cf. Tian, *Beacon Fire*, 150–60), Shen Yue stresses the transformation of literary style in his narrative of literary history: "Literary writers and talents in the more than four hundred years from Han to Wei can be subsumed by three transformations in literary style (*wenti sanbian*)" (*Song shu*, 67.1778).

45. *Liang shu*, 49.690.

46. My analogy of "tidal waves" is partly inspired by Zhong Rong's account of the three poets' prosodic invention: "Wang Yuanchang [i.e., Wang Rong] initiated it, and Xie Tiao and Shen Yue whipped up its waves" (*Shipin jizhu*, 340).

47. See Tang Yongtong, *Han Wei Liang Jin Nan Bei chao fojiaoshi*, 324–27.

48. See Liu, *Menfa shizu yu Yongming wenxue*, 44–48.

49. See Mather, *The Poet Shen Yüeh*, 135–73. For Liang Wudi's Buddhist activities, see Tian, *Beacon Fire*, 52–67.

50. The courtier who made the assertion was Fan Zhen (ca. 450–ca. 515), who was also a member of Jingling's literary coterie. He openly challenged Jingling's Buddhist beliefs, declaring that "there is no Buddha" and further presenting his argument in a treatise entitled "Shenmie lun" (On the Extinction of the Spirit) (*Liang shu*, 48.665–70); despite Jingling's various attempts to refute and silence him—at one point even sending word to him through Wang Rong that he "should have no worry about not being promoted to Vice Director," as long as he "does not ruin it for himself by being strange and contradictory"—he was unmoved and undeterred (*Nan shi*, 57.1421–22; *Liang shu*, 48.665, 670). Fan Zhen's "anti-Buddhist" treatise continued to be viewed as a serious threat by the Buddhist believers in the court, such that when Liang Wudi came to power, he would write "an imperial response" to rebut him, prompting more than sixty courtiers to submit their own responses (see Tian, *Beacon Fire*, 59–62). Shen Yue's "Shen bumie yi" (On the Non-Extinction of the Spirit) (*Taishō*, 52:253b; see Mather, *The Poet Shen Yüeh*, 136–51) was produced upon this occasion.

51. "Shen bumie yi," *Taishō*, 52:253b.

52. Ibid. The emphasis on the difference between "the saint" and "the ordinary person" in Qi-Liang Buddhism is also reflected in Xiao Tong's "Lingzhi jie Erdi yi bing wenda" (*Taishō*, 52:247c), discussed by Whalen Lai in his "Sinitic Understanding of the Two Truths Theory in the Liang Dynasty (502–57)." Lai seems to suggest that the emphasis was the result of the Chinese appropriation of Buddhism, as he comments that "the Chinese Buddhists placed more emphasis on the role of the person" (n. 19) and that truth "becomes relative to the person" and "a function of personality" (p. 345).

53. Elsewhere Shen Yue would write that "Buddha is one who is enlightened (*jue*); one who is enlightened is one who knows (*zhi*)" ("Fozhi buyi zhongshengzhi yi," *Taishō*, 52:252c).

54. "Liudao xiangxu zuo fo yi," *Taishō*, 52:253a. Cf. Mather, *The Poet Shen Yüeh*, 146; Lai, "Beyond the Debate on 'The Immortality Soul,'" 150–51.

55. "Xingshen yi," *Taishō*, 52:253a–b; cf. Mather, *The Poet Shen Yüeh*, 148–49; Lai, "Beyond the Debate," 151–52.

56. Mather, *The Poet Shen Yüeh*, 136.

57. Some give the dates of Harivarman as ca. 250–350. For the *Chengshi lun*, see *Taishō*, 32:239a–373b. Shen Yue came under the influence of several major exponents of the *Chengshi lun*, including Sengrou (431–494) and Huici (434–490), who were the special mentors of Crown Prince Wenhui and the Prince of Jingling, whom he served between 481 and 490. Later he also had frequent contact with Fayun (467–529), another *Chengshi lun* specialist. On the popularity of the *Chengshi lun* during the Southern Dynasties, see Tang, *Han Wei Liang Jin Nan Bei chao fojiaoshi*, 514–26; on its development during the period, see Ren Jiyu, *Zhongguo fojiaoshi*, 3:413–22.

58. Jingling had ordered the compilation of an "abridged" version of the *Chengshi lun* (*Taishō*, 55:78a). On its content, see Lai, "Further Developments of the Two Truths Theory in China"; Chen Shixian, "*Chengshi lun* 'sanxin' yu *Shedachenglun* 'sanxing' sixiang zhi bijiao"; Chang Lei, "*Chengshi lun* zhong mie Sanxin de lilun" and "*Chengshi lun* zhong de Erti sixiang"; Ren, *Zhongguo fojiaoshi*, 3:394–408.

59. 世有二種人．一謂智人．一謂愚人．若不善分別陰界諸入十二因緣等法是名愚人．善分別陰界入等是名智人．(*Taishō*, 32:249a). The *skandha* are the five personality components (*rūpa*, "form"; *vedanā*, "feeling"; *saṃjñā*, "perception"; *saṃskāra*, "action"; *vijñāna*, "knowledge"). The *āyatana* are the twelve sense fields, that is, the six sense organs or faculties (eyes, ears, nose, tongue, body, and mind) and their corresponding objects (sight, sound, smell, taste, touch, and thought). The *dhātu* are the eighteen elements of existence, including the twelve sense fields and the corresponding six consciousnesses (visual, auditory, olfactory, gustatory, tactile, and mental). The *dvādaśāṅgika-pratītya-samutpāda* delineates the chain of causation that leads from rebirth to death: (1) *avidyā* ("ignorance"; *wuming*); (2) *saṃskāra* ("action"; *xing*); (3) *vijñāna* ("knowledge"; *shi*); (4) *nāma-rūpa* ("name and form"; *mingse*); (5) *saḍ-āyatana* ("six sense domains"; *liuchu*); (6) *sparśa* ("contact"; *chu*); (7) *vedanā* ("sensation"; *shou*); (8) *tṛṣṇā* ("lusting"; *ai*); (9) *upādāna* ("grasping"; *qu*); (10) *bhava* ("becoming"; *you*); (11) *jāti* ("birth"; *sheng*); (12) *jarā-maraṇa* ("old age and death"; *laosi*).

60. 輪等和合故名為車。五陰和合故名為人。(*Taishō*, 32:261c). See Note 59 in this chapter for *wuyin* (the five *skandha*).

61. 若爾風中或有香。香應在風中。如香熏油。香應在油中。是事不然。(*Taishō*, 32:263b).

62. Chang, "*Chengshi lun* zhong de Erti sixiang," 3–5.

63. Takakusu, *The Essentials of Buddhist Philosophy*, 77. See also Lai, "Further Developments of the Two Truths Theory in China," 139–61; Chen, "*Chengshi lun* 'sanxin' yu *Shedachenglun* 'sanxing' sixiang zhi bijiao," 3–10; Chang, "*Chengshi lun* zhong mie Sanxin de lilun."

64. *Jiaming xin* is the state of mistaking all perceptions as real and permanent;

faxin is that of, having grasped that all perceptions are unreal, still mistaking the "basic components" of all perceptions (such as the five *skandha*) as real and permanent; and *kongxin* is "an initial nivarnic state," after having grasped that the "basic components" of all perceptions are unreal; it is only after *kongxin* has been extinguished that Nirvāna is truly reached (*Taishō*, 32:327a, 44:513c). See Chen, "*Chengshi lun* 'sanxin' yu *Shedachenglun* 'sanxing' sixiang zhi bijiao," 3–10; Chang, "*Chengshi lun* zhong mie Sanxin de lilun."

65. *Taishō*, 45:4a. Following Tang Yongtong (*Han Wei Liang Jin Nan Bei chao fojiaoshi*, 536), I read the *chai* here as *xi*.

66. "Shen bumie yi," *Taishō*, 52:253c. Cf. Mather, *The Poet Shen Yüeh*, 151; Tian, *Beacon Fire*, 232.

67. *Zhuangzi jishi*, 14.221 : 兼忘天下易, 使天下兼忘我難 ("To totally forget all under Heaven is easy; to make all under Heaven totally forget me is difficult").

68. "Shen bumie yi," *Taishō*, 52:253c. Cf. Mather, *The Poet Shen Yüeh*, 151.

69. Tian, *Beacon Fire*, 229–33.

70. Ibid., 211–59.

Chapter Two

A version of this chapter in the form of an article entitled "Knowing Sound: Poetry and 'Refinement' in Early Medieval China" has been published in *CLEAR* 31 (2009). I thank the editors at *CLEAR* for the permission to reprint.

1. Yang Xiong, *Fayan*, 2.1a. *Chong* ("worm") and *zhuan* ("seal") were two ancient styles of calligraphy.

2. *Nan Qi shu*, 52.900. Cf. Mather, *The Poet Shen Yüeh*, 52.

3. Mair and Mei, "The Sanskrit Origins of Recent Style Prosody," 375–470; a recent response to this article is Hongming Zhang, "Shen Yue's Poetic Metrical Theory and His Poem Composition: A Linguistic Perspective," presented at the 2006 Annual Meeting of the Association for Asian Studies.

4. See, for example, Jiao Ran, *Shi shi*, in *Lidai shihua lun zuojia*, 1:123–24 (for translation, see Mather, *The Poet Shen Yüeh*, 62–63).

5. Shen Yue's and Zhou Yong's tone registers, now lost, were respectively titled *Sisheng pu* (Four Tones Register) and *Sisheng qieyun* (Dividing Rhymes by the Four Tones?). Most scholars believe that the Chinese concept of "four tones" was influenced by, if not based on, the Sanskrit concept of "tones." See Chen Yinque, "Sisheng san wen," in idem, *Jinmingguan conggao chubian*, 328–9; Rao Zongyi, "Yindu Bo'ernixian zhi Weituo sansheng lunlüe: Sisheng wailaishuo pingyi," in idem, *Fanxueji*, 79–92; Mei Tsu-lin, "Tones and Prosody in Middle Chinese and the Origin of the Rising Tone," 86–110.

6. See Mather, *The Poet Shen Yüeh*, 57–60; Lin, *Shen Yue yanjiu*, 231–82.

7. The first rule, called "level head" (*pingtou*), for example, forbids the first two syllables in the first line of a penta-syllabic poem from sharing the same tone as those in its second line; and the second rule, "raised tail" (*shangwei*), states that the last syllable in the first line and that in the second line of a penta-syllabic poem cannot have the same tone; and so on. For a complete listing of these eight rules, see

Kūkai, *Wenjing mifu lun jiao zhu*, ann. Wang Liqi, 400–37; Bodman, "Poetics and Prosody in Early Mediaeval China," 267–320.

8. Mair and Mei, "The Sanskrit Origins of Recent Style Prosody," 380, 436–54.

9. See the entries for the first four and the seventh "defects" (Kūkai, *Wenjing mifu lun jiao zhu*, 404, 407, 412, 419, 432; Bodman, "Poetics and Prosody in Early Mediaeval China," 272, 277, 283, 295, 310, 311); Yoshida Kōichi, "*Bunkyō hifuron* ken dai'ichi 'Shiseiron' ni tsuite," 61–72.

10. *Nan Qi shu*, 52.898.

11. Zhong Rong, *Shi pin jizhu*, 340. Zhong Rong's mention of the two defects only casts more doubt on their attribution to the Yongming poets. He states, "When it comes to 'level,' 'rising,' 'departing' and 'entering,' I am crippled and cannot make use of them; as for 'wasp's waist' and 'crane's knee,' they already exist in the villages." Did he mean Shen Yue and his peers had spread "wasp's waist" and "crane's knee" to "the villages," or did he mean they were not something new from the Yongming poets, since they "already existed in the villages"? The latter reading, in my opinion, is as plausible as the former.

12. This part of Li Yanshou's statement—五字之中，音韻悉異，兩句之內，角徵不同 ("They wanted the sounds and rhymes within the five syllables . . .")—is taken almost verbatim from Shen Yue's essay on poetic prosody, included in full in *Song shu*, and will be cited later in this chapter.

13. *Nan shi*, 48.1195.

14. Liu Yuejin has raised doubt about the authenticity of Shen Yue's "eight defects" (*Menfa shizu yu Yongming wenxue*, 353–63), as has Hongming Zhang ("Shen Yue's Poetic Metrical Theory and His Poem Composition").

15. As will be discussed later in this chapter, Shen Yue referred to a younger poet who had successfully "grasped" his sound patterns as *zhiyin*; other instances in which the term is used in similar ways by the Yongming poets are mentioned in Note 39 to this chapter.

16. *Lüshi Chunqiu zhushu*, 14.1394–95.

17. On the nature of the "four tones" and the two prosodic opposites, "level" and "deflected," see Zhou Fagao, "Shuo pingze," 153–62; Mei, "Tones and Prosody in Middle Chinese," 104–10; Ting Pang-hsin, "Pingze xinkao," 1–15; Zhang Hongming, "Hanyu jintishi shenglü moshi de wuzhi jichu," 185–96.

18. *Nan Qi shu*, 52.899.

19. *Liang shu*, 13.243.

20. See, for example, Mather, *The Poet Shen Yüeh*, 38.

21. *Wenjing mifu lun jiaozhu*, 100–101.

22. Ibid.

23. The transcription for medieval Chinese used here and throughout this chapter is based on David Prager Branner, "Yīntōng: Chinese Phonological Database"; for Branner's discussion of his transcription system, see "A Neutral Transcription System for Teaching Medieval Chinese."

24. This representation of the four tones as, respectively, A, B, C, and D will be used throughout this book.

25. *Liang shu*, 25.375.

26. *Nan Qi shu*, 41.732.

27. Ibid.

28. *Wenjing mifu lun jiaozhu*, 481; see Zhang, "Hanyu Jintishi shenglü moshi," 189.

29. Using various terms to refer to the concept of tones, Shen Yue writes: "You want to have *gong* and *yu* changing in mutation, and the low and the rising alternating with one another. Whenever there are floating sounds at the beginning [of a line], then at the end there must be cutting echoes. In a single line, the sounds and rhymes should all be different, and between the two lines in a couplet, the light and heavy sounds should all contrast with one another. Only those who wittily grasp this principle can begin to talk about refined literature" (*Song shu*, 67.1779). It was common for commentators of this period to use the "five musical notes" (*wuyin*)—*gong, shang, jue, zhi, yu*—to refer to the concept of tones. On the relationship between the concepts "five musical notes" and "four tones," see Zhan Ying, "Sisheng wuyin ji qi zai Han Wei Liuchao wenxue zhi yingyong"; Guo Shaoyu, "Zailun Yongming shengbingshuo," in idem, *Zhaoyushi gudian wenxue lun ji*, 2:190–209; Xia Chengtao, "Sisheng yishuo."

30. Zuckerlandl, *Sound and Symbol*, 169–70. Shen Yue's idea of elevated sound change is very different from that represented by "end-rhyme" (*jieyun*), the most widely practiced prosodic technique in earlier times. End-rhyme was formed by *repeating* a specified rhyme in the final syllables of the lines in a poem (in most cases, only in the final syllables of the even lines). In other words, its underlying principle is that of the repetition and not the changes in sounds. See Shi Huijia, *Gaoseng zhuan*, *Taishō*, 50:414c.

31. *Shi pin jizhu*, 340.

32. This work is cited in full in Shen Yue's biography in the *Liang shu*, 13.236–42; for a complete translation and discussion, see Mather, *The Poet Shen Yüeh*, 176–214. As we will see, this *fu* is a feat in tonal patterning. Additionally, its rhyming pattern is noteworthy. Employing 36 different rhyme categories, it uses one rhyme category in no more than 20 lines at a time, sometimes changing rhyme in as few as two or four lines. Most significantly, no two consecutive rhyme categories are in the same tone. Among the 36 rhyme categories, 11 are in the level tone, 10 in the rising tone, 8 in the falling tone, and 7 in the entering tone; given the fact level-tone syllables are significantly more prevalent than those in the other three tones in medieval Chinese, the fairly even distribution of the four tones in the end-rhymes of this *fu* indicates Shen Yue's conscious effort at making use of all four different tones. The content of this *fu* will be discussed in Chapter Four.

33. *Liang shu*, 33.485.

34. Ibid., 13.240.

35. Ibid., 33.485. This line was one of two that Wang Yun specifically praised according to the account.

36. Mather, *The Poet Shen Yüeh*, 203.

37. *Liang shu*, 13.240.

38. Zhang Hongming, citing Zhang Shilu, points out that the "prolonged" quality of the level tone would become evident only through recitation ("Hanyu Jintishi shenglü moshi," 192). Ting Pang-hsin also observes that "[the level tone] was easy for drawing out the sounds and prolonging them" ("Pingze xinkao," 6).

39. *Liang shu*, 33.485. These words recall a plea that Shen Yue makes at the end of his *Song shu* essay, after proposing his prosodic idea and assailing earlier poets for failing to come to grasp with "sounds and rhymes": "Those in the world who truly know sound (*shi zhi zhiyin zhe*), having the means to obtain it, would know that my words are not mistaken. If there are some who say 'not so,' please await [the judgment of] the wise men in the future" (*Song shu*, 67.1779). They also remind us of the title of a work that Wang Rong is said to have planned to write before he died—"On Knowing Sound" ("Zhiyin lun") (*Shi pin jizhu*, 337).

40. I want to thank an anonymous reviewer of my manuscript for suggesting that I mention this point directly. For examples of how the Yongming poets applied their prosodic principles to the poetic sub-genre commonly known as *yuefu*, see my "Wang Rong's (467–493) Poetics in the Light of the Invention of Tonal Prosody," 184–239. It is also worth noting that the discussion in *Bunkyō hifuron* concerns the prosody of not only *shi*, but also other genres such as *fu*, *song*, and *bi* (see, for example, *Wenjing mifu lun jiaozhu*, 407–8).

41. I follow Stephen Owen's understanding of the *zhi* in *shi yan zhi* as "what is intently on the mind"; see his *Readings in Chinese Literary Thought*, 26–29. For the canonical statement *shi yan zhi* ("poetry expresses what is intently on the mind"), see *Shangshu zhengyi*, 3.79.

42. *Lüshi Chunqiu zhushu*, 14.1394.

43. *Mengzi zhushu*, 13.365.

44. *Song shu*, 67.1779.

45. *Liang shu*, 33.485.

46. Lu Ji, "Wen fu" (*Fu* on Literature), in *Wen xuan*, 17.766–67.

47. I borrow the phrase from Martin Kern, who uses it to discuss the difficulty of envisioning Western Han *fu* as performance texts; in his "Western Han Aesthetics and the Genesis of the *Fu*," 409.

48. Lu Qinli, *XQHWJ*, 2:1661; cf. Mather, *Eternal Brilliance*, 1:225.

49. Lu, *XQHWJ*, 2:1656; cf. Mather, *Eternal Brilliance*, 1:125.

50. *Lunyu zhushu*, 7.89.

51. Lu, *XQHWJ*, 2:1404; cf. Mather, *Eternal Brilliance*, 2:369.

52. It should be noted that these four lines could very well be a fragment that survives from a longer poem.

53. "He Wang Zhongcheng wen qin" 和王中丞聞琴 (Harmonizing with Palace Aide Wang on "Listening to a Zither"), in Lu, *XQHWJ*, 2:1447; cf. Mather, *Eternal Brilliance*, 2:156.

54. Trethewey, *Native Guard*, 14. This is a personal favorite. Once, after hearing the poet recite her poems, I came quite close to "not knowing the taste of meat."

55. *Song shu*, 67.1779.

56. *Nan Qi shu*, 52.900.

57. Ibid.

58. Commenting on the exchange between Lu Jue and Shen Yue, Mather writes: "In criticizing his predecessors so severely, Shen Yue had surely been a bit ungenerous to belittle their 'unwitting' or accidental prosodic successes, as though consciously contrived effects are somehow superior to those that are achieved spontaneously" (*The Poet Shen Yüeh*, 51).

59. "Shen bumie yi," *Taishō*, 52:253c.

60. On the background of this debate, see Mather, *The Poet Shen Yüeh*, 136, 142–45.

61. 佛教所以義奪情靈。言詭聲律。蓋謂即色非有。故擅絕於群家耳。(*Taishō*, 52:40b–c; emphasis added). I take *gui* to mean *bian* ("to transform" or "to mutate"), based on an annotation given by Li Shan for the word (*Wen xuan*, 50.2218).

62. See Tang, *Han Wei Liang Jin Nan Bei chao fojiaoshi*, 179–84.

63. *Taishō*, 50:413b–415c; see Mair and Mei, "The Sanskrit Origins of Recent Style Poetry," 382–88.

64. 巧於轉讀有無窮聲韻 (*Taishō*, 50:414a). *Zhuandu* is to chant or recite the sūtras (*Taishō*, 50:415b).

65. Mair, "Buddhism and the Rise of Written Vernacular," 719. On the Indian musical tradition, including Buddhist chanting, see Rowell, *Music and Musical Thought in Early India*.

66. *Nan Qi shu*, 41.731.

67. 即色非有, 則不外有, 亦不外無. Tang, *Han Wei Liang Jin Nan Bei chao fojiaoshi*, 540.

68. The exponents of the third Truth sought to absorb and transcend the two Truths. See Tang, *Han Wei Liang Jin Nan Bei chao fojiaoshi*, 531–42; Lai, "Further Developments of the Two Truths Theory in China," 139–61.

69. For "mute texts," see Note 47 in this chapter.

Chapter Three

1. Lin Wenyue, "The Decline and Revival of *Feng-ku* (Wind and Bone)," in Lin and Owen, eds., *The Vitality of the Lyric Voice*, 156–59. Cynthia Chennault has made a different argument: "In place of entrenched aristocrats whose concern for craftsmanship symptomized their insulated mentality, I have argued that patronage brought scholars and poets from diverse backgrounds into the salons, and that their art projected the opportunities of a fluid social order" ("Odes on Objects and Patronage," 397).

2. Chennault, "Odes on Objects and Patronage," 332, 334, 376.

3. Lu, *XQHWJ*, 2:1652, 1404, 1451, 1403, 1655, 1657, 1452–53, 1453, 1649, 1652, 1653, 1436, 1656.

4. For a more complete categorization of the things written about in the Yongming poets' *yongwu shi*, see Ami, *Chūgoku chūsei bungaku kenkyū*, 160–66.

5. *Song shu*, 85.2167, 85.2175; the *fu* on the "red parrot" and the "dancing horses" presented by the courtiers in Song Emperor Wen's court, such as those by Xie

Zhuang (421–466), can be found in Yan Kejun, *Quan Song wen*, in idem, *Quan Shanggu Sandai Qin Han Sanguo Liuchao wen*, vol. 3, 34.2625b–26b.

6. Morino Shigeo characterizes the Qi-Liang practice of writing poetry at social gatherings as a kind of literary game; see his "Ryō no bungaku no yūgishō," 27–40.

7. Chennault, "Odes on Objects and Patronage," 331–98.

8. Mather, *The Poet Shen Yüeh*, 102.

9. David R. McCraw has examined the *wutong* imagery in Chinese poetry; see his "Along the Wutong Trail: The Paulownia in Chinese Poetry."

10. *Nan Qi shu*, 40.700, 47.823; *Nan shi*, 21.577; *Zizhi tongjian*, 138.4332–3.

11. Brief biographical information on Yu Xi and Qiu Guobin is given in *Nan shi*, 59.1463.

12. *Nan shi*, 21.578.

13. *Nan Qi shu*, 47.823; *Nan shi*, 21.577.

14. *Nan Qi shu*, 47.825; *Nan shi*, 21.578. For an analysis of Wang Rong's coup d'état, see Liu, *Menfa shizu*, 36–39.

15. *Nan shi*, 21.578; *Nan Qi shu*, 40.701. According to his biography in the *Liang shu*, Shen Yue left for Dongyang in 494, following the troubles in late 493 (*Liang shu*, 13.233), but he might have left earlier, in spring of 493, according to other accounts (see Mather, *The Poet Shen Yüeh*, 88–89).

16. *Nan shi*, 6.169.

17. *Liang shu*, 1.2.

18. Lu, *XQHWJ*, 2:1657; cf. Mather, *Eternal Brilliance*, 1:132.

19. *Shiji*, 39.1635; cf. Mather, *Eternal Brilliance*, 1:132 n2.

20. Lu, *XQHWJ*, 2:1452; cf. Mather, *Eternal Brilliance*, 2:38–39. According to Kong Yingda (574–648), Jin, a later name of Tang, belonged to the *xuyu* ("zodiacal region") of *Shen*, the constellation Triaster (*Chunqiu Zuozhuan zhengyi*, 47.1343; *Xie Xuancheng ji jiao zhu*, ann. Cao Rongnan, 5.389 n4). Mather reads *Shen* as Triaster and *Xu* as "the Barrens," another constellation (*Eternal Brilliance*, 2:38–39 n5).

21. *Shiji*, 39.1635.

22. *Nan shi*, 77.1929.

23. See Kang-i Sun Chang, *Six Dynasties Poetry*, 123–24; Chennault, "Odes on Objects and Patronage," 331–32. For a discussion of the descriptive aesthetic of Xie Lingyun's landscape poetry, see Sun Chang, *Six Dynasties Poetry*, 47–73.

24. A well-known statement on *tiwu* is found in Lu Ji's "Wen fu" (*Wen xuan*, 17.766): "The poem follows from the affections and is sensuously intricate; / Poetic exposition gives the normative forms of things and is clear and bright" 詩緣情而綺靡，賦體物而瀏亮 (translation by Owen, *Readings in Chinese Literary Thought*, 130; for Owen's discussion of *tiwu*, see 131–32).

25. Duan Chengshi, *Youyang zazu*, 18.5a. Wei Jin's biography is in Li Baiyao, *Bei Qi shu*, 40.527. Other than the fact that he was originally from the Liang, not much is known about Chen Zhao; Xu Junfang is even more obscure.

26. The *Hanyu dacidian* cites this comment about the *ruanzao* ("soft dates") by Gao Shiqi (1645–1704): "Sweet in taste and soft" (*wei gan er ruan*).

27. This is how Kong Zhigui (447–501) describes the "green lychees" in his "A

Notice Expressing Gratitude for an Imperial Bestowal of Green Lychees" ("Xie ci sheng lizhi qi"): "Their green leaves like clouds spreading; / Their red fruits like stars shining" 綠葉雲舒，朱實星映 (Yan, *Quan Qi wen*, in idem, *Quan Shanggu Sandai Qin Han Sanguo Liuchao wen*, vol. 3, 19.2899b).

28. Liu Xie, *Wenxin diaolong yizheng*, 3:1747. Cf. Owen, *Readings in Chinese Literary Thought*, 282–83.

29. *Liang shu*, 33.485.

30. Lu, *XQHWJ*, 2:1649; cf. Mather, *Eternal Brilliance*, 1:111.

31. Chennault, "Odes on Objects and Patronage," 333.

32. Lu, *XQHWJ*, 2:1652; cf. Mather, *Eternal Brilliance*, 1:119.

33. Lu, *XQHWJ*, 2:1645–46; cf. Mather, *Eternal Brilliance*, 1:139.

34. Lu, *XQHWJ*, 2:1436; cf. Mather, *Eternal Brilliance*, 2:32.

35. Lu, *XQHWJ*, 2:1451; cf. Mather, *Eternal Brilliance*, 2:34.

36. Lu, *XQHWJ*, 2:1436; cf. Mather, *Eternal Brilliance*, 2:33. The "yellow beaks" refers to young birds.

37. Lu, *XQHWJ*, 1:622. As noted by Lu Qinli, this poem has also been attributed to Bao Zhao (ca. 414–466).

38. Lu, *XQHWJ*, 2:1655; cf. Mather, *Eternal Brilliance*, 1:121.

39. Lu, *XQHWJ*, 2:1404; cf. Mather, *Eternal Brilliance*, 2:450.

40. The *nüluo* is also known as *tusi* ("rabbit floss"). Like the *shuiping* (duckweed), it is often used to express the idea of being "dependent upon" (*ji*), as in the poem "An Ancient Poem on Separation" ("Gu libie") by Jiang Yan (444–505): "Rabbit floss and duckweed—they never leave those that they have come to rely on" (*Wen xuan*, 31.1453). There is a suggestion of loyalty in this idea. The idiom *tusi yanmai* ("rabbit floss and wild oats"), in use in the third century (Wei Shou, *Wei shu*, 66.1472), on the other hand, is a reference to one who has no real substance.

41. Here, Xiao Tiao borrows language from the *Laozi* (*Daode jing*, Section 10, 5): "Carry your restless soul to embrace the One—can you not deviate from this?"

42. Lu, *XQHWJ*, 2:1435; cf. Mather, *Eternal Brilliance*, 2:12–14.

43. For *skandha*, see Chapter One, Note 59.

44. See Zhang Peiheng and Luo Yuming, *Zhongguo wenxue shi*, 386.

45. Lu, *XQHWJ*, 2:1403; cf. Mather, *Eternal Brilliance*, 2:450. While the imagery in the final couplet is of two things reflecting each other, the tones of its syllables also form a "diagonal mirror image," a kind of tonal pattern often utilized by Wang Rong (see Goh, "Tonal Prosody"). In this couplet, this tonal pattern is:

A A C A D
A D C A A

46. *Nan Qi shu*, 48.841.

47. Lu, *XQHWJ*, 2:1469.

48. The two poems (or two sections of a poem) belong to a series of six poems (or a six-part poem), of which only four survive. Lu, *XQHWJ*, 2:1663; cf. Mather, *Eternal Brilliance*, 1:157; Birrell, *New Songs from a Jade Terrace*, 140–41.

49. This poem and the next are the only two that survive from a series of ten poems entitled "Shi yong" (Ten Poems [on Things]). Lu, *XQHWJ*, 2:1652–53; cf.

Mather, *Eternal Brilliance*, 1:120–21; Birrell, *New Songs from a Jade Terrace*, 141–42. There are various other translations for the "flowers" (*hua'er*) in line 4; see Mather, *Eternal Brilliance*, 1:120 n3.

50. See Wang Rong's poem, "Fenghe xianxian" (Respectfully Harmonizing with "Tender and Slender"), where the bird or bird-like pattern on some damask also "comes alive" (Lu, *XQHWJ*, 2:1406; cf. Mather, Eternal Brilliance, 2:457).

51. For a discussion of the manifestation of the Buddhist concept of illusion and illumination in Liang dynasty poetry, see Tian, *Beacon Fire*, 211–59.

52. See Note 49 in this chapter.

53. Tian, *Beacon Fire*, 222.

54. 如瓶轉不止必得住處 (*Taishō*, 32:360b).

Chapter Four

1. Compounds such as "garden grove" (*yuanlin*), "west garden" (*xiyuan*), "north garden" (*beiyuan*), and of course, "fields and gardens," are common in Tao Yuanming's poems about his farming life (Lu, *XQHWJ*, 2:989–1014). For a brief overview of early writings about the garden as a "private" space, see Xiaoshan Yang, *Metamorphosis of the Private Sphere*, 11–12.

2. Mather, *Eternal Brilliance*, 1:239.

3. For an insightful discussion of the idea of "returning to the fields and gardens" in Tao Yuanming's poems, see Xiaofei Tian, *Tao Yuanming and Manuscript Culture*, 95–131. Another Southern Dynasties exemplar of the idea of "retreating"—both in the physical and mental sense—to one's "garden" is Xie Lingyun, whose work will be mentioned in the discussion to follow.

4. *Jin shu*, 33.1006–7, 62.1679. Shi Chong writes about his garden estate in "Preface to 'A Collection of Poems from the Golden Valley Garden'" ("Jin'gu shi xu"; Yan Kejun, *Quan Jin wen*, in *Quan Shanggu Sandai Qin Han Sanguo Liuchao wen*, vol. 2, 33.1651a).

5. *Song shu*, 67.1754.

6. See Note 32 in Chapter Two. Lines 117–124 of the *fu* read: "Among those noble officers of former times, / Few wound their feelings around hills or caves. / Just like the Clustered and Resplendent Terraces of Chu and Zhao, / They often flaunted their excess in trying to surpass each other, / Building their tall gateways to the Northern Tower. / Once having slid the double bolts to enter splendid harems, / Could they ever be "engulfed in tumbleweed and artemisia"? 伊前世之貴仕／罕縈情於丘窟／譬叢華於楚趙／每驕奢以相越／築甲館於銅駝／並高門於北闕／闢重扃於華閨／豈蓬蒿所能沒 (*Liang shu*, 13.238; translation by Mather, *The Poet Shen Yüeh*, 186).

7. *Liang shu*, 13.240.

8. *Nan Qi shu*, 21.401. The same biography in the *Nan Qi shu* also includes another episode involving the prince's obsession with ostentatious construction: he turned a plan to build a "small garden" (*xiaoyuan*) in his Eastern Field (Dongtian) estate into an architectural project so grand that "spectators flocked to the capital city" just to see it (*Nan Qi shu*, 21.401).

9. Ibid., 21.402.

10. Mather, *The Poet Shen Yüeh*, 200 n100.

11. *Liang shu*, 13.240.

12. Ibid., 13.238.

13. *Daode jing*, Section 41, 26; translation by Mather, *The Poet Shen Yüeh*, 187 n58.

14. *Song shu*, 67.1754.

15. As Mark Elvin points out, Xie Lingyun's "*Fu* on Dwelling in the Mountains" is an idealized portrayal of his family estate at "the edge of the mountains along the southern shoreline of Hangzhou Bay" (*The Retreat of the Elephants*, 335). For an account of the garden estates built by the elites during the Six Dynasties, see Liu Shufen, *Liu chao de chengshi yu shehui*, 111–34; Zhu Dawei, *Wei Jin Nan Bei chao shehui shenghuo shi*, 167–74.

16. In her study of Southern Dynasties Jiankang, Shufen Liu points out that "apart from the emperor and crown prince, who lived in the imperial palace, other members of the imperial family lived in lavish residences in suburbs north of the Qinhuai River, where they were neighbors of high officials and other rich and eminent families. The life-styles of these people were extraordinary. Their palatial estates could sell for such huge sums as a million cash or more" ("Jiankang and the Commercial Empire of the Southern Dynasties: Change and Continuity in Medieval Chinese Economic History," in Pearce et al., eds. *Culture and Power in the Reconstitution of the Chinese Realm, 200–600*, 40).

17. *Liang shu*, 13.236.

18. The "Three Goodness" consist of fulfilling one's duties to one's parents, to one's ruler, and to one's elders (*Liji zhengyi*, 20.636–37).

19. *Liang shu*, 13.238.

20. For two interesting old maps that show the locations of Zhongshan (also called Jiangshan) and Jilong shan, which will be mentioned later in this chapter, in relation to Jiankang, see Steinhardt, *Chinese Imperial City Planning*, 76, 78.

21. Mather characterizes Shen Yue's life from 507 to 513, mostly spent in his suburban estate, as a "semiseclusion" (*The Poet Shen Yüeh*, 175); indeed, his biography in the *Liang shu* alludes to at least two occasions near the end of his life, when he had moved to the suburbs, in which Shen Yue still attended on Liang Wudi (*Liang shu*, 13.242–3).

22. "A Letter Written to Liu the Recluse on Behalf of the Prince of Jingling" ("Wei Jingling Wang zhi shu Liu Yinshi," in Yan, *Quan Qi wen*, 24.2925a–b). Another attribution of the letter is to Ren Fang (Yan, *Quan Liang wen*, in *Quan Shanggu Sandai Qin Han Sanguo Liuchao wen*, vol. 3, 43.3201a–b.)

23. On Jingling's Buddhist activities, see Chapter One, 16.

24. For maps of Jilong shan, see Steinhardt, *Chinese Imperial City Planning*, 76, 78.

25. 傾意賓客，天下才學皆遊集焉 (*Nan Qi shu*, 40.694). See Chapter One, 13, for discussion of the Prince of Jingling's literary coterie.

26. *Nan Qi shu*, 40.694.

27. Ibid., 40.692–701.

28. See the discussion of Wang Rong's failed coup in Chapter Three, 42. On Shen Yue's death, see *Liang shu*, 13.242–3.

29. Ibid., 13.238.

30. Sun Chang, *Six Dynasties Poetry*, 137; Yang, *Metamorphosis of the Private Sphere*, 61–63.

31. Lu, *XQHWJ*, 2:1427; cf. Mather, *Eternal Brilliance*, 2:228–29.

32. Lu, *XQHWJ*, 2:1433; cf. Mather, *Eternal Brilliance*, 2:225.

33. Lu, *XQHWJ*, 2:1435; cf. Mather, *Eternal Brilliance*, 2:223–24.

34. In a different poem in which he depicts the more severe weather in Jingzhou, Xie Tiao writes: "Grasses in the wind do not accumulate frost"; the poem will be discussed in Chapter Five.

35. Tao Yuanming, "Yu zi Yan deng shu" (A Letter to My Sons Yan and the Others), in *Song shu*, 93.2289; Yan, *Quan Jin wen*, vol. 3, 2097.

36. Lu, *XQHWJ*, 2:1442; cf. Mather, *Eternal Brilliance*, 2:250–51.

37. *Liang shu*, 13.238.

38. I follow Mather's translation (*The Poet Shen Yüeh*, 189) for the first two lines cited here.

39. *Liang shu*, 13.238.

40. The "carriages and horses" in this line refer to those of officials and aristocrats.

41. Lu, *XQHWJ*, 2:998.

42. Ibid., 2:1395; cf. Mather, *Eternal Brilliance*, 2:347–48.

43. I agree with Mather's suggestion (*Eternal Brilliance*, 2:347 n1) that the locale in the poem is the Prince of Jingling's Western Villa and that the Monastery of Residing-in-Mysticism is located in his estate. The name *diyuan* ("Villa Garden") in the title supports this point. A related observation, as pointed out by Liu Shufen, is that many Buddhist monasteries during the Southern Dynasties "were scattered among the rich suburbs that lay northeast of the city, around Mount Zhong, and between the Xuanyang Gate and the Qinhuai River" ("Jiankang and the Commercial Empire," 41).

44. Mather, *Eternal Brilliance*, 2:347 n2.

45. Ibid., 2:347 n5.

46. My reading of this couplet is different from Mather's. He rendered it as "If even one small inch of shadow [on the sun-dial] may not be detained, / Here by the Orchid steps, how can we sit around and drink?" (*Eternal Brilliance*, 2:282).

47. Mather adopted the variant *qiu* 求 for the first character in this line and translated the line as: "Both [office-] seeking and resolves [to be recluses] we are able to forget" (*Eternal Brilliance*, 2:282).

48. Lu, *XQHWJ*, 2:1456; cf. Mather, *Eternal Brilliance*, 2:282. The three poems in this series all use the *-ak* sound as end-rhymes. Even more interestingly, the three poems collectively formed the following tone pattern with the last syllables of their lines: ADAD/ADAD/CDCD.

49. No. 13 in "Gushi shijiushou" (*Wen xuan*, 29.1348). The translation is by Stephen Owen, *The Making of Early Chinese Classical Poetry*, 187; for more examples

of earlier poems adopting this kind of tone, see Owen's chapter titled "Death and Feast" (178–213).

50. *Zhuangzi jishi*, 6.128 (translation by Mather, *The Poet Shen Yüeh*, 150–51 n43): "To cast off the physical body, banish the senses, be separate from the body and depart from knowledge, to be identified with the Grand Whole—this is what is meant by 'sitting in forgetfulness'" (墮肢體, 黜聰明, 離形去知, 同於大通, 此謂坐忘); for *jianwang*, see Note 67 in Chapter One.

51. See Chapter One, 20.

52. See Note 50 in this chapter.

53. As Tang Yongtong points out, the *ji* in *jise* is *dang* 當 ("now," "this instant," "instantaneous"; *Han Wei Liang Jin Nan Bei chao fojiaoshi*, 182).

54. 即色者。明色不自色。故雖色而非色也。夫言色者。但當色即色。豈待色色而後為色哉。(Sengzhao, "Buzhen konglun," *Taishō*, 45:152a).

55. *Liang shu*, 13.239, 241.

56. Tian, *Beacon Fire*, 196.

57. *Liang shu*, 13.241–42.

58. Lu, *XQHWJ*, 2:1641; cf. Mather, *Eternal Brilliance*, 1:219–20.

59. It was apparently a common practice among rich garden owners in the Jiankang suburbs to call their gardens all kinds of exotic or famous names (see Liu, "Jiankang and the Commercial Empire," 40).

60. Lu, *XQHWJ*, 2:1444; cf. Mather, *Eternal Brilliance*, 2:261–62.

61. Liu Shufen points out that even when they were residing in the capital city, the elites of the Southern Dynasties "retained close ties to their rural roots and maintained a stake in the agricultural production of the large estates they continued to own in rural areas" ("Jiankang and the Commercial Empire," 41).

62. Lu, *XQHWJ*, 2:1641; cf. Mather, *Eternal Brilliance*, 1:237–38.

63. Lu, *XQHWJ*, 2:991.

64. Ibid.

65. See Tian, *Tao Yuanming and Manuscript Culture*, 95–131.

66. Lu, *XQHWJ*, 2:1434–35; cf. Mather, *Eternal Brilliance*, 2:276–77.

67. Lu, *XQHWJ*, 2:1434–35; cf. Mather, *Eternal Brilliance*, 2:276–77.

68. *Chuci buzhu*, 1.18a; *Chuci jiaoshi*, 31; translation by Hawkes, *Ch'u Tz'u*, 25.

69. *Chuci buzhu*, 2.16b; *Chuci jiaoshi*, 226; translation by Hwakes, *Ch'u Tz'u*, 40.

70. *Xie Xuancheng ji jiao zhu*, 258 n10; Mather, *Eternal Brilliance*, 2:277 n5.

71. *Shiji*, 84.2481–91; Hawkes, *Ch'u Tz'u*, 11–19.

Chapter Five

1. "Mid-term restoration" (*zhongxing*) refers to the establishment of the Eastern Jin by members of the Western Jin imperial family and northern émigré families in Jiankang, after they had fled Luoyang (in modern Henan), which was taken over by the Xiongnu. A less flattering term in this case would be *pianan* ("stabilization at one corner").

2. Yan Zhitui, "She wu," *Yanshi jiaxun huizhu*, 72a; cf. Teng, *Family Instructions for the Yen Clan*, 116–17.

3. *Bei Qi shu*, 45.617. Yan Zhitui was a descendent of a northern émigré family from Linyi in Langye (in modern Shandong).

4. See Note 2 in this chapter.

5. Nanjing shi wenwu baoguan weiyuanhui, "Nanjing Qijiashan Dong Jin Xie Kun mu jian bao," 34; see Crowell, "Northern Emigrés," 175–76 n12; Xu Hui et al., *Liu chao wenhua*, 591; Luo Zongzhen, *Liu chao kaogu*, 164.

6. Crowell, "Northern Emigrés," 176 n12. Crowell is reminded of Chiang Kai-shek, who is also "temporarily" buried in Taiwan in the hope of reburying his body on the mainland one day; I, too, am reminded of a more personal incident: a Chinese American student whom I taught five years ago brought the ashes of her late father back to Fuzhou, China, his hometown, even though he had been living in the United States as an immigrant for more than twenty years. Though the situations were obviously different, especially given the politics and political significance of Chiang Kai-shek, the idea and sentiment of "returning to one's native land" in all these cases are the same at the human level.

7. *Jin shu*, 49.1377.

8. Besides better opportunities for political advancement and greater respect in the elite communities (see Chapter One, 9–10), members of northern émigré families in the Eastern Jin could also enjoy lighter or even complete exemption from tax and corvée obligations (Crowell, "Northern Emigrés," 184).

9. Steinbeck, *Of Mice and Men, Cannery Row*, 124–25.

10. 過故鄉而下車，非謂其不忘故耶？(*Shuo yuan*, 10.4a–b).

11. *Song shu*, 11.205. The phrase "feet bound" describes the urgency and difficulty of traveling. "Jing and Yue," which may include Hubei, Zhejiang, and Zhedong, connotes "the south." The "Wild Geese Song" is *Mao* 181. The poem has been read as praise of the officials under King Xuan of Zhou for resettling the people who had been displaced (see Legge, *The Chinese Classics*, 4:293).

12. *Song shu*, 11.205.

13. *Jin shu*, 15.453; cf. Wang Zhongluo, *Wei Jin Nan Bei chao shi*, 348–49, 352–53 n2; see the location of the South Langye Commandery and Linyi in Tan Qixiang, *Zhongguo lishi ditu ji*, 4:27–28. For a detailed discussion of the problem caused by this kind of administrative restructuring, see Crowell, "Northern Emigrés," 174–86.

14. *Nan Qi shu*, 47.817.

15. Crowell, "Northern Emigrés," 187; see 187–208 for his discussion of "residence determination."

16. Yao Silian, *Chen shu*, 1.1.

17. Crowell makes the point that the change in the Chens' native classification "was done voluntarily" ("Northern Emigrés," 189).

18. *Nan Qi shu*, 47.825.

19. The fading of the "northern sentiment" is also reflected by the lack of enthusiasm in the Southern Qi court for Wang Rong's call for an expedition against the north (*Nan Qi shu*, 47:818–21, 828).

20. Tian, *Tao Yuanming and Manuscript Culture*, 59.

21. "Wuliu xiansheng zhuan," in *Song shu*, 93.2286.

22. Du You, *Tongdian*, 16.388.

23. See Chapter One, 11, for a discussion of Shen Yue's view on the recruitment and promotion system.

24. Du You, *Tongdian*, 16.388.

25. Ibid.

26. To be fair, Shen Yue is attempting to address a practical problem in his memorial: "I am always concerned that there are few official positions but yet too many talented people and there is nowhere to place them all" (Du You, *Tongdian*, 16.388); he probably felt he had earned his place in the capital.

27. *Nan Qi shu*, 48.841.

28. For the Eight Friends, see Chapter One, 13.

29. Based on biographical study of Xie Tiao and analysis of his poems, Ami Yūji infers that his home was situated near Jiankang, possibly in Dangtu District, Anhui (*Chūgoku chūsei bungaku kenkyū*, 496–98); Cao Rongnan concedes that Xie Tiao "was probably born in the Southern Dynasty capital Jiankang" (*Xie Xuancheng ji jiao zhu*, 1).

30. For description of Jiankang and its history, see Liu, *Liu chao de chengshi yu shehui*, 35–73; Dien, *Six Dynasties Civilization*, 37–45; Steinhardt, *Chinese Imperial City Planning*, 75–78; Steinhardt et al., *Chinese Architecture*, 66–68; Xu Hui et al., *Liu chao wenhua*, 691–99.

31. See Liu, "Jiankang and the Commercial Empire" and her *Liu chao de chengshi yu shehui*, 195–253.

32. Wang Can (177–217), "Qi ai shi" (Poems on the Seven Sorrows): "Toward the South I climbed the Baling slope; / And, looking back, I gazed toward Chang'an" (*Wen xuan*, 23.1087).

33. Pan Yue (247–300), "Heyang xian" (Heyang Prefecture): "I crane my neck to gaze at the palaces in the capital; / The southward road—one embarks on it by hewing an axe-handle" (*Wen xuan*, 26.1223); cf. Mather, *Eternal Brilliance*, 2:140–41 n2.

34. Lu, *XQHWJ*, 2:1430–31; cf. Mather, *Eternal Brilliance*, 2:140–41.

35. See Tan, *Zhongguo lishi ditu ji*, 4:27–28.

36. "Qi ai shi," in *Wen xuan*, 23.108 7–88; cf. Mather, *Eternal Brilliance*, 2:140–41 n2.

37. "Heyang xian," in *Wen xuan*, 26.1221–24; cf. Mather, *Eternal Brilliance*, 2:140–41 n2.

38. For "Shitou Cheng," see Tan, *Zhongguo lishi ditu ji*, 4:27–28.

39. Lu, *XQHWJ*, 2:1448; cf. Mather, *Eternal Brilliance*, 2:57.

40. Lu, *XQHWJ*, 2:1426–27; cf. Mather, *Eternal Brilliance*, 2:144–45.

41. Lu Ji, "Wei Gu Yanxian zeng fu er shou" (Two Poems Written on Behalf of Gu Yanxiang for His Wife), in *Wen xuan*, 24.1149.

42. See, for example, Lu Ji's "Fu Luo er shou" (Two Poems on Traveling to Luo) and "Fu Luo dao zhong zuo er shou" (Traveling to Luo: Two Poems Written on the Road), in *Wen xuan*, 26.1229–32.

43. Xie Tiao, "Jinglu ye fa" (Setting Out at Night from the Capital Road), in Lu, *XQHWJ*, 2:1430; cf. Mather, *Eternal Brilliance*, 2:126–27.

44. The title given here follows Lu, *XQHWJ*, 1:685; it is given as "Fu Luo ershou" in *Wen xuan*, 26.1230.

45. See *Nan Qi shu*, 47.825–28, and *Liang shu*, 13.232–43; for a brief overview, see Mather, *Eternal Brilliance*, 1:3–4, 2:3–6.

46. Liu, *Wenxin diaolong yizheng*, 3:1502.

47. "Zashi" (Miscellaneous Poem), in *Wen xuan*, 29.1374.

48. Lu, *XQHWJ*, 2:1429; cf. Mather, *Eternal Brilliance*, 2:217–18.

49. For the details of Xie Tiao's route, see Mather, *Eternal Brilliance*, 2:217 n1 and the accompanying map on p. 219.

50. Lu, *XQHWJ*, 2:1430; cf. Mather, *Eternal Brilliance*, 2:126–27. Xie Tiao created the following tone pattern in the final syllables of the lines in this poem: ABDBAB**CB**ABDBAB. Notice that the first six and the last six syllables exhibit the same tone pattern and are separated by "CB" (a falling tone and a rising tone) in the middle.

51. As pointed out in Chapter One, *nian* has the combined meaning of "concentrated thought" (*smṛti*) and "moment" (*kṣaṇa*); in other words, it does not only indicate a state of mind but also a concept of time.

52. *Wen xuan*, 26.1231–32.

53. *Liang shu*, 13.233.

54. For the details of Shen Yue's route, see Mather, *Eternal Brilliance*, 1:162 n1. As Mather points out, Zhufang was the old name for Dantu; see its location in Tan, *Zhongguo lishi ditu ji*, 4:27–28.

55. *Xu*, "silk-tally," "was a document of authentication written on silk and torn in two; one part being retained by the bearer, and the other presented as a credential to the authorities at his destination" (Mather, *Eternal Brilliance*, 1:162 n2).

56. The "late Crown Prince" refers to Xiao Changmao, that is, Crown Prince Wenhui; see Mather, *Eternal Brilliance*, 1:162–63 n3.

57. Imagining the image before Shen Yue's (mind-)eyes, "Handan" can indeed stand for "Jiankang and the dusty world" here (Mather, *Eternal Brilliance*, 1:163 n6).

58. Lu, *XQHWJ*, 2:1636; cf. Mather, *Eternal Brilliance*, 1:161–63.

59. See Chapter Three, 55.

60. As pointed out before, Shen Yue had been on the staff of Prince Wenhui and left for Dongyang to be Grand Warden shortly after the prince's death. By claiming that he was "following the assignment of the late Crown Prince," he could be either suggesting that he was commissioned by the prince to take up the post (Mather, *Eternal Brilliance*, 1:162–63 n3) or simply hinting that he had to leave to avoid the political troubles following the prince's death.

61. "Rosy cloud ambition" refers to the intention to become a recluse.

62. By his "decorated body," Shen Yue is referring to himself as a courtier who is used to living a materially comfortable life.

63. "Traveling to Assume My Post: Via the Roads of Zhufang," see Note 58 in this chapter.

64. Mather, *Eternal Brilliance*, 1:163 n10.

65. *Shiji*, 58.2083.

66. Looking back at his posting to Dongyang in a letter written almost two decades later, Shen Yue alludes to his intention to go into reclusion then: "At the end of the Yongming reign period, when I left the capital city to be the Grand Warden of Dongyang, I was intent on 'stopping when one has enough' (*zhi zu*)" (*Liang shu*, 13.235; for a complete translation of the letter, see Mather, *The Poet Shen Yüeh*, 132–34). For a discussion of Shen Yue's views on reclusion, see Berkowitz, *Patterns of Disengagement*, 171–84; Kamitsuka Yoshiko, "Shin Yaku no initsu shisō."

67. I follow Mather's translation for Cang zhou, a Daoist paradise, as "Glaucous Isles" (*Eternal Brilliance*, 2:217).

68. "Going to Xuancheng Commandery, Leaving Xinlin Port, Proceeding Toward Banqiao," see Note 48 in this chapter.

69. Liu Xiang, *Gu Lienü zhuan*, 2.15a–b.

70. "Setting Out at Night from the Capital Road" (Lu, *XQHWJ*, 2:1430; cf. Mather, *Eternal Brilliance*, 2:126–27).

71. *Nan Qi shu*, 47.825–26.

72. "Wang xinyue shi tongji shi" (Gazing at the New Moon: A Poem for My Fellow Expatriates; Lu, *XQHWJ*, 2:1706). He Xun was one of a number of younger courtier-poets whom Shen Yue had helped promote (see *Liang shu*, 49.693).

73. As discussed in Chapter Four, "hill and garden" is one of Xie Lingyun's four types of worthy "dwellings"; it symbolizes life in reclusion in general.

74. *Ruyue* is the second lunar month (see Mather, *Eternal Brilliance*, 2:100 n4).

75. Lu, *XQHWJ*, 2:1433; cf. Mather, *Eternal Brilliance*, 2:99–101. I use Mather's translation of the official titles in the poem's title. The four persons named in the title are Xie Tiao's fellow officials on the Prince of Sui's staff in Jiangling. See Mather's note 1 for their identity.

76. "Setting Up My Residence" (see Chapter Four, 65–66).

77. These are lines 13 and 14 of "Exilic Feelings at the End of Winter: Presented to Consulting Aide Xiao, Administrator for Cultivated Fields Yu, and Two Attendants-in-Ordinary, Liu and Jiang." See Note 75 in this chapter.

78. Lu, *XQHWJ*, 2:1428; cf. Mather, *Eternal Brilliance*, 2:102–3.

79. On the term *qiaocai* ("wood-gatherers"), Mather comments that it is "a playful designation for the frugal lifestyle of Xie and his 'exile' colleagues in Jiangling" (*Eternal Brilliance*, 2:103 n5); see his note for the source of the term.

80. "In Reply to Wang Deyuan, Grand Warden of Jin'an," see pp. 86–87 in this chapter.

81. See Tan, *Zhongguo lishi ditu ji*, 4:34–35.

82. "'Double-eared' merits" is "a metaphor for good administration" and "'three-winters' post" refers to Xie Tiao's appointment as literary tutor (Mather, *Eternal Brilliance*, 2:89 n5 and n6).

83. "Da Zhang Qixing" 答張齊興 (A Reply to Zhang, Grand Warden of Qixing), in Lu, *XQHWJ*, 2:1426; cf. Mather, *Eternal Brilliance*, 2:88–89.

84. The phrase "golden waves" refers to the moonlight. The "Ostrich Tower" and

Jianzhang Palace were both Han Emperor Wu's palace buildings. The Jade Rope refers to two of the stars forming the Great Dipper. The Tripod Gate was the south gate of Jiaru, an ancient city; Mather suggests that "it seems to represent the central southern gate of Jiankang" here (*Eternal Brilliance*, 2:129 n11). King Zhao's Mound, located northwest of Jiangling, was where King Zhao of Chu was buried.

85. Lu, *XQHWJ*, 2:1426; cf. Mather, *Eternal Brilliance*, 2:128–29.

86. For King Zhao's Mound, see Note 84 in this chapter.

87. *Jin shu*, 75.1986.

88. *Song shu*, 2.30.

89. On the family graves of the Wangs from Linyi in Langye, see Luo, *Liu chao kaogu*, 106–12, 159–63.

90. "Zhongzhi," in *Yanshi jiaxun huizhu*, 134; cf. Teng, *Family Instructions for the Yen Clan*, 211.

91. *Nan Qi shu*, 47.824, 827.

Chapter Six

1. *Xiaoxie caotang za lun shi*, in Guo Shaoyu, *Qing shihua xubian*, 1:913.

2. *Chen shu*, 1.1.

3. *Nan Qi shu*, 48.840.

4. Ibid., 21.401.

5. Lu, *XQHWJ*, 2:1405; cf. Mather, *Eternal Brilliance*, 2:467. This poem is also attributed to Xiao Yi (508–554), but I believe the attribution to Wang Rong is more plausible (see my "Tonal Prosody," 64 n17).

6. For a brief discussion of pre-Tang poems on rocks, see Yang, *Metamorphosis of the Private Sphere*, 94–98.

7. As I have discussed before ("Tonal Prosody," 64–66), the tone pattern of this poem, like its wording, is "reversible."

8. On Tang and Song literati's obsession with "fake mountains and fake rivers," see Yang, *Metamorphosis of the Private Sphere*.

9. *Sui shu*, 33.983. Only portions of this work have survived; see Yan Kejun, *Quan Song wen*, in idem, *Quan Shanggu Sandai Qin Han Sanguo Liuchao wen*, vol. 3, 33.2616a–b.

10. *Song shu*, 93.2279.

11. "Hua shanshui xu" (Preface to a Painted Landscape), in Yan Kejun, *Quan Song wen*, 20.2546a. For a complete translation of this preface, see Bush and Shih, *Early Chinese Texts on Painting*, 36–38. Xiaofei Tian has also translated and discussed the preface (see her *Tao Yuanming and Manuscript Culture*, 28–31, and "Seeing with the Mind's Eye," 91).

12. One *ren* is about 8 feet.

13. "Hua shanshui xu," in Yan Kejun, *Quan Song wen*, 20.2546a.

14. *Song shu*, 93.2279.

15. "Hua shanshui xu," in Yan Kejun, *Quan Song wen*, 20.2545–46. Cf. Tian, *Tao Yuanming and Manuscript Culture*, 30.

16. "Roaming the Villa Garden after Listening to a Lecture at the Monastery of

Residing-in-Mysticism: Writing in Seven Rhymes at the Command of the Director of Instruction," see Chapter Four, 68–69.

17. Liu Yiqing, *Shishuo xinyu jian shu*, 145. The comment cited is the version that appears in Liu Xiaobiao's annotation.

18. Sun Chang, *Six Dynasties Poetry*, 52.

19. Ibid., 64: "In sharp contrast to the temporal movement in an actual progressive journey, the visual images of landscape in Hsieh's poetry are synchronically balanced. For his is a device of parallelism where things are viewed and juxtaposed as necessary correlations"; also see pp. 52–53 and 62–73 of her book.

20. Lu, *XQHWJ*, 2:1424; cf. Mather, *Eternal Brilliance*, 2:230–32.

21. See Mather, *Eternal Brilliance*, 2:231 n1.

22. The one "bereft of limbs" is Shu, "whose chin was buried in his navel and whose shoulders hunched higher than the top of his head. [. . .] When the king called up the troops (in preparation for war), the man bereft of limbs bared his arms and wandered freely among the others (confident of not being conscripted)" (*Zhuang zi jishi*, 4.82, 83; translation by Mather, *Eternal Brilliance*, 2:231 n2).

23. Chennault, "The Poetry of Hsieh T'iao," 89.

24. For an example, see Xie Lingyun's "Shanju fu," *Song shu*, 67.1754–72.

25. These plant names have appeared in the most famous earlier *fu*, such as "Zixu fu" by Sima Xiangru, "Xijing fu" by Zhang Heng (78–139), and "Wudu fu" by Zuo Si (fl. ca. 300), all three of which are collected in the *Wen xuan* (7.351, 2.65, 5.212).

26. Shangzi is the recluse Shang Chang (fl. 54), whose name is given as Xiang Chang in Fan Ye, *Hou Han shu*, 83.2758–59; after all his children were married, he wandered into the Five Sacred Peaks and disappeared. Master Bing is Bing Manrong (fl. ca. 1), who refused a salary over six hundred bushels when he was in office and eventually left office of his own accord (*Han shu*, 72.3083).

27. *Wen xuan*, 30.1397.

28. "Chu qu jun," in *Wen xuan*, 26.1244 and Lu, *XQHWJ*, 2:1171. For Shangzi and Master Bing, see Note 26 in this chapter.

29. See Mather, *Eternal Brilliance*, 2:147 n1.

30. Lu, *XQHWJ*, 2:1468–69.

31. "You shan," see Note 20 and the discussion on pp. 104–7 in this chapter.

32. "He Liu Hui 'Ru Pipaxia wang Jipuji'" (Harmonizing with Liu Hui's "Entering the Lute Gorge, Gazing at Heaped-Rocks Rapids"), in Lu, *XQHWJ*, 2:1443; cf. Mather, *Eternal Brilliance*, 2:146–47.

33. In the first two lines of this poem, Xie Tiao writes, "In the past I waited upon the Prince; / And was there [at the Heaped-Rocks Rapids] while roaming through Jing and Han" 昔余侍君子／歷此遊荊漢 (Lu, *XQHWJ*, 2:1443).

34. I read the *gu* here as *hu* 弧.

35. Cited here are lines 3 to 10 of the poem, in Lu, *XQHWJ*, 2:1636; Mather, *Eternal Brilliance*, 1:164.

36. Mather, *Eternal Brilliance*, 1:164 n1.

37. These are lines 5 to 8 of "You Jingting shan" (Roaming on Mount Jingting), in Lu, *XQHWJ*, 2:1424–25; Mather, *Eternal Brilliance*, 2:233–34.

38. "Deng Xuanchang lou" (Ascending the Loft of Mystic Exultation), in Lu, *XQHWJ*, 2:1634; Mather, *Eternal Brilliance*, 1:171–72.

39. The Xuanchang lou, believed to have been built on Shen Yue's instructions when he was Grand Warden of Dongyang (in modern Jinhua, Zhejiang), was later renamed Bayong lou after his "Bayong shi" (Eight Songs; in Lu, *XQHWJ*, 2:1663–69; Mather, *Eternal Brilliance*, 1:173–99). The "northern mountains" in line 1 are said to be the Gold Foriate whose range is north of Dongyang city. The "river" in line 4 is the Dongyang River, which converges with the Yongkang River upstream and the Beigang downstream; the "three tributaries" in line 7 probably refer to these three rivers, all of which flow into the Gu River. See Mather, *Eternal Brilliance*, 1:171 n1–4.

40. While the view depicted in these four lines changes dramatically, the sound change in their syllables is also elevated to the utmost—each line utilizes all four tones in a different way, accentuating the sense of tonal change:

DACAB
CBDAA
AABCD
DBACA

41. "He Xu Ducao chu Xinting zhu" (Harmonizing with Xu of the Capital Ministry: Departing from Xinting Shore), in Lu, *XQHWJ*, 2:1442; Mather, *Eternal Brilliance*, 2:93.

42. "He Wang Zhuzuo Bagong shan" (Harmonizing with Editor Wang Rong: The Eight Retainers Mountain), in Lu, *XQHWJ*, 2:1440–41; cf. Mather, *Eternal Brilliance*, 2:84–85.

43. Lu, *XQHWJ*, 2:1384. Liu Huan (434–489) was a highly respected Confucian scholar of Qi; Prince Sui's poem, along with four others, including one by Xie Tiao and one by Shen Yue, were harmonized with a poem written on the same occasion by the Prince of Jingling. On Prince Sui's involvement in the literary culture of the Yongming era, see Ami, *Chūgoku chūsei bungaku kenkyū*, 35–40.

44. Lu, *XQHWJ*, 2:1425; cf. Mather, *Eternal Brilliance*, 2:271.

45. "Shang Xiang du Pipaji shi" (Crossing the Pipa Rapids on My Way Up to the Xiang River), in Lu, *XQHWJ*, 2:1470.

46. *Chen shu*, 1.1.

47. According to the *Wen xuan* annotation, the Shibi Jingshe was a study in the valley (*Wen xuan*, 22.1044), although *jingshe* could also be a Buddhist monastery; the poem is also in Lu, *XQHWJ*, 2:1165.

48. *Chuci jiao shi*, 232–35; cf. Hawkes, *Ch'u Tz'u*, 41–42.

49. Translation by Hawkes, *Ch'u Tz'u*, 42.

50. *Chuci buzhu*, 7.3a; *Chuci jiao shi*, 296: "When the Canglang's waters are clear, I can wash my capstrings in them; / when the Canglang's waters are muddy, I can wash my feet in them" 滄浪之水清兮, 可以濯吾纓, 滄浪之水濁兮, 可以濯吾足.

51. "Xin'an jiang zhi qing qianshen jian di yi jingyi youhao" (The Xin'an River Is Extremely Clear; Shallow or Deep, the Bottom Can be Seen: Writing to My

Friends and Associates in the Capital), in Lu, *XQHWJ*, 2:1635; cf. Mather, *Eternal Brilliance*, 1:166. This river "rises in western Zhejiang, flowing eastward to join the Gu River at Jiande, where the two combine it to become the Zhe, which continues in a northeasterly direction until it empties into Hangzhou Bay" (Mather, *Eternal Brilliance*, 1:166 n1).

52. "You Jingting shan," in Lu, *XQHWJ*, 2:1424–25; cf. Mather, *Eternal Brilliance*, 2:233–34.

53. *Nan Qi shu*, 3.62. In Buddhism, *āraṇyaka* is to "leave home" and live a pure Buddhist life in a Sangha.

54. "Setting Out Early from Mount Ding," in Lu, *XQHWJ*, 2:1636; cf. Mather, *Eternal Brilliance*, 1:164. "Culling the triple-blooming polypores" is an image in the "Nine Songs" of *Chuci*; and the "Nine Immortals" are "nine varieties of 'transcendent beings'" (see Mather, *Eternal Brilliance*, 1:164 n8 and n9).

55. "Jiang you Xiangshui, xun Gouxi," in Lu, *XQHWJ*, 2:1425; Mather, *Eternal Brilliance*, 2:271.

56. Mather, *Eternal Brilliance*, 2:272 n6.

57. Lu, *XQHWJ*, 2:1455–56; Mather, *Eternal Brilliance*, 2:281.

58. This poem has been dated to Xie Tiao's Xuancheng period—his so-called "happier time" (Mather, *Eternal Brilliance*, 2:281 n1).

59. *Song shu*, 93.2279. According to his biography, Zong Bing always "forgot to return" when he went into the mountains and rivers; one time his older brother had to force him to end his visit to Mount Lu. He lived in poverty and turned down several official appointments.

60. *Song shu*, 93.2279.

61. "Shibi jingshe huan hu zhong zuo," in *Wen xuan*, 22.1044; Lu, *XQHWJ*, 2:1165.

62. Lu, *XQHWJ*, 2:1383.

Epilogue

1. See pp. 29-30 and Note 41 in Chapter Two for my discussion of the concept of *zhi* in *shi yan zhi* and of how Shen Yue's poetics reflects a new interpretation of this traditional paradigm. As pointed out there, I follow Owen's understanding of *zhi*.

2. Liu Xie, *Wenxin diaolong yizheng*, 7.1276.

3. Ibid.

4. In his chapter entitled "Shenglü" (Sounds and Prosody), Liu Xie characterizes poetic prosody as "the sound that sprouts from my mind-heart," further implying that it is the externalization of an inner feeling or thought; see my "Tonal Prosody," 59–60.

5. *Quan Tang shi*, 4:125.1250e.

6. Pauline Yu saw "an implicit denial of the visual" in this Wang Wei poem, adding that, "this is not surprising, however, when the philosophical and religious underpinnings, with their emphasis on intuitive rather sensuous perception, are considered" (*The Poetry of Wang Wei*, 155).

7. "Going to Xuancheng Commandery, Leaving Xinlin Port, Proceeding toward Banqiao," see Chapter Five, 89.

8. "Traveling to Assume My Post: Via the Roads of Zhufang," see Chapter Five, 90–91.

9. In the "level versus deflected tones" prosody, the three tones called "rising," "departing," and "entering" are grouped together as the "deflected" tone and seen in contrast to the "level" tone. Instead of using the four-way contrast among the level, rising, departing, and entering tones, it uses the two-way contrast between the level and the deflected tones; in that sense, it is simpler. The earliest appearance of the terms *ping* and *ze* (or *ce*) as a pair of prosodic concepts has been traced to Yin Fan's preface to the *Heyue yingling ji* (dated 753); see Mair and Mei, "The Sanskrit Origins of Recent Style Poetry," 409.

10. That is, rising/level/entering/level/rising/level/entering/level.

11. 沈約有聲無韻, 有色無華。(Lu Shiyong, *Gushi jing*, 12a).

12. See Wang Yunxi and Gu Yisheng, eds., *Zhongguo wenxue piping tongshi*, 4:557–66.

13. This phrase is derived from Kern's phrase; see Chapter Two, Note 69.

Selected Bibliography

Abrams, M. H. *A Glossary of Literary Terms.* New York: Holt, Rinehart and Winston, 1981.

Ackerman, Diane. *A Natural History of the Senses.* New York: Vintage Books, 1991.

Allen, Joseph Roe. *In the Voice of Others: Chinese Music Bureau Poetry.* Michigan Monographs in Chinese Studies vol. 63. Ann Arbor: Center for Chinese Studies, University of Michigan, 1992.

Ami Yūji 綱祐次. "Nanchō shidaifu no seishin no inchimen—Shin Yaku ni tsuite" 南朝士大夫の精神の一面, 沈約について. *Shibun* 30 (1961): 13–23.

———. *Chūgoku chūsei bungaku kenkyū: Nan Sei Eimei jidai o chūshin to shite* 中國中世文學研究：南齊永明時代を中心として. Tokyo: Shinjusha, 1960.

Ban Gu 班固 (32–92). *Han shu* 漢書. Rpt. Beijing: Zhonghua shuju, 1995.

Baxter, William Hubbard. *A Handbook of Old Chinese Phonology.* Berlin: Mouton de Gruyter, 1992.

Bear, Peter M. "The Lyric Poetry of Yü Hsin." Ph.D. diss., Yale University, 1969.

Berkowitz, Alan J. *Patterns of Disengagement: The Practice and Portrayal of Reclusion in Early Medieval China.* Stanford, CA: Stanford University Press, 2000.

Birrell, Anne. *Games Poets Play: Readings in Medieval Chinese Poetry.* Cambridge, Eng.: McGuinness China Monographs, 2004.

———, trans. *New Songs from a Jade Terrace: An Anthology of Early Chinese Love Poetry, Translated with Annotations and an Introduction.* London: George Allen & Unwin, 1982.

Bishop, John L., ed. *Studies in Chinese Literature.* Cambridge, MA: Harvard University Press, 1965.

Bodman, Richard Wainwright. "Poetics and Prosody in Early Mediaeval China: A Study and Translation of Kūkai's *Bunkyo Hifuron.*" Ph.D. diss., Cornell University, 1978.

Branner, David Prager. "A Neutral Transcription System for Teaching Medieval Chinese." *Tang Studies* 17 (1999): 1–169.

———. "Tonal Prosody in Chinese Parallel Prose." *JAOS* 123 (2003): 93–119.

———. "Yīntōng: Chinese Phonological Database." http://americanorientalsociety.org/yintong/public/.

Bush, Susan, and Christian Murck, eds. *Theories of the Arts in China*. Princeton, NJ: Princeton University Press, 1983.

Bush, Susan, and Hsio-yen Shih, eds. *Early Chinese Texts on Painting*. Cambridge, MA: Harvard University Press, 1985.

Buswell, Robert E., ed. *Chinese Buddhist Apocrypha*. Honolulu: University of Hawai'i Press, 1990.

Cai Zhongxiang 蔡鐘翔 et al. *Zhongguo wenxue lilun shi* 中國文學理論史. Beijing: Beijing chubanshe, 1991. 5 vols.

Cai, Zong-qi, ed. *A Chinese Literary Mind: Culture, Creativity, and Rhetoric in Wenxin diaolong*. Stanford, CA: Stanford University Press, 2001.

———. *Configurations of Comparative Poetics: Three Perspectives on Western and Chinese Literary Criticism*. Honolulu: University of Hawai'i Press, 2002.

———. *The Matrix of Lyric Transformation*. Michigan Monographs in Chinese Studies vol. 75. Ann Arbor: Center for Chinese Studies, University of Michigan, 1996.

Cao Daoheng 曹道衡. *Han Wei Liu chao wen jingxuan* 漢魏六朝文精選. Nanjing: Jiangsu guji chubanshe, 1992.

———. "Lun Dong Jin Nanchao zhengquan yu shizu de guanxi ji qi dui wenxue de yingxiang" 論東晉南朝政權與士族的關係及其對文學的影響. *Wenxue yichan* 5 (2003): 29–38.

———. *Nanchao wenxue yu Beichao wenxue yanjiu* 南朝文學與北朝文學研究. Nanjing: Jiangsu guji chubanshe, 1999.

———. *Zhonggu wenxueshi lunwenji xubian* 中古文學史論文集續編. Taibei: Wenjin chubanshe, 1994.

———, and Liu Yuejin 劉躍進. *Nan Bei chao wenxue biannianshi* 南北朝文學編年史. Beijing: Renmin wenxue chubanshe, 2000.

———, and Shen Yucheng 沈玉成. *Nan Bei chao wenxueshi* 南北朝文學史. Beijing: Renmin wenxue chubanshe, 1991.

Chang, Garma Chen-chi. *The Buddhist Teaching of Totality: The Philosophy of Hwa-yen Buddhism*. University Park: Pennsylvania State University Press, 1971.

Chang Lei 常蕾. "*Chengshi lun* zhong de Erti sixiang" 成實論中的二諦思想. *Wutaishan yanjiu* 4 (2006): 3–8.

———. "*Chengshi lun* zhong mie Sanxin de lilun" 成實論中滅三心的理論. *Wutaishan yanjiu* 1 (2006): 20–25.

Chappell, David W., ed. *Buddhist and Taoist Practice in Medieval Chinese Society*. Honolulu: University of Hawai'i Press, 1987.

Chen Hong 陳洪. *Fojiao yu Zhongguo gudian wenxue* 佛教與中國古典文學. Tianjin: Tianjin renmin chubanshe, 1993.

Chen Kejian 陳克艱. "Weishi de jiegou—*Chengweishi lun* chudu" 唯識的結構—成唯識論初讀. *Shilin* 2 (2003): 1–3.

Ch'en, Kenneth K. S. *Buddhism in China: A Historical Survey*. Princeton, NJ: Princeton University Press, 1964.

Chen, Mathew Y. "The Primacy of Rhythm in Verse: A Linguistic Perspective." *Journal of Chinese Linguistics* 8 (1980): 15–41.

Chen Qingyuan 陳慶元, ann. *Shen Yue ji jiao jian* 沈約集校箋. Hangzhou: Zhejiang guji chubanshe, 1995.

Chen Shixian 陳世賢. "*Chengshi lun* 'sanxin' yu *Shedacheng lun* 'sanxing' sixiang zhi bijiao" 成實論 "三心" 與攝大乘論 "三性" 思想之比較. *Zhengguan zazhi* 28 (2004): 1–30.

Chen Shunzhi 陳順智. "Sisheng fuyi" 四聲復議. In *Wei Jin Nan Bei chao wenxue yu sixiang xueshu yantaohui lunwen ji* 魏晉南北朝文學思想學術研討會論文集. Taibei: Wenjing chubanshe, 2001. 4:289–324.

———. *Wei Jin Nan Bei chao shixue* 魏晉南北朝詩學. Changsha: Hunan renmin chubanshe, 2000.

Chen Xinxiong 陳新雄. "Shengyun yu wenqing zhi guanxi—yi Dongpo shi wei li" 聲韻與文情之關係—以東坡詩為例. *Shengyun luncong* 9 (August 2000): 117–46.

Chen Yinque 陳寅恪. *Jinmingguan conggao chubian* 金明館叢稿初編. Shanghai: Shanghai guji chubanshe, 1982.

———. *Wei Jin Nan Bei chao shi jiangyanlu* 魏晉南北朝史講演錄. Hefei: Huangshan shushe, 1999.

Chen Yunji 陳允吉. "Zhonggu qiyan shiti de fazhan yu foji fanyi" 中古七言詩體的發展與佛偈翻譯. *Zhonghua wenshi luncong* (1993): 201–25.

Cheng Tsai-fa 鄭再發. "Hanyu de judiao yu wenxue de jiezou" 漢語的句調與文學的節奏. *Shengyun luncong* 9 (2000): 147–58.

Cheng Zhangcan 程章燦. *Shizu yu Liu chao wenxue* 世族與六朝文學. Haerbin: Heilongjiang jiaoyu chubanshe, 1998.

———. *Wei Jin Nan Bei chao fu shi* 魏晉南北朝賦史. Nanjing: Jiangsu guji chubanshe, 2001.

Chennault, Cynthia L. "Odes on Objects and Patronage during the Southern Qi." In Kroll and Knechtges, eds., *Studies in Early Medieval Chinese Literature and Cultural History.* 331–98.

———. "The Poetry of Hsieh T'iao (A.D. 464–499)." Ph.D. diss., Stanford University, 1979.

Chou Chao-ming. "Hsieh T'iao and The Transformation of Five-character Poetry." Ph.D. diss., Princeton University, 1986.

Chuci buzhu 楚辭補注. Ann. Hong Xingzu 洪興祖 (1090–1155). Taibei: Taiwan Zhonghua shuju, 1972.

Chuci jiao shi 楚辭校釋. Ann. Wang Siyuan 王泗原. Beijing: Renmin jiaoyu chubanshe, 1990.

Chunqiu Zuozhuan zhengyi 春秋左傳正義. In Li Xueqin, ed., *Shisanjing zhushu.* Vol. 7.

Coblin, W. South. "The *Chiehyunn* System and the Current State of Chinese Historical Phonology." *JAOS* 123.2 (2003): 377–83.

Crowell, William G. "Northern Emigrés and the Problems of Census Registration under the Eastern Jin and the Southern Dynasties." In Dien, ed., *State and Society in Early Medieval China.* 171–209.

Dao Xuan 道宣 (596–667). *Guang Hongming ji* 廣弘明集. In *Taishō shinshū daizōkyō* (hereafter *Taishō*). 52:425a–707a.

Daode jing 道德經. *Zhuzi jicheng* ed.

De Woskin, Kenneth. *A Song for One or Two: Music and the Concept of Art in Early China*. Michigan Papers in Chinese Studies no. 42. Ann Arbor: University of Michigan, 1982.

Dien, Albert E. "Civil Service Examinations: Evidence from the Northwest." In Pearce et al., eds., *Culture and Power in the Reconstitution of the Chinese Realm, 200–600*. 99–124.

———. *Six Dynasties Civilization*. New Haven, CT: Yale University Press, 2007.

———, ed. *State and Society in Early Medieval China*. Stanford, CA: Stanford University Press, 1990.

Ding Fubao 丁福保, comp. *Qing shihua* 清詩話. Beijing: Zhonghua shuju, 1963.

Ding Fulin 丁福林. *Dong Jin Nanchao de Xie shi wenxue jituan* 東晉南朝的謝氏文學集團. Haerbin: Helongjiang jiaoyu chubanshe, 1998.

Dobson, W. A. C. H. "The Origin and Development of Prosody in Early Chinese Poetry." *T'oung Pao* LIV (1968): 231–50.

Downer, G. B., and A. C. Graham. "Tonal Patterns in Chinese Poetry." *Bulletin of the School of Oriental and African Studies, University of London* 26.1 (1963): 145–48.

Du Xiaoqin 杜曉勤. *Qi Liang shige xiang Tang shige de shanbian* 齊梁詩歌向唐詩歌的嬗變. Taibei: Shangding wenhua chubanshe, 1996.

Du You 杜佑 (734–812), comp. *Tongdian* 通典. Beijing: Zhonghua shuju, 1988. 5 vols.

Duan Chengshi 段成式 (ca. 803–863). *Youyang zazu* 酉陽雜俎. *SBCK* ed.

Elvin, Mark. *The Retreat of the Elephants: An Environmental History of China*. New Haven, CT: Yale University Press, 2004.

Fan Ye 范曄 (398–445). *Hou Han shu* 後漢書. Rpt. Beijing: Zhonghua shuju, 2001.

Fan Ziye 范子燁. *Zhonggu wenren shenghuo yanjiu* 中古文人生活研究. Ji'nan: Shandong jiaoyu chubanshe, 2001.

Fang Xuanling 房玄齡 (579–648) et al., comps. *Jin shu* 晉書. Beijing: Zhonghua shuju, 1974.

Feng Chengji 馮承基. "Lun Yongming shenglü—sisheng" 論永明聲律—四聲. *Dalu zazhi yuwen congshu* 2.4 (1965): 303–7.

———. "Zai lun Yongming shenglü—babing" 再論永明聲律—八病. *Dalu zazhi yuwen congshu* 2.4 (1966): 308–12.

Feng Weina 馮惟訥 (1512–1572), comp. *Gushi ji* 古詩紀. *Siku quanshu zhenben* ed.

Finch, Annie. *The Ghost of Meter: Culture and Prosody in American Free Verse*. Ann Arbor: University of Michigan Press, 2000.

Foguang shan wenjiao jijinhui 佛光山文教基金會 et al., eds. *Wenxue yu foxue guanxi* 文學與佛學關係. Taibei: Taiwan xuesheng shuju youxian gongsi, 1994.

Frye, Northrop, ed. *Sound and Prosody*. New York: Columbia University Press, 1967.

Fujii Mamoru 藤井守. "Ō Yū no 'Saku shusai bun' ni tsuite" 王融 の「策秀才文」について. In *Obi hakase taikyū kinen ronbunshū: Chūgoku bungaku ronshū* 小尾博士退休紀念文論集: 中國文學論集. Kyoto: Dai'ichi gakushusha, 1976.

Ge Hong 葛洪 (ca. 283–363). *Xijing zaji* 西京雜記. Beijing: Zhonghua shuju, 1985.

Ge Xiaoyin 葛曉音. "Guanyu shixing yu jiezou de yanjiu: Songpu Youjiu jiaoshou fangtan lu" 關於詩型與節奏的研究—松浦友久教授訪談錄. *Wenxue yichan* 4 (2002): 131–35.

———. *Han Tang wenxue de shanbian* 漢唐文學的嬗變. Beijing: Beijing daxue chubanshe, 1995.

———. *Shanshui tianyuan shipai yanjiu* 山水田園詩派研究. Shenyang: Liaoning daxue chubanshe, 1993.

———, ed. *Xie Lingyun yanjiu lunji* 謝靈運研究論集. Guilin: Guangxi shifan daxue chubanshe, 2001.

Gernet, Jacques. *Buddhism in Chinese Society: An Economic History (5th to 10th c.)*. Trans. Franciscus Verellen. New York: Columbia University Press, 1995.

Goh, Meow Hui. "Knowing Sound: Poetry and 'Refinement' in Early Medieval China." *CLEAR* 31 (2009): 45–69.

———. "Tonal Prosody in Three Poems by Wang Rong." *JAOS* 124.1 (2004): 59–68.

———. "Wang Rong's (467–493) Poetics in the Light of the Invention of Tonal Prosody." Ph.D. diss., University of Wisconsin-Madison, 2004.

Gregory, Peter N., ed. *Sudden and Gradual: Approaches to Enlightenment in Chinese Thought*. Honolulu: University of Hawai'i Press, 1987.

Guan Xiong 管雄. "Shenglülun de fasheng he fazhan ji qi zai Zhongguo wenxueshi shang de yingxiang" 聲律論的發生和發展及其在中國文學史上的影響. In Zhongguo gudai wenxue lilun xuehui, ed., *Gudai wenxue lilun yanjiu*. 3:18–45.

———. *Wei Jin Nan Bei chao wenxue shi lun* 魏晉南北朝文學史論. Nanjing: Nanjing daxue chubanshe, 1998.

Gui Qing 歸青. *Nanchao Gongti shi yanjiu* 南朝宮體詩研究. Shanghai: Shanghai guji chubanshe, 2006.

Guo Maoqian 郭茂倩 (1041–1099). *Yuefushi ji* 樂府詩集. Beijing: Zhonghua shuju, 1998.

Guo Shaoyu 郭紹虞, comp. *Qing shihua xubian* 清詩話續編. Shanghai: Shanghai guji chubanshe, 1983. 2 vols.

———. "Shenglüshuo xukao: Guanyu *Shenglei Yunji* de wenti" 聲律說續考—關於聲類韻集的問題. In Zhongguo gudai wenxue lilun xuehui, ed., *Gudai wenxue lilun yanjiu*. 3:1–17.

———. *Zhaoyushi gudian wenxue lunji* 照隅室古典文學論集. Shanghai: Shanghai guji chubanshe, 1983.

Guo Xiliang 郭錫良. *Hanzi guyin shouce* 漢字古音手冊. Beijing: Beijing daxue chubanshe, 1986.

Hawkes, David, trans. *Ch'u Tz'u (The Songs of the South): An Ancient Chinese Anthology*. London: Oxford University Press, 1959.

Holcombe, Charles. *In the Shadow of the Han: Literati Thought and Society at the Beginning of the Southern Dynasties*. Honolulu: University of Hawai'i Press, 1994.

Hong Shunlong 洪順隆. *You yinyi dao gongti* 由隱逸到宮體. Taibei: Wenshizhe chubanshe, 1984.

Hong Xingzu 洪興祖 (1070–1135). *Chu ci buzhu* 楚辭補註. Beijing: Zhonghua shuju, 1993.

Hu Dalei 胡大雷. *Gongti shi yanjiu* 宮體詩研究. Beijing: Shangwu yinshuguan, 2004.

———. *Zhonggu wenxue jituan* 中古文學集團. Guilin: Guangxi shifan daxue, 1996.

Hu Dehuai 胡德懷. *Qi Liang wentan yu Si Xiao yanjiu* 齊梁文壇與四蕭研究. Nanjing: Nanjing daxue chubanshe, 1997.

Huang Xianian 黃夏年. "*Chengshi lun* er ti" 成實論二題. *Shijie zongjiao yanjiu* 2 (1995): 41–47.

Hucker, Charles O. *A Dictionary of Official Titles in Imperial China*. Stanford, CA: Stanford University Press, 1985.

Huo Songlin 霍松林. "Jianlun Jintishi gelü de zheng yu bian" 簡論近體詩格律的正與變. *Wenxue yichan* (2003): 104–17.

Jiao Ran 皎然 (730–799). *Shishi* 詩式. In Chang Zhenguo 常振國 and Jiang Yun 降雲, eds., *Lidai shihua lun zuojia* 歷代詩話論作家. Changsha: Hunan renmin chubanshe, 1984.

Jing Shuhui 景蜀慧. *Wei Jin shiren yu zhengzhi* 魏晉詩人與政治. Taibei: Wenjin chubanshe, 1991.

Kamitsuka Yoshiko 神塚淑子. "Shin Yaku no initsu shisō" 沈約の隱逸思想. *Nihon Chūgoku gakkaihō* 31 (1979): 105–8.

Kao, Yu-kung, and Tsu-lin Mei. "Meaning, Metaphor, and Allusion in T'ang Poetry." *HJAS* 38.2 (1978): 281–356.

———. "Syntax, Diction, and Imagery in T'ang Poetry." *HJAS* 31 (1971): 51–136.

———. "Tu Fu's 'Autumn Meditations': An Exercise in Linguistics Criticism." *HJAS* 28 (1968): 44–80.

Karlgren, Bernhard (Gao Benhan 高本漢). *Hanwen dian* 漢文典. Eds. and trans. Pan Wuyun 潘悟雲 et al. Shanghai: Shanghai cishu chubanshe, 1997.

Kern, Martin. "Western Han Aesthetics and the Genesis of the *Fu*." *HJAS* 63.2 (2003): 383–437.

Knechtges, David R. "Culling the Weeds and Selecting Prime Blossoms: The Anthology in Early Medieval China." In Dien, ed., *Culture and Power in the Reconstitution of the Chinese Realm, 200–600.* 200–41.

———, trans. and ann. *Wen Xuan or Selections of Refined Literature*. Princeton, NJ: Princeton University Press, 1982, 1987, 1996. Vols. 1–3.

Kōzen Hiroshi 興善宏. "Cong sisheng babing dao sisheng eryuanhua" 從四聲八病到四聲二元化. *Zhonghua wenshi luncong* 47 (1991): 101–15.

———. "Enshi no keisei to Shin Yaku" 艶詩の形成と沈約. *Nihon Chūgoku gakkaihō* 24 (1971): 114–34.

Kroll, Paul W. "The Quatrains of Meng Hao-Jan." *Monumenta Serica* 31 (1974–1975): 344–74.

———, and David R. Knechtges, eds. *Studies in Early Medieval Chinese Literature and Cultural History: In Honor of Richard B. Mather and Donald Holzman*. Provo, UT: T'ang Studies Society, 2003.

Kūkai 空海 (774–835). *Wenjing mifu lun jiao zhu* 文鏡秘府論校註. Ann. Wang Liqi 王利器. Beijing: Zhongguo shehui kexue chubanshe, 1983.

Kumārajīva 鳩摩羅什 (344–413), trans. *Chengshi lun* 成實論 (*Satyasiddhiśāstra*; by Harivarman [ca. 310–390]). *Taishō*, 32:239a–373b.

Lai, Whalen. "Beyond the Debate on the 'Immortality of the Soul': Recovering an Essay by Shen Yüeh." *Oriental Culture* 19.2 (1981): 138–57.

———. "Chou Yung vs. Chang Jung (on Sunyata): The Pen-wu Mo-yu Controversy in Fifth-Century China." *Journal of the International Association of Buddhist Studies* 1.2 (1979): 23–44.

———. "Emperor Wu of Liang on the Immortal Soul, Shen Pu Mieh." *JAOS* 101.2 (1981): 167–75.

———. "Further Developments of the Two Truths Theory in China: The Ch'eng-shih Tradition and Chou Yung's San-tsung-lun." *Philosophy East and West* 30.2 (1980): 139–61.

———. "Sinitic Understanding of the Two Truths Theory in the Liang Dynasty (502–557): Ontological Gnosticism in the Thoughts of Prince Chao-ming." *Philosophy East and West* 28.3 (1978): 339–51.

———. "Yung and the Tradition of the Shih." *Religious Studies* 21 (1986): 181–203.

Laozi jiao shi 老子校釋. Col. and ann. Zhu Qianzhi 朱謙之. Beijing: Zhonghua shuju, 1963.

Legge, James, trans. *The Chinese Classics with a Translation, Critical and Exegetical Notes, Prolegomena, and Copious Indexes*. Hong Kong: Hong Kong University Press, 1960. 5 vols.

Li Baiyao 李百藥 (565–648). *Bei Qi shu* 北齊書. Beijing: Zhonghua shuju, 1972.

Li Fang 李昉 (925–996) et al., comps. *Taiping guangji* 太平廣記. Rpt. Beijing: Zhonghua shuju, 1995. 10 vols.

Li ji zhengyi 禮記正義. In Li Xueqin, ed., *Shisanjing zhu shu*. Vol. 6.

Li Sanrong 李三榮. "Yu Xin 'Xiaoyuan fu' diyiduan de yinyun jiqiao" 庾信小園賦第一段的音韻技巧. *Shengyun luncong* 3 (May 1991): 25–39.

Li Xinkui 李新魁. "Yinyunxue yu Zhongguo gudai wenhua de yanjiu" 音韻學與中國古代文化的研究. In *Li Xinkui yuyanxue lunji* 李新魁語言學論集. Beijing: Zhonghua shuju, 1994. 437–58.

Li Xueqin 李學勤, ed. *Shisanjing zhushu* 十三經注疏. Beijing: Beijing daxue chubanshe, 1999. 13 vols.

Li Yanshou 李延壽 (fl. 600), comp. *Nan shi* 南史. Rpt. Beijing: Zhonghua shuju, 1997.

Li, Wai-Yee. "Between 'Literary Mind' and 'Carving Dragons': Order and Excess in *Wenxin diaolong*." In Zong-qi Cai, ed., *A Chinese Literary Mind: Culture, Creativity, and Rhetoric in* Wenxin diaolong. 193–225.

Liang Sen 梁森. *Xie Tiao yu Li Bai guankui* 謝朓與李白管窺. Beijing: Renmin wenxue chubanshe, 1995.

Liezi jishi 列子集釋. Ann. Yang Bojun 楊伯俊. Hong Kong: Taiping shuju, 1965.

Lin Jiali 林家驪. *Shen Yue yanjiu* 沈約研究. Hangzhou: Hangzhou daxue chubanshe, 1999.

Lin, Shuen-fu, and Stephen Owen, eds. *The Vitality of the Lyric Voice: Shih Poetry from the Late Han to the T'ang*. Princeton, NJ: Princeton University Press, 1986.

Lin Wenyue 林文月. *Xie Lingyun ji qi shi* 謝靈運及其詩. Taibei: Guoli Taiwan daxue wenxueyuan, 1966.

Liu, J. Y. James. *Chinese Theories of Literature*. Chicago: University of Chicago Press, 1975.

Liu Shipei 劉師培. *Zhongguo Zhonggu wenxue shi jiangyi* 中國中古文學史講義. Shanghai: Shanghai guji chubanshe, 2000.

Liu, Shufen. "Jiankang and the Commercial Empire of the Southern Dynasties: Change and Continuity in Medieval Chinese Economic History." In Pearce et al., eds., *Culture and Power in the Reconstitution of the Chinese Realm, 200–600*. 35–52.

———— 劉淑芬. *Liu chao de chengshi yu shehui* 六朝的城市與社會. Taibei: Xuesheng shuju, 1992.

Liu Xiang 劉向 (ca. 77 B.C.E.–ca. 6 C.E.). *Gu lienü zhuan* 古烈女傳. *SBCK* ed.

Liu Xie 劉勰 (ca. 465–522). *Wenxin diaolong yizheng* 文心雕龍義証. Ann. Zhan Ying 詹鍈. Rp. Shanghai: Shanghai guji chubanshe, 1999. 3 vols.

————. *Wenxin diaolong zhushi* 文心雕龍注釋. Ann. Zhou Zhenfu 周振甫. Beijing: Renmin wenxue chubanshe, 2002.

Liu Xu 劉煦 (887–946) et al., comps. *Jiu Tang shu* 舊唐書. Beijing: Zhonghua shuju, 1975.

Liu Yiqing 劉義慶 (403–444). *Shishuo xinyu jian shu* 世說新語箋註. Ann. and comm. Xu Zhen'e 徐震堮. Beijing: Zhonghua shuju, 2001. 2 vols.

————. *Shishuo xinyu jian shu* 世說新語箋註. Ann. Liu Xiaobiao 劉孝標 (462–521). Shanghai: Shanghai guji chubanshe, 1996.

Liu Yuejin 劉躍進. *Menfa shizu yu Yongming wenxue* 門閥世族與永明文學. Beijing: Sanlian shudian, 1996.

————, and Fan Ziye 范子燁, comps. *Liuchao zuojia nianpu jiyao* 六朝作家年譜輯要. Haerbin: Heilongjiang jiaoyu chubanshe, 1999. 2 vols.

Loewe, Michael, ed. *Early Chinese Texts: A Bibliographical Guide*. Early China Special Monograph Series no. 2. Berkeley: Society for the Study of Early China and the Institute of East Asian Studies, University of California, 1993.

Lotz, John. "Elements of Versification." In Wimsatt, ed., *Versification: Major Language Types*. 1–21.

Lu Qinli 逯欽立 (1910–1973), comp. *Xian Qin Han Wei Jin Nan Bei chao shi* 先秦漢魏晉南北朝詩. Rpt. Beijing: Zhonghua shuju, 1995. 3 vols.

Lu Shiyong 陸時雍 (fl. 1633). *Gushi jing* 古詩鏡. *Siku quanshu zhenben* ed. Taibei: Taiwan Shangwu yinshuguan, 1976.

Lu Xun 魯迅 (1881–1936). *Jiwai ji shiyi* 集外集拾遺. In *Lu Xun quanji* 魯迅全集. Vol. 7. Beijing: Renming wenxue chubanshe, 1961.

———. *Wei Jin fengdu ji qita* 魏晉風度及其他. Shanghai: Shanghai guji chubanshe, 2000.

Lu Zhiwei 陸志韋. "Shilun Du Fu lüshi de gelü" 試論杜甫律詩的格律. *Wenxue pinglun* 4 (1962): 13–35.

Lunyu zhushu 論語注疏. In Li Xueqin, ed., *Shisanjing zhushu*. Vol. 10.

Luo Xinben 羅新本. "Liang Jin Nanchao de xiucai, xiaolian chaju" 兩晉南朝的秀才，孝廉察舉. *Lishi yanjiu* 3 (1987): 116–23.

Luo Yuming 駱玉明, and Zhang Zongyuan 張宗原. *Nan Bei chao wenxue* 南北朝文學. Hefei: Anhui jiaoyu chubanshe, 1998.

Luo Zongqiang 羅宗強. *Wei Jin Nan Bei chao wenxue sixiang shi* 魏晉南北朝文學思想史. Beijing: Zhonghua shuju, 1996.

Luo Zongzhen 羅宗真. *Liu chao kaogu* 六朝考古. Nanjing: Nanjing daxue chubanshe, 1996.

Lüshi Chunqiu zhu shu 呂氏春秋注疏. Ann. Wang Liqi 王利器. Chengdu: Bashu shushe, 2002. 4 vols.

Lusthaus, Dan. *Buddhist Phenomenology: A Philosophical Investigation of Yogācāra Buddhism and the Ch'eng Wei-shih lun*. London: RougtledgeCurzon, 2002.

Mair, Victor H. "Buddhism and the Rise of the Written Vernacular in East Asia: The Making of National Languages." *JAS* 53.3 (1994): 707–51.

———, ed. *The Columbia History of Chinese Literature*. New York: Columbia University Press, 2001.

———, and Tsu-lin Mei. "The Sanskrit Origins of Recent Style Prosody." *HJAS* 51.2 (1991): 375–470.

Mao Hanguang 毛漢光. *Liang Jin Nan Bei chao shizu zhengzhi zhi yanjiu* 兩晉南北朝士族政治之研究. Taibei: Zhongguo xueshu zhuzuo jiangzhu weiyuanhui, 1966. 2 vols.

Mao Jiapei 茆家培, and Li Zilong 李子龍. *Xie Tiao yu Li Bai yanjiu* 謝朓與李白研究. Beijing: Renmin wenxue chubanshe, 1995.

Mao Shi zhengyi 毛詩正義. In Li Xueqin, ed., *Shisanjing zhu shu*. Vol. 3.

Mather, Richard B., trans. and ann. *The Age of Eternal Brilliance: Three Lyric Poets of the Yung-ming Era (483–493)*. Leiden: Brill, 2003. 2 vols.

———. "The Life of the Buddha and the Buddhist Life: Wang Jung's (468–93) 'Songs of Religious Joy' (*FA-LE TZ'U*)." *JAOS* 107.1 (1987): 31–38.

———. *The Poet Shen Yueh (441–513): The Reticent Marquis*. Princeton, NJ: Princeton University Press, 1988.

———, trans. *Shih-shuo Hsin-yu: A New Account of Tales of the World*. Ann Arbor: Center for Chinese Studies, University of Michigan, 2002.

———. "Wang Jung's 'Hymns on the Devotee's Entrance into the Pure Life.'" *JAOS* 106.1 (1986): 79–98.

McCraw, David R. "Along the Wutong Trail: The Paulownia in Chinese Poetry." *CLEAR* 10.1 (1988): 81–107.

Mei Tsu-lin. "Tones and Prosody in Middle Chinese and the Origin of the Rising Tone." *HJAS* 30 (1970): 86–110.

Mengzi zhu shu 孟子注疏. In Li Xueqin, ed., *Shisanjing zhushu*. Vol. 11.

Miao, Ronald C. "Palace-Style Poetry: The Courtly Treatment of Glamour and Love." In Ronald C. Miao, ed., *Studies in Chinese Poetry and Poetics*. Vol. 1. San Francisco: Chinese Materials Center, Inc., 1978. 1–42.

Morino Shigeo 森野繁夫. "Ryō no bungaku no yūgishō" 梁の文學の遊戲性. *Chūgoku chūsei bungaku kenkyū* 6 (1967): 27–40.

Mou Yuanxiang 牟願相 (1760–1811). *Xiaoxie caotang za lun shi* 小澥草堂雜論詩. In Guo Shaoyu, ed., *Qing shihua xubian*. 1:911–24.

Nanjing shi wenwu baoguan weiyuanhui 南京市文物保管委員會. "Nanjing Qijiashan Dong Jin Xie Kun mu jian bao" 南京戚家山東晉謝鯤墓簡報. *Wenwu* 6 (1965): 34–35.

Nienhauser, William H., Jr., ed. *The Indiana Companion to Traditional Chinese Literature*. Rpt. Taibei: SMC Publishing Inc., 1986.

Norman, Jerry. *Chinese*. Cambridge, Eng.: Cambridge University Press, 1988.

Ouyang Xiu 歐陽修 (1007–1072) et al., comps. *Xin Tang shu* 新唐書. Beijing: Zhonghua shuju, 1975.

Ouyang Xun 歐陽詢 (fl. ca. 625), comp. *Yiwen leiju* 藝文類聚. Col. Wang Shaoying 汪紹楹. Beijing: Zhonghua shuju, 1965.

Owen, Stephen. *The Making of Early Chinese Classical Poetry*. Cambridge, MA: Harvard University Asia Center, 2006.

———. *Readings in Chinese Literary Thought*. Cambridge, MA: Council on East Asian Studies, Harvard University, 1992.

———. *Traditional Chinese Poetry and Poetics: Omen of the World*. Madison: University of Wisconsin Press, 1985.

Paul, Diana Y. *Philosophy of Mind in the Sixth-Century China: Paramartha's Evolution of Consciousness*. Stanford, CA: Stanford University Press, 1984.

Pearce, Scott, et al., eds. *Culture and Power in the Reconstitution of the Chinese Realm, 200–600*. Cambridge, MA: Harvard University Asia Center, 2001.

Pi Rixiu 皮日休 (ca. 834–ca. 883). *Songling ji* 松陵集. *Siku quanshu zhenben* ed.

Pulleyblank, E. G. *Middle Chinese: A Study in Historical Phonology*. Vancouver: University of British Columbia Press, 1984.

Quan Tang shi 全唐詩. Comps. Peng Dingqiu 彭定球 (1645–1719) et al. Rpt. Beijing: Zhonghua shuju, 1985. 25 vols.

Rao Zongyi 饒宗頤. *Fanxueji* 梵學集. Shanghai: Shanghai guji chubanshe, 1993.

Ren Jiyu 任繼愈 et al. *Zhongguo fojiaoshi* 中國佛教史. Rpt. Beijing: Zhongguo shehui kexue chubanshe, 1997. 3 vols.

Rowell, Lewis. *Music and Musical Thought in Early India*. Chicago: University of Chicago Press, 1992.

Schaberg, David. *A Patterned Past: Form and Thought in Early Chinese Historiography*. Cambridge, MA: Harvard University Asia Center, 2001.

Sengyou 僧祐 (435–518). *Hongming ji* 弘明集. *Taishō*, 52:1a–96b.

Sengzhao 僧肇 (384–414). "Zhao lun" 肇論. *Taishō*, 45:150a–61b.

Shangshu zhengyi 尚書正義. In Li Xueqin, ed., *Shisanjing zhu shu*. Vol. 2.

Shapiro, Karl, and Robert Beum. *A Prosody Handbook*. New York: Harper & Row, 1965.

Shen Deqian 沈德潛 (1673–1769). *Shuoshi zuiyu* 說詩晬語. *SBBY* ed.

Shen Yue 沈約 (441–513), comp. *Song shu* 宋書. Rpt. Beijing: Zhonghua shuju, 2000.

Shen Yue ji jiao jian 沈約集校箋. Col. and ann. Chen Qingyuan 陳慶元. Hangzhou: Zhejiang guji chubanshe, 1995.

Shi Fengyu 施逢雨. "Danju lühua—Yongming shenglü yundong zou xiang lühua de yige guanjian guocheng" 單句律化—永明聲律運動走向律化的一個關鍵過程. *Qinghua xuebao* 29.3 (1999): 301–20.

Shi Guanhai 石觀海. *Gongti shipai yanjiu* 宮體詩派研究. Wuhan: Wuhan daxue chubanshe, 2003.

Shi Huijiao 釋慧皎 (497–554). *Gaoseng zhuan* 高僧傳. *Taishō*, 50:322c–423a.

Shih Chang-qing. *The Two Truths in Chinese Buddhism*. Delhi: Motilal Banarsidass Publishers, 2004.

Shimizu Yoshio 清水凱夫. "Shen Yue 'babing' zhenwei kao" 沈約八病真偽考. In *Liu chao wenxue lunwenji* 六朝文學論文集. Trans. Han Guoji 韓國基. Chongqing: Chongqing chubanshe, 1989. 194–211.

———. "Shen Yue shenglü lunkao—tantao pingtou, shangwei, fengyao, hexi" 沈約聲律論考—探討平頭, 上尾, 蜂腰, 鶴膝. In *Liu chao wenxue lunwenji*. Trans. Han Guoji. 212–38.

———. "Shen Yue yunniu sibing kao—kaocha dayun, xiaoyun, bangniu, zheng-niu" 沈約韻紐四病考—考察大韻, 小韻, 傍紐, 正紐. In *Liuchao wenxue lunwenji*. Trans. Han Guoji. 239–70.

Shisanjing zhushu (see under Li Xueqin).

Shuo yuan 說苑. *SBCK* ed.

Sibu beiyao 四部備要. Taibei: Taiwan Zhonghua shuju, 1965–1966.

Sibu congkan 四部叢刊. Shanghai: Shangwu yinshuguan, 1929–1934.

Sima Guang 司馬光 (1019–1086). *Zizhi tongjian* 資治通鑑. Ann. Hu Sanxing 胡三省 (1230–1302). Beijing: Guji chubanshe, 1956.

Sima Qian 司馬遷 (ca. 145–ca. 87 B.C.E.). *Shiji* 史記. Rpt. Beijing: Zhonghua shuju, 2002.

Soothill, W. E., and L. Hodous. *A Dictionary of Chinese Buddhist Terms: With Sanskrit and English Equivalents and a Sanskrit-Pali Index*. London: K. Paul, Trench, Trubner, 1937.

Steinbeck, John. *Of Mice and Men, Cannery Row*. London: Penguin Books, 1965.

Steinhardt, Nancy Shatzman et al. *Chinese Architecture*. New Haven, CT: Yale University Press, 2002.

———. *Chinese Imperial City Planning*. Honolulu: University of Hawaiʻi Press, 1999.

Stewart, Susan. *On Longing: Narratives of the Miniature, the Gigantic, the Souvenir, the Collection*. Durham, NC: Duke University Press, 1993.

———. *Poetry and the Fate of the Senses*. Chicago: University of Chicago Press, 2002.

Strassberg, Richard E. *Inscribed Landscapes: Travel Writing from Imperial China*. Berkeley: University of California Press, 1993.

Sun Chang, Kang-i. *Six Dynasties Poetry*. Princeton, NJ: Princeton University Press, 1986.

Sun Changwu 孫昌武. *Fojiao yu Zhongguo wenxue* 佛教與中國文學. Shanghai: Shanghai renmin chubanshe, 1988.

Taishō shinshū daizōkyō (see under Takakusu Junjirō).

Takagi Masakazu 高木正一. "Liuchao lüshi zhi xingcheng (shang)" 六朝律詩之形成 (上). Trans. Zheng Qingmao. *Dalu zazhi* 13.9 (1956): 17–18.

———. "Liuchao lüshi zhi xingcheng (xia)" 六朝律詩之形成 (下). Trans. Zheng Qingmao 鄭清茂. *Dalu zazhi* 13.10 (1956): 24–32.

Takakusu Junjiro. *The Essentials of Buddhist Philosophy*. 3rd ed. Honolulu: Office Appliance Co., 1956.

Takakusu Junjirō 高楠順次郎 and Watanabe Kaikyoku 渡邊海旭, eds. *Taishō shinshū daizōkyō* 大正新修大藏經. Tokyo: Taishō Issaikyō Kankō kai, 1924–1932. 85 vols.

Tan Qixiang 譚其驤, comp. *Zhongguo lishi ditu ji* 中國歷史地圖集. Beijing: Zhongguo ditu chubanshe, 1996. 8 vols.

Tanaka, Kenneth K. *The Dawn of Chinese Pure Land Buddhist Doctrine*. Albany, NY: SUNY Press, 1990.

Tang Changru 唐長孺. *Wei Jin Nan Bei chao shi luncong* 魏晉南北朝史論叢. Shijiazhuang: Hebei jiaoyu chubanshe, 2002.

———. *Wei Jin Nan Bei chao Sui Tang shi san lun—Zhongguo fengjian shehui de xingcheng he qianqi de bianhua* 魏晉南北朝隋唐史三論—中國封建社會的行程和前期的變化. Wuhan: Wuhan daxue chubanshe, 1996.

Tang Yongtong 湯用彤. *Han Wei Liang Jin Nan Bei chao fojiaoshi* 漢魏兩晉南北朝佛教史. Beijing: Beijing daxue chubanshe, 1997.

Teng Ssu-yü. *Family Instructions for the Yen Clan (Yen-shih chia-hsün by Yen Chih-t'ui): An Annotated Translation with Introduction*. Leiden: Brill, 1968.

Tian Yuqing 田余慶. *Dong Jin menfa zhengzhi* 東晉門閥政治. Beijing: Beijing daxue chubanshe, 2000.

Tian Xiaofei. *Beacon Fire and Shooting Star: The Literary Culture of the Liang (502–557)*. Cambridge, MA: Harvard University Asia Center, 2007.

———. "Illusion and Illumination: A New Poetics of Seeing in Liang Dynasty Court Literature." *HJAS* 65.1 (2005): 7–56.

———. "Seeing with the Mind's Eye: The Eastern Jin Discourse of Visualization and Imagination." *Asia Major* 18.2 (2005): 67–102.

———. *Tao Yuanming and Manuscript Culture: The Record of a Dusty Table*. Seattle: University of Washington Press, 2005.

Ting Pang-hsin 丁邦新. "Cong shengyunxue kan wenxue" 從聲韻學看文學. *Zhongwai wenxue yuekan* 37 (1975): 128–47.

———. "Pingze xinkao" 平仄新考. *Zhongyang yanjiuyuan lishi yuyan yanjiusuo jikan* 47 (1975): 1–15.

Trethewey, Natasha. *Native Guard*. Boston: Mariner, 2007.

Tsukamoto, Zenryū. *History of Early Chinese Buddhism: From Its Introduction to the Death of Hui-Yuan*. Trans. Leon Hurvitz. Tokyo: Kodansha, 1985.

Ulving, Tor, ed. *Dictionary of Old and Middle Chinese: Bernhard Karlgren's* Grammata Serica Recensa *Alphabetically Arranged*. Goteborg: Acta Universitatis Gothoburgensis, 1997.

Wang Kaiyun 王凱運 (1833–1916), comp. *Badai shi xuan* 八代詩選. Rpt. Taibei: Guangwen shuju, 1970. 2 vols.

Wang Li 王力. *Hanyu shilü xue* 漢語詩律學. Shanghai: Shanghai jiaoyu chubanshe, 2002.

———. "Nan Bei chao shiren yong yun kao" 南北朝詩人用韻考. In *Wang Li yunyanxue lunwen ji* 王力語言學論文集. Beijing: Shangwu yinshuguan, 2000. 1–58.

Wang Lin 王琳. *Liu chao cifu shi* 六朝辭賦史. Haerbin: Helongjiang jiaoyu chubanshe, 1998.

Wang Mingsheng 王鳴盛 (1722–1798). *Shiqi shi shangque* 十七史商榷. Taibei: Dahua shuju, 1977.

Wang Yao 王瑤. *Zhonggu wenxueshi lun* 中古文學史論. Beijing: Beijing daxue chubanshe, 1998.

Wang Yunxi 王運. "Cong wenlun kan Nanchao ren xinmu zhong de wenxue zhengzong" 從文論看南朝人心目中的文學正宗. In *Dangdai xuezhe zixuan wenku: Wang Yunxi juan* 當代學者自選文庫: 王運熙卷. Hefei: Anhui jiaoyu chubanshe, 1998.

———. "Wenzhilun yu Zhongguo zhonggu wenxue piping shi" 文質論與中國中古文學批評史. *Wenxue yichan* 5 (2002): 4–10.

———, and Gu Yisheng 顧易生, eds. *Zhongguo wenxue piping tongshi—Wei Jin Nan Bei chao juan* 中國文學批評通史—魏晉南北朝卷. Shanghai: Shanghai guji chubanshe, 1996. 6 vols.

Wang Zhongluo 王仲犖. *Wei Jin Nan Bei chao shi* 魏晉南北朝史. Rpt. Shanghai: Renmin chubanshe, 1998. 2 vols.

Watson, Burton, trans. *The Complete Works of Chuang-tzu*. New York: Columbia University Press, 1968.

Wei Gengyuan 魏耕原. *Xie Tiao shi lun* 謝朓詩論. Beijing: Zhongguo shehui kexue chubanshe, 2004.

Wei Shou 魏收 (506–572). *Wei shu* 魏書. Beijing: Zhonghua shuju, 1974.

Wei Zheng 魏徵 (580–643). *Sui shu* 隋書. Beijing: Zhonghua shuju, 1973.

Wilhelm, Richard, and Cary F. Baynes, trans. *The I Ching*. Princeton, NJ: Princeton University Press, 1973.

Williams, Miller. *Patterns of Poetry: An Encyclopedia of Forms*. Baton Rouge: Louisiana State University Press, 1986.

Wimsatt, W. K., Jr. *The Verbal Icon: Studies in the Meaning of Poetry*. Lexington: University of Kentucky Press, 1954.

———. *Versification: Major Language Types*. New York: Modern Language Association, 1972.

Wu Fusheng. *The Poetics of Decadence: Chinese Poetry of the Southern Dynasties and Late Tang Periods*. Albany, NY: SUNY Press, 1998.

Wu Huaidong 吳懷東. *Du Fu yu Liu chao shige guanxi yanjiu* 杜甫與六朝詩歌關係研究. Hefei: Anhui jiaoyu chubanshe, 2002.

Wu Meisun 吳眉孫. "Sisheng shuo" 四聲說. In Wu Wenqi 吳文祺, ed., *Zhonghua wenshi luncong zengkan—Yuyan wenzi yanjiu zhuanji* 中華文史論叢增刊—語言文字研究專輯. Shanghai: Shanghai guji chubanshe, 1982. 1:41–8.

Wu Xianning 吳先寧. *Bei chao wenhua tezhi yu wenxue jincheng* 北朝文化特質與文學進程. Beijing: Dongfang chubanshe, 1997.

Wu Xiaoping 吳小平. *Zhonggu wuyanshi yanjiu* 中古五言詩研究. Nanjing: Jiangsu guji chubanshe, 1998.

Wu Yun 吳雲, ed. *Wei Jin Nan Bei chao wenxue yanjiu* 魏晉南北朝文學研究. Beijing: Beijing chubanshe, 2001.

Xia Chengtao 夏承燾. "Sisheng yishuo" 四聲議說. *Zhonghua wenshi luncong* 5 (1964): 223–30.

Xiao Tong 蕭統 (501–531), comp. *Wen xuan* 文選. Rpt. Shanghai: Shanghai guji chubanshe, 1997.

Xiao Zixian 蕭子顯 (489–537), comp. *Nan Qi shu* 南齊書. Rpt. Beijing: Zhonghua shuju, 1997.

Xie Xuancheng ji jiao zhu 謝宣城集校註. Ann. Cao Rongnan 曹融南. Shanghai: Shanghai guji chubanshe, 2001.

Xie Yunfei 謝雲飛. *Wenxue yu yinlü* 文學與音律. Taibei: Dongda tushu gongsi, 1978.

Xiong Deji 熊德基. "Liu chao haozu kao" 六朝豪族考. In *Liu chao shi kaoshi* 六朝史考實. Beijing: Zhonghua shuju, 2000. 305–23.

Xu Hui 許輝 et al. *Liu chao wenhua* 六朝文化. Nanjing: Jiangsu guji chubanshe, 2001.

Xu Ling 徐陵 (507–583), comp. *Yutai xinyong jian zhu* 玉臺新詠箋註. Ann. Wu Zhaoyi 吳兆宜 (fl. 1672), with emendations by Cheng Yan 程琰 (fl. 1774). Changchun: Jilin renmin chubanshe, 1999.

Yan Buke 閻步克. "Wei Jin de chaoban, guanpin, he weijie" 魏晉的朝班、官品和位階. *Wei Jin Nan Bei chao Sui Tang shi* 2 (2001): 2–18.

Yan Kejun 嚴可均 (1762–1843), ed. *Quan Shanggu Sandai Qin Han Sanguo Liu chao wen* 全上古三代秦漢三國六朝文. Beijing: Zhonghua shuju, 1958. 4 vols.

Yan Zhitui 顏之推 (531–591). *Yanshi jiaxun huizhu* 顏氏家訓彙注. Ann. Zhou Fagao 周法高. Taibei: Zhongyang yanjiuyuan, 1960. 4 vols.

Yang, Xiaoshan. *Metamorphosis of the Private Sphere: Gardens and Objects in Tang-Song Poetry*. Cambridge, MA: Harvard University Asia Center, 2003.

Yang Xiong 揚雄 (53 B.C.E.–18 C.E.). *Fayan* 法言. *SBCK* ed.

Yao Silian 姚思廉 (d. 637). *Chen shu* 陳書. Rpt. Beijing: Zhonghua shuju, 1997.

——— et al., comps. *Liang shu* 梁書. Rpt. Beijing: Zhonghua shuju, 1997.

Yao Zhenli 姚振黎. *Shen Yue ji qi xueshu yanjiu* 沈約及其學術研究. Taibei: Wenshizhe chubanshe, 1989.

Yoshida Kōichi 吉田辛一. "*Bunkyō hifuron* ken dai'ichi 'Shiseiron' ni tsuite" 文鏡秘府論卷第一「四聲論」について. *Shoshigaku* 17.2 (1941): 45–52, 17.3 (1941): 61–72.

Yu Naiyong 余迺永. *Xin jiao huzhu Song ben Guang yun* 新校互註宋本廣韻. Shanghai: Shanghai cishu chubanshe, 2002.

Yu, Pauline. *The Poetry of Wang Wei: New Translations and Commentary*. Bloomington: Indiana University Press, 1980.

———. *The Reading of Imagery in the Chinese Poetic Tradition*. Princeton, NJ: Princeton University Press, 1987.

Zhan Ying 詹鍈. "Sisheng wuyin ji qi zai Han Wei Liu chao wenxue zhi yingyong" 四聲五音及其在漢魏六朝文學之應用. *Zhonghua wenshi luncong* 3 (1963): 163–92.

Zhang Hongming 張洪明. "Hanyu jintishi shenglü moshi de wuzhi jichu" 漢語近體詩聲律模式的物質基礎. *Zhongguo shehui kexue* 4 (1987): 185–96.

———. "Shen Yue's Poetic Metrical Theory and His Poem Composition: A Linguistic Perspective." Unpublished.

Zhang Peiheng 章培恆, and Luo Yuming 駱玉明. *Zhongguo wenxue shi* 中國文學史. Rpt. Shanghai: Fudan daxue chubanshe, 1999.

Zhang Xuhua 張旭華. "Nanchao jiupin zhongzhengzhi de fazhan yanbian ji qi zuoyong" 南朝九品中正制的發展演變及其作用. *Zhongguoshi yanjiu* (1998): 49–60.

Zhao Erxun 趙爾巽 (1844–1927) et al., comps. *Qingshi gao* 清史稿. Hong Kong: Xianggang wenxue yanjiushe, 1960? 2 vols.

Zhong Rong 鍾嶸 (466–518). *Shi pin jizhu* 詩品集注. Ed. Cao Xu 曹旭. Rpt. Shanghai: Shanghai guji chubanshe, 1996.

Zhongguo gudai wenxue lilun xuehui 中國古代文學理論學會, ed. *Gudai wenxue lilun yanjiu* 古代文學理論研究. Shanghai: Shanghai guji chubanshe, 1981.

Zhou Fagao 周法高. "Shuo pingze" 說平仄. *Zhongyang yanjiuyuan lishi yuyan yanjiusuo jikan* 13 (1948): 153–62.

Zhou Jianjiang 周建江. *Beichao wenxueshi* 北朝文學史. Beijing: Zhongguo shehui kexue chubanshe, 1997.

Zhou Yi *zhushu ji buzheng* 周易註疏及補正. Ed. Yang Jialuo. Taibei: Shijie shuju, 1968.

Zhou Yiliang 周一良. "Lun Liang Wudi ji qi shidai" 論梁武及其時代. In *Wei Jin Nan Bei chao shi lunji* 魏晉南北史論集. Beijing: Beijing daxue chubanshe, 1997. 338–68.

Zhou Zumo 周祖謨. "Wei Jin yin yu Qi Liang yin" 魏晉音與齊梁音.
    Zhonghua wenshi luncong 23.3 (1982): 167–89.
Zhu Dawei 朱大渭 et al. *Wei Jin Nan Bei chao shehui shenghuo shi* 魏晉南北朝
    社會生活史. Beijing: Zhongguo shehui kexue chubanshe, 1998.
Zhu Qianzhi 朱謙之. *Zhongguo yinyue wenxueshi* 中國音樂文學史. Beijing:
    Beijing daxue chubanshe, 1989.
Zhuangzi jishi 莊子集釋. *Zhuzi jicheng* ed.
Zhuzi jicheng 朱子集成. Shanghai: Shanghai shudian, 1986.
Zuckerlandl, Victor. *Sound and Symbol: Music and the External World*. Trans.
    Willard R. Trask. New York: Pantheon Books, 1956.

Character List

Bagong shan　八公山
bai zai yanzhong yi　敗在眼中矣
Bao Zhao　鮑照
Bayong lou　八詠樓
Bayong shi　八詠詩
Bayou　八友
Beigang　北港
beiyuan　北園
bi　筆
bian　變
bing　病
Bing Manrong　邴曼容
Bo Ya　伯牙
Boshi　伯始
Bubing xiaowei　步兵校尉
buer shengse　不邇聲色
Bunkyō hifuron　文鏡秘府論
buxiu zhi shengshi　不朽之盛事
buzhi rouwei　不知肉味
Cao Cao　曹操
Cao Zhi　曹植
chai[xi]fa mingkong　拆[析]法明空
Chang zai ren wai shang　暢哉人外賞
Chen Baxian　陳霸先
Chen Da　陳達
Chen Zhao　陳昭
Cheng　成
chengbang　城傍
Chengshi　成實
Chengshi lun　成實論
Chenguo Yangxia ren ye　陳國陽夏人也

Chenliu   陳留
chenwang   塵網
chi yingwu   赤鸚鵡
Chu qu jun   初去郡
chujia   出家
ciyun   辭韻
congrong hu ren ye zhijian   從容乎人野之閒
cou   湊
cu   麤
Da Zhang Qixing   答張齊興
dangshi cizong   當世辭宗
Dangtu   當塗
Dantu   丹徒
dayin xisheng, daxiang wuxing   大音希聲, 大象無形
de   得
Deng Xuanchang lou   登玄暢樓
Dian lun Lun wen   典論論文
diaochong zhuanke   雕蟲篆刻
ding   定
Dongjun   東君
Dongtian   東田
Dongyang   東陽
Dongyuan   東園
dun   頓
En xing   恩倖
Erdi   二諦
fa xin   法心
fan   凡
Fan Yun   范雲
Fan Zhen   范縝
Fang Jinggao   房景高
Fayun   法雲
Fei   淝
Fenghe xianxian   奉和纖纖
Fengshan   封禪
fengyao   蜂腰
Fozhi buyi zhongshengzhi yi   佛知不異眾生知義
fu   賦
Fu Luo dao zhong zuo er shou   赴洛道中作二首
Fu Luo er shou   赴洛二首
Fu Yue   傅說
Gao Shiqi   高士奇
gao xia di ang   高下低昂
gong   宮

Gongti　宮體
Gu　谷
Gu libie　古離別
guanzhe　觀者
gudao　古道
gui　歸
gui gongzi　貴公子
guigong zisun　貴公子孫
Guoyu　國語
Guozi xue　國子學
Gushi shijiushou　古詩十九首
guxiang　故鄉
Han　漢
han ling　含靈
hanmen　寒門
hanren　寒人
Hanyu da cidian　漢語大詞典
He Liu Hui 'Ru Pipaxia wang Jipuji shi'　和劉繪 "入琵琶峽望積布磯詩"
He shi　荷詩
He Wang Zhuzuo Bagong shan　和王著作八公山
He Xu Ducao chu Xinting zhu　和徐都曹出新亭渚
He Xun　何遜
hexi　鶴膝
Heyang xian　河陽縣
Hu Guang　胡廣
Hua shanshui xu　畫山水序
huan　還
huang　荒
Huang Xian　黃憲
hui　晦
Huici　慧次
ji　寄
Ji Zang　吉藏
jiaming　假名
jiaming xin　假名心
Jiande　建德
Jiang Yan　江淹
Jiangcheng　江乘
Jiangling　江陵
Jiangshan　蔣山
Jiankang　建康
jianwang　兼忘
jianzhao　兼照
Jiaoju fu　郊居賦

jiaoyuan　郊園
jiashan jiashui　假山假水
jiazang　假髒
Jibuji　積布磯
jie shengse　戒聲色
jieyun　結韻
jijie chengzan　擊節稱贊
Jilong shan　雞籠山
jilü　羈旅
jilü zhi yuanqu　羈旅之怨曲
Jin　晉
Jingu shi xu　金谷詩序
Jingu yuan　金谷園
jing　精
Jing　荊
Jingling　竟陵
Jinglu ye fa　京路夜發
jingshi　經師
Jingting　敬亭
jingyi　京邑
jingyi renshi　京邑人士
Jingzhou　荊州
Jinhua　金華
jise　即色
Jiuge　九歌
Jiujiang　九江
jiwu　即物
ju buyi zhi di　居不疑之地
jue　覺 (one who is enlightened)
jue　角 (a musical term)
junzi xiaoren　君子小人
kong　空
kong xin　空心
Kong Yingda　孔穎達
Kong Zhigui　孔稚珪
ku　酷
Kuang Heng　匡衡
Kūkai　空海
Langye　琅邪
Langye Linyi ren ye　琅邪臨沂人也
Laozi　老子
lei　類
li　力
Li Bai　李白

li de　立德
li gong　立功
li yan　立言
lian　聯
Liang shu　梁書
Liang Wudi　梁武帝
Liang Xiaowang　梁孝王
Libu Shangshu　吏部尚書
Liji　禮記
Lingzhi jie Erdi yi bing wenda　令旨解二諦義並問答
Linyi　臨沂
Lisao　離騷
Liu Hui　劉繪
Liu Shanjing　劉善經
Liu Xie　劉勰
Liu Xizong　劉係宗
Liu Yi　劉毅
Liu Yilong　劉義隆
Liu Yu　劉彧 (Song Mingdi)
Liu Yu　劉裕 (Song Wudi)
Liu Zhen　劉瑱
Liudao xiangxu zuo fo yi　六道相續作佛義
liuyu　流寓
Lu Chui　陸倕
Lu Ji　陸機
Lu Jue　陸厥
Lu Xun　魯迅
Luo Xinben　羅新本
Luoyang　洛陽
Lüshi　律詩
Lüshi Chunqiu　呂氏春秋
mei　昧
ming　銘
Mingdi　明帝
Mou Yuanxiang　牟願相
mu　歋
Nan Langye Jun　南琅邪郡
Nan Qi shu　南齊書
nian　念
nüluo　女蘿
Pan Yue　潘岳
pianan　偏安
pin　品
pingtou　平頭

Qi   齊
Qi ai shi   七哀詩
Qi Wudi   齊武帝
qiaoyan   巧言
qiaoyan lingse   巧言令色
qiaozhi   僑置
qilu dongxi   岐路東西
qingxing   情性
qishan   奇山
Qiu Guobin   丘國賓
qiuyuan   丘園
Qixing   齊興
Qu   曲
Qu Yuan   屈原
Qushui shi xu   曲水詩序
Ren bi Shen shi   任筆沈詩
Ren Fang   任昉
rencai   人才
rongchang   冗長
ru   儒
san buxiu   三不朽
Sanlun   三論
Sengrou   僧柔
Sengzhao   僧肇
shan fenbie   善分別
Shang   商
shang   商
Shang Chang   尚長
Shang Xiang du Pipaji shi   上湘度琵琶磯詩
Shangfu   尚父
shangwei   上尾
shanju   山居
Shanju fu   山居賦
shanshui fu   山水賦
shanshui zhi mei, shi ren yingjie buxia   山水之美，使人應接不暇
Shanyin   山陰
Shao   韶
She wu   涉務
shen bumie   神不滅
Shen bumie yi   神不滅義
Shen Deqian   沈德潛
Shen Xiuwen   沈休文
Shen Yue   沈約
sheng   聖

shengbing　聲病
shengpu　聲譜
shengse　聲色
Shenmie lun　神滅論
shi　史 (historical learning)
shi　士 (the gentry)
shi　詩 (poetry)
shi yan zhi　詩言志
Shi Yi　史佚
Shi yong　十詠
shi zhi zhiyin zhe　世之知音者
Shige zhi di　詩歌之敵
Shiji　史記
Shining　始寧
Shishuo xinyu　世說新語
Shoushi zuiyu　說詩晬語
shu　庶
Shudu　叔度
shuiping　水萍
Shuyu　叔虞
si　似 (semblance)
si　思 (conscious thought)
sili　思力
Sima　司馬
Sima Qian　司馬遷
Sima Xiangru　司馬相如
sisheng　四聲
sisheng babing　四聲八病
Sisheng pu　四聲譜
Sisheng qieyun　四聲切韻
song　頌
Song Bian　宋弁
Song shu　宋書
Song Wendi　宋文帝
Song Wudi　宋武帝
Sudi　俗諦
Sui　隋
sui jia yan　遂家焉
Taifu　太傅
Taigong　太公
Taishou　太守
Tan Qian　曇遷
tan Xiaozhu zhi buwu　歎蕭主之不悟
Tang　唐

Tao Qian　陶潛
Tao Yuanming　陶淵明
taolian　陶練
tianyuan shi　田園詩
tianyuan shiren　田園詩人
ting zhi buwen ming yue xi, bo zhi bude ming yue wei
　　　聽之不聞名曰希, 博之不得名曰微
tiwu　體物
tong yu Datong　同於大通
tongji　同羈
tuduan　土斷
tusi　兔絲
tusi yanmai　兔絲燕麥
waiwu　外無
waiyou　外有
wang　忘
Wang Can　王粲
Wang Deyuan　王德元
wang gui　忘歸
Wang Jian　王儉
Wang Jingze　王敬則
Wang Mang　王莽
wang nian　忘念
Wang Rong　王融
Wang Sengda　王僧達
Wang xinyue shi tongji shi　望新月示同羈詩
Wang Yun　王筠
Wang Zan　王讚
Wang Zijing　王子敬
Wei　魏
wei gan er ruan　味甘而軟
Wei Gu Yanxian zeng fu er shou　為顧彥先贈婦二首
Wei Jin　尉瑾
Wei Jingling Wang zhi shu Liu Yinshi　為竟陵王致書劉隱士
Wei Shou　魏收
wei zai shengse gouma zhijian de wanwu　位在聲色狗馬之間的玩物
Wei Zhun　魏準
weimiao yinsheng　微妙音聲
Wen fu　文賦
wen shi　文史
Wenhui　文惠
wenti sanbian　文體三變
wenxue　文學
wenzhang jingzuo zhi daye　文章經國之大業

wo yi you zhi　臥以遊之
wu sheng wu xiu　無聲無臭
wuchang　無常
Wudu fu　吳都賦
Wuliu xiansheng zhuan　五柳先生傳
wuma　舞馬
Wuxing　吳興
Wuxing Changcheng Xiaruo li ren ye　吳興長城下若里人也
xian　賢 (the worthy one)
xian　顯 (to show oneself)
xiang　鄉
Xiang Chang　向長
xiangli　鄉里
Xiangyang ling　襄陽令
xiangyi　鄉邑
xianzhe　賢者
xiao　曉
Xiao Changmao　蕭長懋
Xiao Chen　蕭琛
Xiao Luan　蕭鸞
Xiao Yan　蕭衍
Xiao Yi　蕭繹
Xiao Ze　蕭賾
Xiao Zhaoye　蕭昭業
Xiao Ziliang　蕭子良
Xiao Zilong　蕭子隆
Xiao Zixian　蕭子顯
xiaolian　孝廉
Xiaoxie caotang za lun shi　小澥草堂雜論詩
xiaoyuan　小苑
Xidi　西邸
Xie ci sheng lizhi qi　謝賜生荔枝啓
Xie Kun　謝鯤
Xie Lingyun　謝靈運
Xie Tiao　謝朓
Xie Xuan　謝玄
Xie Zhuang　謝莊
Xijing fu　西京賦
Xin'an　新安
xinbian　新變
Xing Zicai　邢子才
xingchen　倖臣
xingqing　性情
Xingshen yi　形神義

xingsi   形似
xiu   修
Xiwang Mu   西王母
xiyan   禊宴
xiyuan   西園
Xu Junfang   徐君房
xuan   玄
Xuanchang lou   玄暢樓
Xuancheng   宣城
xuyu   虛域
Yan Yannian   顏延年
Yan Zhitui   顏之推
Yang Jian   楊堅
Yang Xiong   揚雄
yanqi   巖棲
yanzhi zhangjiao, wei zi tuze, xian shi shiren zhi zhi
       言志章教, 惟資塗澤, 先失詩人之旨
Yao Cha   姚察
ye   野
yi   義
yi gui yi jian   以貴役賤
yi nian er jian   一念而兼
yi nian wei cheng   一念未成
yi zhi yi yu   以智役愚
yin   因 (*hetu*)
yin   隱 (hiding)
ying shanshui   營山水
Yingchuan   潁川
yinsheng yu nüse   淫聲與女色
yinyan   吟研
yinyun   音韻
yiwen   藝文
Yongkang   永康
Yongming   永明
Yongming ti   永明體
Yongshou sheng   永壽省
yongwu shi   詠物詩
You Jingting shan   遊敬亭山
You mingshan zhi   遊名山志
youxian   優閑
Youyang zazu   酉陽雜俎
youyuan   遊園
yu   羽
Yu Gaozhi   庾杲之

Yu Xi　虞羲
Yu Xin　庾信
Yu zi Yan deng shu　與子儼等書
Yuan　園 (garden)
yuan　緣 (*pratyaya*)
yuanlin　園林
yuefu　樂府
Zixu fu　子虛賦
Zong Bing　宗炳
Zuo Si　左思
Zuo zhuan　左傳
zuowang　坐忘
yan　嚴
yu　愚
Yulin　鬱林
yuxiang zhu Fo　玉像諸佛
zaihu wenzhang, mihuan fanjiu, ruo wu xinbian, buneng daixiong
　　　在乎文章，彌患凡舊·若無新變，不能代雄
Zashi　雜詩
Zhang Heng　張衡
Zhang Hua　張華
Zhang Rong　張融
Zhang Shilu　張世祿
zhao　照
Zhe　浙
Zhendi　真諦
zheng　箏
Zheng Tan　鄭覃
Zhenglu jishi　征虜記室
zhi　徵 (a musical term)
zhi　志 (what is intently on the mind)
zhi　止 (*śamatha*)
zhi　知 (to know)
Zhi Dun　支遁
zhi wu cheng xing　指物呈形
zhi zu　止足
zhicu　直促
zhiyin　知音
Zhiyin lun　知音論
zhiyin zhe　知音者
Zhong Rong　鍾嶸
Zhong Ziqi　鍾子期
Zhonghui　仲虺
Zhongshan　鍾山

Zhongwen da cidian　中文大辭典
zhongxing　中興
Zhongzhi　終制
Zhou　周
Zhou Han zhi dao　周漢之道
Zhou She　周捨
Zhou Yong　周顒
Zhu yuan　竹園
Zhufang　朱方

Index

"About to Set Out from the Shitou Fortress, I Ascend the Beacon-Fire Loft" ("Jiang fa Shitou shang Fenghuolou") (Xie Tiao), 86

"About to Travel to Xiang River, I First Seek Out Fish-hook Creek" ("Jiang you Xiangshui, xun Gouxi") (Xie Tiao), 114–15, 117–18

Ami Yūji, 129n3, 147n29

"Ancient Poem on Separation, An" ("Gu libie") (Jiang Yan), 141n40

appraisals (*song*), 40

"Ascending the Loft of Mystic Exultation" ("Deng Xuanchang lou") (Shen Yue), 112–13, 152n38

āyatana, 18, 134n58

babing ("eight defects"), 22–24, 120, 135n7

Bao Zhao, 2

Bayou (Eight Friends), 13–14, 84

bing ("[poetic] defect"), 22

Bing Manrong, 107, 116, 151n26

Bo Ya, 24, 29–30

Buddhism: Chan, 123; Chengshi school, 18–19, 69, 121; Fan Zhen's anti-Buddhism, 133n50; garden (*yuan*) in struggle for Enlightenment, 6; garden poetry and, 68–72; influence in Southern Dynasties courts, 5, 16–20, 37, 38, 121; on refinement (*jing*), 20, 36; saint and ordinary person distinguished in, 17, 133n52; Sanskrit origins of Chinese tonal prosody, 21–22; on spirit not becoming extinct, 36; *śūnyatā*, 20, 71; Western Paradise of Amitābha Buddha, 69,

73; "worthy one" (*xianzhe*) concept, 17–18, 121; in Xie Tiao's "A Lecture and Exposition on an Autumn Night," 52

"Building Fences along the Rapids in the Tree Garden South of the Field" ("Tiannan shuyuan jiliu zhiyuan") (Xie Lingyun), 107

Bunkyōhifuron (Kūkai), 22

Cannery Row (Steinbeck), 81

Cao Cao (Emperor Wu of Wei), 11

Cao Pi, 3–4

Cao Zhi, 36

Chan Buddhism, 123

Chen Baxian (Emperor Wu of Chen), 83, 101, 115

Chen Da, 101, 115

Chen shu, 83

Chen Zhao, 46, 140n25

Cheng of Zhou, King, 44

Chengshi lun (*Satyasiddhiśāstra*) (Harivarman), 18–19, 56, 134n57, 134n58

Chengshi school of Buddhism, 18–19, 69, 121

Chennault, Cynthia L., 5, 42, 106, 139n1

Chiang Kai-shek, 146n6

Chuci, 78, 115

"Climbing Three-Peaks Mountain at Dusk, Gazing Back toward Capital City" ("Wan deng Sanshan huan wang Jingyi") (Xie Tiao), 85–86

Confucianism: and individual talent, 10, 121; on the "soundless and odorless" (*wu sheng wu xiu*), 2; worldview underlies early medieval Chinese poetry, 20

Confucius: captivation by *Shao* music, 34; on "glib speech and pleasing appearance," 21; on *shengse* ("sound and sight"), 2. *See also* Confucianism
court literati (*gongting wenren*), 120
court poets (*gongting shiren*), 120
"Courtyard Rain: Responding to an Imperial Command" ("Tingyu ying zhao") (Shen Yue), 47–48
crane's knee (*hexi*), 23, 136n11
Crowell, William G., 81, 146n6
Crown Prince Wenhui, *see* Wenhui, Crown Prince (Xiao Changmao)
cu ("crudity"), 35–36

deflected (*ze*) tones, 123, 154n9
departing (*qu*), 23, 24, 29, 136n11, 154n9
Dien, Albert E., 131n28
"Dongjun" (*Chuci*), 115
Double Forgetting (*jianwang*), 20, 71
dvādaśāṅgika-pratītya-samutpāda, 18, 134n58

eight defects, see *babing* ("eight defects")
Eight Friends, see *Bayou* (Eight Friends)
Elvin, Mark, 143n15
end-rhyme (*jieyun*), 137n30
entering (*ru*), 23, 24, 29, 136n11, 154n9
"Entering the Lute Gorge, Gazing at Heaped-Rocks Rapids" ("Ru Pipaxia wang Jibuji shi") (Liu Hui), 108–10, 118
Erdi (Two Truths), 38
examination system, 12, 131n28
"Exilic Feelings at the End of Winter" ("Dong xu jihuai") (Xie Tiao), 94–95, 144n34

fa xin ("dharma mind"), 19, 134n64
Fan Ning, 98
Fan Yun, 13, 43
Fan Zhen, 133n50
Fang Jinggao, 15
fengyao ("wasp's waist"), 23, 136n11
four tones, see *sisheng* ("four tones")
fu, 4, 21, 33, 40, 41, 58
"*Fu* on Dwelling in the Mountains" ("Shanju fu") (Xie Lingyun), 58, 143n15
"*Fu* on Living in the Suburbs" ("Jiaoju fu")

(Shen Yue), 27–29, 58–59, 61, 63–64, 67, 73–74, 137n32, 142n6
Fu Yue, 10, 130n17

Gaoseng zhuan (Huijiao), 37
garden, see *yuan* ("garden")
"Gathering at Night with Fellow Expatriates" ("Tongji yeji") (Xie Tiao), 95–96
"Gazing at Ease from My Lofty Study in the Xuancheng Commandery: In Reply to Legal Counsel Lü" ("Junnei gaozhai xianwang da Lü Facao") (Xie Tiao), 65
"Going Down to the Capital on a Temporary Assignment" ("Zan shi xia du") (Xie Tiao), 96–97
"Going to Xuancheng Commandery, Leaving Xinlin Port, Proceeding toward Banqiao" ("Zhi Xuancheng jun chu Xinlin pu xiang Banqiao") (Xie Tiao), 89, 92–93, 123
Golden Valley Garden (Jin'gu yuan), 58, 142n4
Gongti, see Palace style (*Gongti*)
gongting shiren, see court poets (*gongting shiren*)
gongting wenren, see court literati (*gongting wenren*)
Gu Yanxian, 87
guxiang ("hometown"), 6, 81–83, 98–99

Harivarman, 18–19, 134n57
"Harmonizing with Editor Wang Rong: The Eight Retainers Mountain" ("He Wang Zhuzuo Bagong shan") (Xie Tiao), 113
"Harmonizing with Libationer Shen's 'Strolling Through the Garden'" ("He Shen Jijiu 'Xing yuan'") (Xie Tiao), 75–76
"Harmonizing with Liu Hui's 'Entering the Lute Gorge, Gazing at Heaped-Rocks Rapids'" ("He Liu Hui 'Ru Pipaxia wang Jipuji'") (Xie Tiao), 109–10
"He shi" ("Poem on the Lotus") (Zhang Hua), 49–50, 51
He Xun, 94
Hexi, see crane's knee (*hexi*)
Hometown, see *guxiang* ("hometown")

Hu Guang, 10, 130n18
Huan Tan, 122
Huang Xian, 10, 131n18
Huici, 134n57
Huijiao, 37

illusion, seeing as, 51–56
"In Reply to Wang Deyuan, Grand
    Warden of Jin'an" ("Chou Wang Jin'an
    Deyuan") (Xie Tiao), 86–87
"In the Middle Garden of Merit Officer Ji"
    ("Ji Gongcao zhong yuan") (Xie Tiao),
    70–72, 144n48
individual talent (*rencai*), 9–16; dynamic
    between worthy one and, 20; literary
    distinction for measuring, 12–14;
    measuring, 11–12; Shen Yue on, 10–11,
    121; of Yongming poets, 12–13
inscriptions (*ming*), 40

Ji Zang, 19
Jia Yi, 122
jiaming xin ("mind of provisional reality"),
    19, 134n64
Jiang Yan, 12, 141n40
Jiankang, 84–88; as capital of Southern Dy-
    nasties, 4; contradictory attitudes toward,
    121; expatriates from, 94–96; as lost, re-
    gained, then wiped out, 99; returning to,
    96–99; Shen Yue on elite men gathering
    in, 83–84; traveling from, 88–93
Jianwang, *see* Double Forgetting
    (*jianwang*)
Jieyun, *see* end-rhyme (*jieyun*)
jilü ("temporarily residing in a foreign
    place"), 80, 81, 82, 83, 99
Jin shu, 81
jing ("refinement"), 20, 35–39, 123–24
Jingling, Prince of, *see* Prince of Jingling
    (Xiao Ziliang)
Jin'gu yuan (Golden Valley Garden), 58,
    142n4

karma, 17, 69
Knechtges, David R., 131n27
knowing sound, see *zhiyin* ("knowing
    sound")
kong xin ("mind of emptiness"), 19, 134n64

Kong Zhigui, 101, 140n27
Kuang Heng, 1
Kūkai, 22

Lai, Whalen, 133n52
landscape painting, 102–3, 111, 118
landscape poetry, 6, 100–119; approaching
    as specific experience, 108–10; balanced
    approach to, 104–7, 118; to bring back
    the mountains and rivers, 101–4; exiting
    the landscape, 115–19; moving in, 110–11
Laozi, 82
Laozi, 60, 61, 141n41
"Lecture and Exposition on an Autumn
    Night, A" ("Qiuye jiangjie") (Xie Tiao),
    52
level (*ping*), 23, 24, 29, 123, 136n11, 154n9
Li Bai, 8
Li Yanshou, 23, 136n12
Liang shu, 8, 16, 129n3
Liang Wudi (Xiao Yan): asks what "four
    tones" are, 25; aspires to be Buddhist
    king, 17, 133n50; in Eight Friends
    (*Bayou*), 13, 14; recruitment system
    under, 11, 131n24; Shen Yue dies after
    audience with, 63; Shen Yue drafts edict
    legitimizing, 14; and Wang Rong's plot,
    43; on Wenhui's extravagance, 59
Liang Xiaowang, 92
liangwang ("double forgetting"), 71
Liji, 2
Lin Jiali, 130n12
"Listening to Gibbons' Cries at Stone Dike
    Rapids" ("Shitanglai ting yuan") (Shen
    Yue), 31–32
literary distinction: gains importance,
    9; talent measured by, 12–14;
    transcendental value of, 14–15;
    Yongming poets attain as youths, 9,
    12–13
literature: denunciation of pure artistry
    in, 21, 36; literary history as constructed
    in Southern Dynasties, 15–16; poetry as
    deeply woven into court culture, 120;
    shi yan zhi ("poetry expresses what is
    intently in the mind" paradigm), 122.
    See also literary distinction
Liu Huan, 113–14, 152n43

Liu Hui, 53, 54, 108–10, 114, 118
Liu Shanjing, 25
Liu Shufen, 145n61
Liu Xie, 46, 88–89, 122, 153n4
Liu Xin, 122
Liu Xizong, 45
Liu Yi, 11, 131n20
Liu Yilong (Song Wendi), 131n27
Liu Yu (Song Wudi), 10, 98, 130n13, 132n39
Liu Yuejin, 136n14
Liu Zhen, 114
lively spirit (*shen*), 123
"lively spirit and reverberating resonance"
    (*shenyun*), 123
Lu Chui, 13
Lu Ji, 30, 36, 87, 88, 90, 140n24, 147n42
Lu Jue, 21, 35, 36
Lu Shiyong, 123
Lu Xun, 4
Lu Yun, 122
Luo Xinben, 12
Lüshi ("Regulated poetry"), 9
Lüshi Chunqiu, 24, 29–30

Mair, Victor H., 21–22
"Making a Palindromic Poem in the Back
    Garden" ("Huoyuan zuo huiwenshi")
    (Wang Rong), 102
Mather, Richard B., 7, 28, 69, 117, 139n58,
    143n21, 144n43, 149n79
Mei Cheng, 122
Mei Tsu-lin, 21–22
Ming, Emperor (Xiao Luan), 42, 43
ming, see inscriptions (*ming*)
Mou Yuanxiang, 100
"Moving My Mat to the Zither Room:
    Writing at the Instruction of the
    Director of Instruction" ("Yi xi qinshi
    ying Situ jiao") (Wang Rong), 34–35
Mundane Truth (*Sudi*), 38, 72
"Myth" (Tretheway), 35

Nan Qi shu, 16, 59, 82, 83, 101, 132n44,
    142n8
Nan shi, 43
"nature and feeling" (*xingqing*), 2
nian ("thought-instant"), 19–20, 36–37, 90,
    121, 148n51

"Nine Ranks System," 11, 131n20
Northern Dynasties, 4, 14–15
"novelty and transformation" (*xinbian*),
    15–16

"On Azure Moss" ("Yong qingtai") (Shen
    Yue), 48
"On Bamboos" ("Yong zhu") (Xie Tiao), 49
"On Embroidery along the Collar"
    ("Lingbian xiu") (Shen Yue), 54–55
"On New Lotuses: By Imperial
    Command" ("Yong xinhe yingzhao shi")
    (Shen Yue), 50–51
"On Return Route, Overlooking the Isle"
    ("Huantu lin zhu") (Xie Tiao), 118
"On the Dodder" ("Yong nüluo") (Wang
    Rong), 51
"On the Non-Extinction of the Spirit"
    ("Shen bumie yi") (Shen Yue), 71
"On the Pear Tree's Flowers above the
    Pond" ("Yong chishang lihua") (Wang
    Rong), 52–53
"On the Rambler Rose" ("Yong
    Qiangwei") (Xie Tiao), 48–49
"On the Snow: By Imperial Command"
    ("Yong xue yingling") (Shen Yue), 48
"On the Twelve-Stringed Zither" ("Yong
    zheng shi") (Shen Yue), 33–34
"On the Wind" ("Yong feng") (Xie Tiao),
    48
"On the Wutong" ("Yong wutong") (Shen
    Yue), 42, 44, 45

Palace style (*Gongti*): Buddhist concepts
    in, 20; as pleasure poems, 8; Shen
    Yue's "The Sandals beneath Her Feet"
    categorized with, 55, 91; Yongming style
    compared with, 8–9
"Passing the Tomb of Liu Huan" ("Jing
    Liu Huan muxia") (Prince Sui), 113–14,
    152n43
personal worth: new hybrid concept of, 5,
    9, 16, 20, 121. *See also* individual talent
ping, see level (*ping*)
"Poem Composed while Returning to the
    Lake from the Stone Wall Study, A"
    ("Shibi jingshe huan hu zhong zuo")
    (Xie Lingyun), 115, 119

"Poem Written in the Eastern Palace, A" ("Donggong zuo shi") (Lu Ji), 88
poems on things, see *yongwu shi* ("poems on things")
poetic defect, see *bing* ("[poetic] defect")
"poetry expresses what is intently in the mind" (*shi yan zhi*) paradigm, 122
"Preface to Poems on the Qu River" (Wang Rong), 15, 132n41
"Preface to 'Strolling in My Estate'" ("Xing zhai shi xu") (Prince of Jingling), 119
Prince of Jingling (Xiao Ziliang): Buddhist activities of, 16, 62, 133n50; death of, 14, 43, 62–63; Eight Friends (*Bayou*) of, 13, 84; "Preface to 'Strolling in My Estate,'" 119; Wang Rong attempts to enthrone, 42, 43, 63; Western Villa of, 13, 60–61, 62, 84, 144n43; Zhou Yong at literary gatherings of, 25
Prince Sui (Xiao Zilong): death of, 14; "Passing the Tomb of Liu Huan," 113–14, 152n43; Xie Tiao serves, 13, 43, 94; Xie Tiao's farewell letter to, 93
Prince Yulin (Xiao Zhaoye), 42, 43
"Professing Sickness, I Return to My Garden" ("Yi bing huan yuan") (Xie Tiao), 77–78

Qi Wudi (Xiao Ze), 5, 13, 15, 26, 42–43, 45, 117
Qiu Guobin, 43
qu, see departing (*qu*)
Qu Yuan, 78

Record of Traveling in Famous Mountains (*You mingshan zhi*) (Xie Lingyun), 102
recruitment system, 10–12
refinement, see *jing* ("refinement")
Regulated poetry, see *Lüshi* ("Regulated poetry")
Ren Fang, 12, 13, 14, 132n42
rencai, see individual talent (*rencai*)
resemblance in form (*xingsi*), 46–47, 104
residence determination (*tuduan*), 82–83, 98
"Respectfully Harmonizing with 'Tender and Slender'" ("Fenghe xianxian") (Wang Rong), 142n50

"Responding to 'On the Pear Tree's Flowers above the Pond'" ("He 'Yong chishang lihua'") (Liu Hi), 53, 54
"Reviewing Matters in My Lofty Study" ("Gaozhai shi shi") (Xie Tiao), 65
rising (*shang*), 23, 24, 136n11, 154n9
"Roaming on Mount Jingting" ("You Jingting shan") (Xie Tiao), 111–12, 119
"Roaming the Mountains" ("You shan") (Xie Tiao), 104–7, 116–17
"Roaming the Villa Garden" ("Qixuan si ting jiang bi you diyuan") (Wang Rong), 68–69, 71, 72, 144n43
ru, see entering (*ru*)

san buxiu ("three eternities"), 132n38
"Sandals beneath Her Feet, The" ("Jiaoxia lü") (Shen Yue), 55, 91
Sanlun school of Buddhism, 19
seeing, 40–56; as happening, 47–51; as illusion, 51–56; observation's importance in court environment, 42–46; *xingsi*, see resemblance in form (*xingsi*)
Sengrou, 134n57
Sengzhao, 72
"Setting Out at Night on the Capital Road" ("Jinglu yefa") (Xie Tiao), 89–90
"Setting Out Early from Mount Ding" ("Zao fa Ding shan") (Shen Yue), 110–11, 117
"Setting Up a North-facing Window Recently: Harmonizing with Retainer He" ("Xin zhi beichuan he He Congshi") (Xie Tiao), 66–67
"Setting Up My Residence" ("Zhizhai") (Xie Tiao), 65–66
shang, see rising (*shang*)
Shangzi, 107, 116, 151n26
Shen, see lively spirit (*shen*), 123
Shen Deqian, 2–4
Shen Qingzhi, 130n9
Shen Yue
literary characteristics and views of: *babing* ("eight defects") in poetry of, 22–24; on conscious thought in literature, 30, 35–36, 139n58; on interaction of *sisheng* ("four tones"), 24; on *jing* ("refinement"), 35–36; Li

Bai on, 8; literary distinction attained as youth, 9; Lu Shiyong's criticism of, 123; as master of poetic "sounds and rhymes," 38; Mou Yuanxiang on landscape poetry of, 100; on *nian* ("thought-instant"), 19–20, 36–37, 90, 121; on prejudice toward his new poetic form, 21; "Ren Fang's prose and Shen Yue's poetry," 14; "Setting Out Early from Mount Ding," 110–11, 117; *sisheng* ("four tones") begin to be used by, 16; sound poems of, 31, 33; on those who know sound as understanding him, 138n39; on tone difference as guideline for poetry, 26–27, 137n29; on transformation of literary style, 132n44; on "worm carving and seal engraving" criticism, 21, 36; on *xingsi* ("resemblance in form"), 47; as Yongming poet, 7; *zhi* aesthetic contrasted with, 30

personal characteristics and views of: away from capital city, 88, 90–93; Buddhist practice of, 16–20; Chengshi school as influence on, 18, 134n57; on commoners and gentry, 11, 131n23; conflicting desires of, 72–73; Crown Prince Wenhui favors, 12–13; death of, 63; drafts edict legitimizing Liang Wudi, 14; among Eight Friends (*Bayou*) in Prince of Jingling's coterie, 13–14, 84; on elite men gathering in capital city, 83–84, 147n26; Emperor Wu of Qi compares to Liu Xizong, 45; family background of, 9; on "individual talent" (*rencai*), 10–11, 121; intends to go into reclusion, 149n66; known in Northern Wei, 132n42; leaves capital after death of Prince of Jingling, 43, 140n15; lives beyond Yongming period, 7; long life of, 7, 14; on northern émigrés as "those living in a drift," 82; ostentatious garden rejected by, 58–60; semiseclusion of, 61, 143n21; social advancement of, 10, 130n12; on spirit not becoming extinct, 17, 36, 71; suburban estate

of, 57, 60–61, 84; on taming nature, 63–64; on "worthy one" (*xianzhe*), 17–18, 121, 133n53; in Xiao Yan's ascension to throne, 43

works of: "Ascending the Loft of Mystic Exultation," 112–13, 152n38; "Courtyard Rain: Responding to an Imperial Command," 47–48; "*Fu* on Living in the Suburbs," 27–29, 58–59, 61, 63–64, 67, 73–74, 137n32, 142n6; "Listening to Gibbons' Cries at Stone Dike Rapids," 31–32; "On Azure Moss," 48; "On Embroidery along the Collar," 54–55; "On New Lotuses: By Imperial Command," 50–51; "On the Non-Extinction of the Spirit," 71; "On the Snow: By Imperial Command," 48; "On the Twelve-Stringed Zither," 33–34; "On the Wutong," 42, 44, 45; "The Sandals beneath Her Feet," 55, 91; "Six Recollections," 53–54; *Song shu*, 10, 11, 26, 30, 35, 103, 137n29; "Spending the Night in the Eastern Garden," 76–77; "Strolling Through the Garden," 74–75; "Traveling to Assume My Post: Via the Roads of Zhufang," 90–92, 123; "The Xin'an River Is Extremely Clear," 116

shengpu ("tone register"), 22, 135n5
shengse ("sound and sight"), 1–6; Buddhist process of refinement and, 20; Confucius on, 2; defining, 1–2; in *fu* poetry, 4; negative connotations of, 1; in Regulated poetry (*Lüshi*), 9; as sensual pleasure, 1, 129n4; Shen Deqian on Southern Dynasties poetry and, 2–4. *See also* seeing; sound
shenyun, see "lively spirit and reverberating resonance" (*shenyun*)
Shi Chong, 58, 142n4
shi yan zhi, see "poetry expresses what is intently in the mind" (*shi yan zhi*) paradigm
Shi Yi, 44, 45
Shiji, 44
Shishuo xinyu, 104
Shoushi zuiyu (Shen Deqian), 2

Shufen Liu, 143n16

Shuyu, 44–45

Sima Qian, 44–45

Sima Xiangru, 15

sisheng ("four tones"): conscious thought in use of, 30; Emperor Wu of Liang's question about, 25; excitement caused by introduction of, 24, 26; modern sensibility no longer hears, 124; origins of, 135n5; in refined sound, 36; Shen Yue on interaction of, 24; in Wang Wei's "Written while Crossing the Yellow River to Qinghe," 123; in Yongming poets' new prosody, 5, 16, 22, 23, 39, 120; Zhou Yong's use of, 25–26

"Six Recollections" ("Liu yi") (Shen Yue), 53–54

skandha, 18, 134n59

song, see appraisals (*song*)

Song Bian, 15

Song shu (Shen Yue), 10, 11, 26, 30, 35, 103, 137n29

Song Wendi, *see* Liu Yilong (Song Wendi)

Song Wudi, *see* Liu Yu (Song Wudi)

sound, 21–39; grasping in Yongming poetry, 31–35; Yongming style as about perfection of, 8. *See also zhiyin* ("knowing sound")

sound and sight, *see shengse* ("sound and sight")

sounds and rhymes, *see yinyun* ("sounds and rhymes")

Southern Dynasties: Buddhism's influence in, 5, 16–20, 121; capital city of, 4; component dynasties of, 2; as era of political dysfunction and military weakness, 4; individual talent in advancement in, 9–16; literary history as constructed in, 15–16; northern émigrés in, 80; rivalry with northern states, 14–15, 132n39; Shen Deqian on *shengse* and poetic decline in, 2–4

"Spending the Night in the Eastern Garden" ("Su Dongyuan") (Shen Yue), 76–77

Steinbeck, John, 81

"Strolling Through the Garden" ("Xing yuan") (Shen Yue), 74–75

Sudi (Mundane Truth), 38, 72

Sui Wendi (Yang Jian), 4

Sun Chang, Kang-i, 64

śūnyatā, 20, 71, 113

Taigong (Lü Shang; Jiang Shang), 10, 130n17

Tan Qian, 37

Tang Yongtong, 38

Tao Yuanming (Tao Qian): "Field and Garden Poetry" (*tianyuan shi*) of, 68; on his place of origin, 83; on north-facing windows, 66; on returning to the fields and gardens, 77, 142n3; Shen Deqian on, 2–3; "When the mind is far, the place is naturally remote," 67–68, 69; Yongming poets influenced by, 57; *yuan* as used by, 57, 142n1

thought-instant, *see nian* ("thought-instant")

three eternities, *see san buxiu* ("three eternities")

Tian Xiaofei, 8, 20

Tian Yuqing, 130n12

tone register (*shengpu*), 22, 135n5

travel poems, 6, 88–93

"Traveling to Assume My Post: Via the Roads of Zhufang" ("Xun yi Zhufang daolu") (Shen Yue), 90–92, 123

"Traveling to Luo: Two Poems Written on the Road (No. 2)" (Fu Luo daozhong er shou") (Lu Ji), 90

Tretheway, Natasha, 35

Tuduan, see residence determination (*tuduan*)

Two Truths, see *Erdi* (Two Truths)

Ultimate Truth, see *Zhendi*

"Wandering in the East Hall: On the Wutong" ("You Dongtang yong tong") (Xie Tiao), 42, 44, 45

Wang Deyuan, 86

Wang Jian, 26

Wang Rong

    literary characteristics and views of: dodder as fascination of, 45; "Let it roam—appreciation outside the human real!," 68, 103; literary distinction attained as youth, 9; literary reputation of, 15; and Ren Fang's prose, 14; *sisheng* ("four tones") begin to be used by, 16; as Yongming poet, 7

personal characteristics and views of: ancestral hometown of, 82; Buddhist practice of, 16; careful observation lacking in, 42–43; death coincides with end of Yongming period, 7, 14; edict to enthrone Prince of Jingling prepared by, 42, 63; among Eight Friends (*Bayou*) in Prince of Jingling's coterie, 13–14, 84; Emperor Wu of Qi compares to Liu Xizong, 45; episode with Fang Jinggao and Song Bian, 15, 132n40; execution of, 42–43, 99; family background of, 9; graves of ancestors of, 98; native identity of, 98; premonition about Xiao Yan, 43; Prince of Jingling as fond of, 13

works of: "Making a Palindromic Poem in the Back Garden," 102; "Moving My Mat to the Zither Room: Writing at the Instruction of the Director of Instruction," 34–35; "On the Dodder," 51; "On the Pear Tree's Flowers above the Pond," 52–53; "Preface to Poems on the Qu River," 15, 132n41; "Respectfully Harmonizing with 'Tender and Slender,'" 142n50; "Roaming the Villa Garden," 68–69, 71, 72, 144n43; "Zhiyin lun" ("On Knowing Sound") planned by, 138n39

Wang Sengda, 10
Wang Wei, 122–23, 153n6
Wang Yun, 27, 29, 30, 36
Wang Zan, 88–89
Wang Zijing, 104
wasp's waist, see *fengyao* ("wasp's waist")
Wei Shou, 132n42
Wei Zhun, 43
Wenhui, Crown Prince (Xiao Changmao): death of, 14, 42; ostentatious estate of, 58–59, 142n8; Prince of Jingling's

relationship with, 62; rock garden of, 101; Shen Yue in service of, 12–13, 91, 148n56, 148n60
Wenxin diaolong (Liu Xie), 88–89
Western Paradise of Amitābha Buddha, 69, 73
"what is intently on the mind," see *zhi*
worthy one (*xianzhe*), 17–18; dynamic between individual talent and, 20; Shen Yue on, 17–18, 121, 133n53
"Written while Crossing the Yellow River to Qinghe" ("Du He dao Qinghe zuo" (Wang Wei), 122–23, 153n6
Wu of Chen, Emperor, see Chen Baxian (Emperor Wu of Chen)
Wu of Qi, Emperor, see Qi Wudi (Xiao Ze)
Wu of Song, Emperor, see Liu Yu (Song Wudi)
Wu of Wei, Emperor, see Cao Cao (Emperor Wu of Wei)
wutong tree, 42

xianzhe, see worthy one (*xianzhe*)
Xiao Changmao, see Wenhui, Crown Prince (Xiao Changmao)
Xiao Chen, 13
Xiao Luan, see Ming, Emperor (Xiao Luan)
Xiao Tong, 133n52
Xiao Yan, see Liang Wudi (Xiao Yan)
Xiao Ze, see Qi Wudi (Xiao Ze)
Xiao Zhaoye, see Prince Yulin (Xiao Zhaoye)
Xiao Ziliang, see Prince of Jingling (Xiao Ziliang)
Xiao Zilong, see Prince Sui (Xiao Zilong)
Xiao Zixian, 16, 22–23, 62, 84, 132n44
Xiaoxie caotang za lun shi (Mou Yuanxiang), 100
Xie Kun, 81, 83, 98
Xie Lingyun: artificial frames in poems of, 64; "Building Fences along the Rapids in the Tree Garden South of the Field," 107; on dwelling types, 60, 63; "*Fu* on Dwelling in the Mountains," 58, 143n15; as known in the north, 132n42; "A Poem Composed while Returning to the Lake from the Stone Wall Study," 115, 119; *Record of Traveling in Famous Mountains,*

102; rejection of ostentatious garden, 58; on retreating to the garden, 142n3; "scanning the landscape" method, 104, 118; Shen Deqian on poetic traits of, 2, 3; Xie Tiao's "Roaming the Mountains" and, 104, 106–7; Yongming poets influenced by, 6, 57, 101

Xie Tiao

literary characteristics and views of: artificial frames in poems of, 64–65; composes about object seen from his seat at social gathering, 45; literary distinction attained as youth, 9; melancholic quality of work of, 48; as sensitive observer of "old sheaths," 49, 71; *sisheng* ("four tones") begin to be used by, 16; as Yongming poet, 7

personal characteristics and views of: ancestor Xie Kun, 81, 83, 98; away from capital city, 88, 89–90; Buddhist practice of, 16; among Eight Friends (*Bayou*) in Prince of Jingling's coterie, 13–14, 84; execution for court intrigue, 43, 99; family background of, 9; on his existence as courtier, 87–88; hometown of, 84, 147n29; on Jiankang as in the center, 84–85; *jilü* experienced by, 83; lives beyond Yongming period, 7; as "man of Yangxia in the Commandery of Chen," 83, 98; marriage to daughter of Wang Jingze, 10; premature death of, 14; Prince Sui as fond of, 13; returning to the capital, 96–97

works of: "About to Set Out from the Shitou Fortress, I Ascend the Beacon-Fire Loft," 86; "About to Travel to Xiang River, I First Seek Out Fish-hook Creek," 114–15, 117–18; "Climbing Three-Peaks Mountain at Dusk, Gazing Back toward Capital City," 85–86; "Exilic Feelings at the End of Winter," 94–95, 144n34; "Gathering at Night with Fellow Expatriates," 95–96; "Gazing at Ease from My Lofty Study in the Xuancheng Commandery: In Reply to Legal Counsel Lü," 65; "Going Down to the Capital on a Temporary Assignment," 96–97; "Going to Xuancheng Commandery, Leaving Xinlin Port, Proceeding toward Banqiao," 89, 92–93, 123; "Harmonizing with Editor Wang Rong: The Eight Retainers Mountain," 113; "Harmonizing with Libationer Shen's 'Strolling Through the Garden,'" 75–76; "Harmonizing with Liu Hui's 'Entering the Lute Gorge, Gazing at Heaped-Rocks Rapids,'" 109–10; "In Reply to Wang Deyuan, Grand Warden of Jin'an," 86–87; "In the Middle Garden of Merit Officer Ji," 70–72, 144n48; "A Lecture and Exposition on an Autumn Night," 52; "On Bamboos," 49; "On Return Route, Overlooking the Isle," 118; "On the Rambler Rose," 48–49; "On the Wind," 48; "Professing Sickness, I Return to My Garden," 77–78; "Reviewing Matters in My Lofty Study," 65; "Roaming on Mount Jingting," 111–12, 119; "Roaming the Mountains," 104–7, 116–17; "Setting Out at Night on the Capital Road," 89–90; "Setting Up a North-facing Window Recently: Harmonizing with Retainer He," 66–67; "Setting Up My Residence," 65–66; "Wandering in the East Hall: On the Wutong," 42, 44, 45

Xie Xuan, 113

Xie Zhuang, 139n5

"Xin'an River Is Extremely Clear" ("Xin'an jiang zhi qing") (Shen Yue), 116

Xinbian, see "novelty and transformation" (*xinbian*)

Xing Zicai, 132n42

Xingqing, see "nature and feeling" (*xingqing*)

Xingsi, see resemblance in form (*xingsi*)

Xu Junfang, 46, 140n25

Yan Yanzhi, 2, 15

Yan Zhitui, 80, 99
Yang Jian, *see* Sui Wendi (Yang Jian)
Yang, Xiaoshan, 64
Yang Xiong, 21
Yao Cha, 12
Yin Fan, 154n9
yinyun ("sounds and rhymes"), 25
Yongming poets
    literary characteristics and views of:
        babing ("eight defects") in poetry of,
        22–24, 120, 135n7; contexts important
        to poetics of, 5, 7–20; criticized as
        "superfluous" or "severe," 38–39;
        diminutive grasping of, 69, 121–24;
        enthusiasm aroused by, 27; grasping
        sound in poetry of, 31–35; on *jing*
        ("refinement"), 20, 35–39, 123–24;
        keen interest in observing things,
        5; landscape poetry of, 6, 100–119;
        literary distinction attained as
        youths, 9, 12–13; physical smallness of
        subjects of, 45; seeing as happening
        in, 47–51; *sisheng* ("four tones") in
        poetry of, 5, 16, 22, 23, 120; travel
        poems of, 6, 88–93; Xie Lingyun as
        influence on, 6, 57, 101; *yongwu shi*
        ("poems on things") of, 40–56; *yuan*
        ("garden") in poetry of, 5–6, 57–79;
        zhiyin ("knowing sound") in, 21–39
    members of, 7
    personal characteristics and views of:
        Buddhism's influence in, 5, 16–20,
        37, 38, 68–72, 121; as courtier-
        poets, 4–5, 6, 38, 40, 56, 57–58, 94,
        97, 116, 117, 119, 120–21; among
        Eight Friends (*Bayou*) in Prince of
        Jingling's coterie, 13–14; leave capital
        city behind, 6, 80–99; new ideal of
        personal worth of, 20
    See also Shen Yue; Wang Rong; Xie Tiao
Yongming style (*Yongming ti*): as about
    perfection of sound, 8; *Liang shu* on,
    8, 129n3; Palace style compared with,
    8–9; seen as ornate and superfluous, 8;
    Yongming poets as originators of, 7, 8
yongwu fu, 41
yongwu shi ("poems on things"), 40–56;

endings of Yongming, 55; lingering,
    penetrating quality of Yongming, 49–51;
    narrow focus of, 40; for negotiating
    personal merit, 42; physical smallness
    of subjects of, 45; sampling of titles
    of, 41; seeing as illusion in, 51–56; as
    social verse, 41–42; why the poets were
    captivated by, 55–56; on *wutong* tree,
    42; *xingsi* ("resemblance in form")
    associated with, 46–47; Yongming poets
    popularize, 5
Youyang zazu, 46
Yu Gaozhi, 62
Yu, Pauline, 153n7
Yu Xi, 43
Yu Xin, 15, 46, 132n42
yuan ("garden"), 57–79; conflicting forces
    in, 72–77; exotic names for, 145n59;
    between the human and wilderness,
    60–63, 79; naturalistic, 63–67; rejection
    of ostentatious, 58–60; returning to,
    77–79; vacating, 67–72; varieties of, 57;
    of Wenhui, 58–59, 142n8; withdrawal
    from officialdom to, 5–6
Yulin, Prince, *see* Prince Yulin (Xiao
    Zhaoye)

Ze, see deflected (*ze*) tones
Zhang Hongming, 136n14
Zhang Hua, 49–50, 51
Zhang Rong, 37
Zhendi (Ultimate Truth), 38, 72
Zheng Tan, 4
zhi ("what is intently on the mind"),
    29–30, 56, 122
Zhi Dun, 37
zhiyin ("knowing sound"), 24–30; on
    difference between refinement and
    crudity, 35–36
Zhong Rong, 9, 23, 27, 132n44, 136n11
Zhong Ziqi, 24, 29–30
Zhonghui, 1
Zhou She, 25
Zhou Yong, 22, 25–26, 37–38
Zhuangzi, 68, 69
Zhuangzi, 71, 107
Zong Bing, 102–3, 104, 111, 118, 153n59